Margaret Mahler

Margaret Mahler

A Biography of
the Psychoanalyst

ALMA HALBERT BOND

McFarland & Company, Inc., Publishers
Jefferson, North Carolina, and London

LIBRARY OF CONGRESS CATALOGUING-IN-PUBLICATION DATA

Bond, Alma Halbert.
     Margaret Mahler : a biography of the psychoanalyst / Alma
Halbert Bond.
         p.   cm.
     Includes bibliographical references and index.

     ISBN 978-0-7864-3355-1
     softcover : 50# alkaline paper ∞

     1. Mahler, Margaret S.   2. Psychoanalysts — Biography.
3. Infant psychology.   4. Child analysis.   I. Title.
BF719.B66   2008
150.19'5092 — dc22 [B]   2008015998

British Library cataloguing data are available

On the cover: Margaret Mahler, 1940; background ©2008 PhotoSpin.
Front cover by TG Design.

Manufactured in the United States of America

McFarland & Company, Inc., Publishers
   Box 611, Jefferson, North Carolina 28640
      www.mcfarlandpub.com

To the memory of Margaret Mahler,
a wise and remarkable psychoanalyst,
researcher, theorist, and teacher
who was all too human.

Acknowledgments

My gratitude to:

Anni Bergman, for her cooperation in discussing her experiences with Margaret Mahler, and for sending me her paper, "Revisiting Rapprochement."

Maria Nardone, for sharing her personal photographs of Dr. Mahler, many of which are reproduced in this book.

Raquel Berman, for allowing me to include her interview with Dr. Mahler, which was first presented at the "1st Symposium Margaret Mahler: The Separation-Individuation Process in Childhood Development — Preventive Aspects" held in Mexico D.F. Mexico, with the participation of Dr. Margaret Mahler (by video), Dr. Raquel Berman (by video), Dr. Annie Bergman, Dr. Louise Kaplan and Dr. Calvin Settlage on November 30 through December 2, 1979 (funded by the Mexican Association of Psychoanalytic Psychotherapy).

Judy Mars (Columbia) for Karlen Lyons-Ruth's article, "Rapprochement or Approchement: Mahler's Theory Reconsidered from the Vantage Point of Recent Research on Early Attachment Relationships."

Lydia Kordalewsky, Anne Mansfield, Dory Knoll, and Trish Reilly early readers of the manuscript. Arline Zaks and Lois Barrowcliff for their extensive critiques of one of the final versions.

A special thanks to Frank Hernadi for his thorough critique of the manuscript and his many wonderful suggestions.

To Bluma Swerdloff, Mary Marshall Clark and Rebecca Solomon (Columbia Oral History) for first making accessible to me Dr. Swerdloff's oral history of Margaret Mahler, and particularly to Dr. Swerdloff for allowing me to use her personal copy of the history.

To Dr Dravai Istvan, for his descriptions of Sopron.

Denise Galatas, Southern Mutual Help Association, Inc., for her information on Sister Anne

Catherine Bizalion, the first recipient of the Gray Panthers Margaret S. Mahler Award.

Anna Kovacs, for sending me A. Harrach's memorial eulogy in Hungary for Margaret Mahler.

Balazs E. Pataki, for his definition of *numerus clausus*.

Gyorgy Gergely, for sending me his article, "Reapproaching Mahler: New Perspectives." JAPA 48/4

Dr. Lotte Koehler, for the chapter of her autobiography dealing with her relationship with Margaret Mahler.

Ulrike May Tolson, for contacting Thomas Aichhorn in regard to the correspondence between Mahler and Professor Rosa Dworschak.

Thomas Aichhorn, for graciously sending me copies of the correspondence between Mahler and August Aichhorn, and the letters between Professor Rosa Dworschak and Margaret Mahler.

Yale University, Archives and Manuscripts, for allowing me to access the contents of the Margaret S. Mahler Collection, and for sending copies of many folders, cassettes, and photographs. I particularly appreciate the assistance given me by Diane E. Kaplan, archivist, and her assistant, Danelle Moon.

George Gardner (archives technician) at Glasgow University Archive Services, Glasgow, Scotland, for forwarding me information on the *Queen Mary*.

My friend and colleague, Dr. Mary Bruce, for her suggestion on improving the title.

My heartfelt thanks to:

My former agent, Nancy Hertz, of the Crow's Nest Literary Agency, for her painstakingly thorough critique of the manuscript, and for her contagious enthusiasm for the book.

Phil Stokes, for giving me permission to use his excellent World War II chronology, which helped immeasurably in the writing of this book.

My limitless gratitude to Margaret Mahler's many wonderful colleagues and friends who kindly shared their memories and insights into her character. The list, which sounds like a modern day *Who's Who of Psychoanalysis*, includes: Drs. Leo Rangell, Jacob Arlow, Henri Parens, Anni Bergman, John McDevitt, Fred Pine, Harold Blum, Helen Gediman, Leo Madow, Kitty LaPerriere, Patricia Nachman, Ruth Lax, Peter Neubauer, Emanuel Furer, Lotte Koehler, Louise Kaplan, Maria Nardone, Darline Levy, Edgar L. Lipton, Patsy Turrine, Joyce Edward, Karen Berberian (the daughter of Selma

Kramer), Jeremy Berberian, Maria and Martin Bergmann, Arlene and Arnold Richards, Helen and Donald Meyers, Bernard Pacella, Samuel Ritvo, Morton Reiser, Irving Sternschein, Judith Smith, Sylvia Brody, Ernst Abelin, Anne-Marie Sandler, Lucia Wright, Ava Bry Penman, Bluma Swerdloff, Raquel Berman, Ulrike May Tolson, and John Singletary, president of the Margaret Mahler Foundation in Philadelphia. I would also like to thank Mahler's coworkers, Helen Fogarassy, Bernice Apter, Joan Jackson, and Anita Kolek, for their generosity in entrusting me with their illuminating memories and comments, and Frank Hernadi for sharing his information about Hungary. I also would like to thank Sam Vaknin for giving his permission to quote from his web article, "Malignant Self Love — Narcissism Revisited. http://samvak.tripod.com. I am especially grateful to Margaret Mahler, herself, for her permissions to Bluma Swerdloff to use her research materials, who was kind enough to share her insights with me. And a very special thank you to my son, Jonathan Halbert Bond, CEO, former president, and cofounder of Kirschenbaum, Bond, and Partners, for his generosity in publicizing my books and allowing me the use of K&B facilities in the preparation of this book.

Contents

Preface

John Steinbeck, in *Journal of a Novel*,[1] a book dedicated to his little sons, wrote that in *East of Eden,* he is going to tell them "one of the greatest, perhaps the greatest story of all — the story of good and evil, of strength and weakness, of love and hate, of beauty and ugliness." He says he wants to show them that these emotions are inseparable, that neither can exist without the other, and creativity is born from their coupling.

With Steinbeck's intent, if not his talent, I want to tell the story of Margaret Mahler, which encompasses her shortcomings as well as her strengths. Boswell, when asked by a friend of Samuel Johnson to soften his portrayal of the "asperities ... [of] our virtuous and most revered departed friend," replied that "he would not cut off his claws, nor make a tiger a cat, to please anybody."[2] Nor would I. Instead, I would like to paint a portrait of the complete Margaret Mahler, and to show how, out of the *sturm und drang* of separation-individuation struggles, in the midst of the Holocaust, the great horror of the twentieth century, she was able to create one of the great theories of psychoanalysis.

Her dear friend, Darline Levy, wrote Mahler,[3] "I will never forget a beautiful little passage in a letter you wrote to me, at the end of last summer.... Darling Darline — if you can accept me with my great weaknesses and dependencies?? Would you want to...? The greatest human strengths are rooted in and develop out of great weaknesses and dependencies."

After all, wasn't it *rapprochement* she was pleading for from Darline? Isn't it *rapprochement* of her strengths and her weaknesses that we can offer as a final gift to the memory of Margaret Mahler? Like Walt Whitman, who said to his biographer,[4] "Be sure to write about me honest; whatever you do, do not prettify me: include all the hells and damns," I think Margaret Mahler would have liked that.

Nevertheless, despite my philosophy of wanting to paint a true portrait of Margaret Mahler, an unexpected phenomenon happened in the writing of this book. Perhaps because I am an analyst of many years' experience, the interviewees tended to speak freely to me of their feelings about Margaret Mahler. Or it may be that they just needed to discharge their pent up hostility. As a result, much anger toward her burst forth during the original interviews. After being granted a publishing contract by McFarland, I returned to the subjects to obtain permission to use their interviews in my manuscript. To my dismay, a few people changed their minds altogether and refused to allow me to include their remarks at all, while almost unanimously the interviewees wished to change their original contributions. Many edited their remarks for style, but most simply wished to remove vitriolic remarks from their stories. As a result, Dr. Mahler appears a bit, shall we say, "gentler" in the finished book than in the first spontaneous interviews, although I trust the flavor of the interviewees' rage comes through despite the widespread extractions. Perhaps this phenomenon tells us more about human nature than it does about Margaret Mahler.

The development may not be so strange after all, when viewed in the context of the universal wish of people to appear "nice." It has at least one precedent. Masud Khan was a psychoanalyst who, like Mahler, inspired strong feelings of love and hate in his colleagues, friends, and analysands. In *False Self: The Life of Masud Khan*,[5] the wonderful definitive biography of Khan by Linda Hopkins, there were at least 80 references by her interviewees indicating reluctance to express their feelings in print, such as "an anonymous analyst said..." or "according to a person who does not wish to be identified...." Unfortunately, such caution is necessary in the framework of today's litigious world.

Prologue (1938)

Imagine this scene, if you will. It is October 1938. Margaret Mahler, a forty-one-year-old Hungarian psychoanalyst (later to become the great infant researcher, theorist, and teacher of child analysis) leans over the bow of a majestic ocean liner as gulls squawk overhead. Giant waves crash against the ship's sides. The spray flies up over the railing and drenches her hat and coat. Her damp face stings in the wind, but she refuses to join her husband inside their warm cabin. There is too much to see as the great ship slowly slides its way out of the Liverpool harbor, leaving Europe behind in its wake. The Paul Mahlers have set sail for America on the *Queen Mary*, narrowly escaping with their lives from the great horror of the twentieth century, the Holocaust.

What overwhelming emotions Margaret must have felt as the mighty ship slipped further and further away from the homeland that had cast her out, and

Margaret Mahler at age 43 in 1940, two years after she arrived in the U.S.

Margaret and Paul Mahler in approximately 1940 when love was still in bloom.

relentlessly carried her toward the vast unknown. She certainly must have experienced great relief by escaping from the constant threat to their lives and, at the same time, anguish and grief for her lost homeland and the parents and sister she might never see again, and guilt at the thought of her good fortune, in contrast to that of loved ones she was leaving behind.

Her mind, in all likelihood, was teeming with questions as the powerful ship forged its way across the widening miles. Would she ever be able to exorcize the harrowing scenes of Nazi Germany that were chiseled into her mind? Would she even want to? How could she possibly make a living in the new land when she didn't speak the language? Would she have trouble learning English? Languages never were her strong point. Would psychoanalysis be practiced the same way in America as it was in Europe? She had heard rumors to the contrary. Would she be so overcome with grief and longing for her lost family that she wouldn't be able to work at all? If so, who would take care of her in the strange land? Certainly not her husband, for he was lucky if he could look after himself. Would Paul even be able to find a job, or would he remain unemployed, as he had been in London? Would their old friends help, as they had in England? Would they have enough money for food? For rent? She would kill herself before being relegated to the realms of charity. Where would they live (for they had no idea of the novel terrain)? Would Americans snobbishly reject the "greenhorns" as less than equals? More to the point, would *she* like the brash, money hungry Americans that she, as a cultured European woman, disparaged?

All these questions must have flooded Margaret's mind as she reeled under the boundlessness of the mid-ocean skies. If she dared put aside her guilt, her heart would have overflowed with hope for the start of a new day. It is not difficult to imagine how much of the ordinarily peaceful ocean voyage she spent working through these feelings. Then, as the great ship inches its way into New York's harbor, once again Margaret eagerly leans over the bow of the *Queen Mary*— this time reveling in the sight of the Land of the Free. She was never to lose the feelings of joy and gratitude she experienced as the great ocean liner entered New York Harbor. Romantic feelings about the Statue of Liberty were to remain with her for the rest of her life.[1]

1

The Early Years

The Schoenbergers (1897–1911)

Margaret Schoenberger was born to an upper middle class Jewish family on May 10, 1897, in Sopron, Hungary, some eight years after the birth of a baby boy named Adolf Schickelgruber, later known as Adolf Hitler, in Braunau-am-Inn, Austria, approximately two hundred and ten miles away. Sopron, a charming city known as the ancient jewel of the country, is located along the Austrian-Hungarian border at the foot of the Alps, forty miles from Vienna. The ambiance of the town is perhaps more Austrian than Hungarian. There are quiet little streets of the historical city center, unique buildings and many monuments of the Middle Ages, as well as a plethora of museums which have given it the nickname of "museum town." If you want to take a rest, you can always find a park overlooking acres of gardens to sit in. You can stroll along paths, read on benches, and smell the fresh flowers. The citizens are famous for their hospitality.

There is a lively cultural life in the city, including a tradition of art, music, and theatre. All types of famous artists who come to Vienna make a side visit to the little Hungarian border town. In addition to its high culture, the natural surroundings, the mountainsides with woods, springs, and the air of the Alps make Sopron an ideal place for mental and physical recreation.

Margaret Mahler was a true daughter of Sopron in her gracious hospitality, her love of art, music, and theatre, her pursuit of the intellectual life, and her extensive use of the cultural life of her adopted city of New York. Like her fellow Sopronians who knew how to enjoy their town's cul-

7

Margaret called her mother, Eugenia Wiener Schoenberger, "a beautiful lady." She is pictured here around 1927.

tural assets, Mahler made good use of the artistic resources of Manhattan, frequently attending museums, concerts, ballets, and the theatre, even late in her life when she required the use of a wheelchair. She adored the woods, and greatly enjoyed her view of Central Park and grew trees herself at her beloved country home in Brookfield, Connecticut. She carried with her into New York City many of the attributes of a Sopronian. A connoisseur and collector of art, she was a gracious and perfectionistic hostess who made sure that every detail of her service was correct. Once, when Bluma Swerdloff came to have tea with her, the housekeeper brought a cup and saucer that didn't match, and Mahler had an absolute fit. Swerdloff said,[1] "Don't get yourself upset about it. It isn't important." Mahler replied, "In my house we do it right."

The Gustztav Schoenbergers lived in a complex of apartment houses in Sopron called *Gyoery Palota* (Palais of the Railroad Company), where executives of the famous railroad that ran through the town once lived. The complex no longer exists. The community, which was replete with tennis courts and gardens, provided an excellent social life for its young people. The Schoenbergers' apartment itself was probably not too different from Margaret's large European style apartment in the El Dorado, which overlooked the trees of Central Park. Her cherished Connecticut home of Brookfield, surrounded with the woods she loved, may well have brought back

Margaret Schoenberger at age five in 1902.

memories of the natural surroundings of Sopron, with its silent forests of oak, poplar, and beech trees, its pinewoods and chestnut groves.

The parents of Margaret's mother, Eugenia Wiener Schoenberger, were born in Lakenbach, a German-speaking Schwabish town. Although Eugenia had been educated in a Hungarian school, she spoke only German with her parents, and as a result never really mastered Hungarian. Since Hungarian was Margaret's native tongue, the language difficulty was only one of the basic issues separating mother and child. All her life, Margaret complained that people often found her hard to understand. This difficulty began at her mother's knee, long before she emigrated to the United States.

Margaret, or Margit, as she was then called, was born to the nineteen-year-old Eugenia Wiener Schoenberger nine months and ten days after Eugenia's wedding. Eugenia felt very put upon by her pregnancy, as she considered herself too young to be a mother. Apparently she blamed Margit for the mishap, and had as little to do with her as possible. As a result, the future student of symbiosis was left to work out her own destiny on that score, as a normal symbiotic process and its resolution could not have developed with so rejecting a mother.

In startling contrast, when Suzannah was born four years later, Eugenia fell in love with the child and made no secret about which little girl was her favorite. Margaret dealt with the pain of longing by behaving in kind and substituting her father for her mother. Once, she sat watching her mother nurse her sister and heard her say, "I suckle you, I love you, I adore you. I live only for you." Margaret's heart was shattered. She retaliated with, "And I was born by my Papa, not my mother!" She said later that the remark reminded her of Pallas Athene, who in the Greek legend sprang fully grown from the head of Zeus, her father. Pallas Athene, of course, grew up to become the goddess of arts and the embodiment of intelligence. The incident, which left the little girl bursting with envy and rage, was the prototype of the myriad scenes of mothers and babies she was to observe in decades to come. "I believe my mother and sister were the first mother-child relationship I investigated," she said. Here we see the Repetition Compulsion[2] at work. What the little girl of four couldn't tolerate she tried to master over the years by repeating the scene over and over again.

Dr. Karen Berberian, the child psychologist daughter of Dr. Selma Kramer, Mahler's student and close friend, personally saw the repetition in action. She said in an interview with me,[3] "I remember when my son Josh was an infant, I was breast feeding him and Mahler came and watched intently. I think I passed the test, but it was kind of creepy."

Mahler told an anecdote which demonstrates the intensity of the terrible sibling rivalry she experienced. When Suzannah was around two years

Margaret and Suzannah Schoenberger in 1902. Margaret was six and Suzannah was four.

old, she picked up a hot iron and held it to her cheek. Mrs. Schoenberger became hysterical and twirled around the room with the sobbing child. Margit was delighted, as well as contemptuous. She said, "How could she be so dumb as to put a hot iron to her cheek?"

Mahler never overcame the sibling rivalry of her childhood, and continued to act it out all her life with certain junior colleagues and children, such as Jeremy Beberian, the grandson of Dr. Kramer. Jeremy said,[4] "Mahler ignored me, she definitely wasn't grandmotherly to me at all. If anything, she was very cold. She adored my brother, which would have been fine with me if it wasn't that he got all the amenities. I didn't like the fact that she loved my brother and not me. Just because she was a great analyst doesn't mean she was a great person. Her contribution to the world seems very significant, but her contribution as a human being was pretty menial. I liked everybody who liked me, and she didn't."

Mahler's demonstration of favoritism in at least one instance extended even to her tiny research subjects. A brother and sister were subjects at Masters Children's Center. Their mother complained to a friend of mine, "Mahler gave presents to all the boys but not to the girls."

Margaret's sister, Suzannah Schoenberger, in about 1927.

Margaret had another screen memory in which her mother, who was nursing her sister, developed a breast abscess. The mean-spirited woman informed her older daughter while she was nursing Suzannah that she had not breast fed Margaret. The remark set off a paroxysm of rage in the child, in which she angrily thought the abscess served her mother right, to have had that little creature chewing up her breast. This bout of rage was the forerunner of the frequent outbreaks that were to plague Mahler and her colleagues all her life.

Not surprisingly, Margit was a sickly infant and a poor sleeper. It was her father and a nurse who were up with her at night, not her mother. Mahler thought perhaps she slept badly because she had so many unusual difficulties in her early childhood, with two parents who had very dissimilar characters. She saw them as compatible in that they really needed each other, although Mahler never understood why. As a result, she said in her seventies that her Oedipus complex was still not completely resolved. But her father needed her mother very much, and her mother also needed her father, which must have pleased as well as dismayed the child.

Margaret said,[5] "My mother was a beautiful, in many respects lovable, very sick woman. She certainly did not mean to become pregnant in the first act of her marriage, and have a girl child nine months and ten days after the marriage ceremony. I was put into the arms of a wet nurse, who was dismissed when I was five months old because she stole something. That is hearsay, but a fact, so that my sleep was disturbed. In my second year of life, I was tremendously vigilant, so that my new nurse would carry me back and forth in the room."

One night when her nurse was walking her up and down trying to put her to sleep, Dr. Schoenberger said to the woman, "Why don't you put her in her crib?" The woman replied, "How can I? She stares like a lynx." The nurse was indeed prophetic, as befitting the caretaker of an embryonic genius. The watchful lynx is a creature said to be able to "see through the thickest darkness and immediately tell truth from error,"[6] a description of the adult Mahler as felicitous as any ever conceived. Lynx cubs, however, are more fortunate in their choice of mother than Margit Schoenberger was. The female wildcat usually remains close to her offspring throughout their first winter. Unlike the lynx, Mahler suspected that she was watchful because she thought her mother wanted to kill her. Elsewhere, she said[7] she really had a need to be vigilant, to look, to see, and to understand, and that the necessity was a great liability to her pleasurable emotional life, even if an asset to her scientific career.

Margaret felt that her surplus of curiosity was biologically determined and accompanied by a zeal to investigate and to influence others to do the same. This was borne out by another screen memory concerning vision which took place perhaps a year later. The child, who had been told of the birth of kittens in a neighbor's attic, snuck in to see them. To her horror, she found the kittens' eyes sealed shut. To Margaret the watcher, not to see was the worst nightmare she could imagine, so she picked up the kittens one by one and pried open their eyes. She said later that she was completely unaware of the danger to her own eyes on the part of the mother cat, who might have attacked her instinctively in defense of her young. She told Dr. Peter Neubauer, "That is what I wanted to do all my life, to see what one could do for development." Mahler saw that the germs of her first articles, "Pseudoimbecility: A Magic Cap of Invisibility,"[8] and "Les Infants Terrible,"[9] lay hidden in this episode.

H.L. Mencken[10] once said that curiosity motivates one of the most useful beings the human race has yet produced, the scientific investigator. Certainly that was true of Margaret Mahler. Mencken concluded that what actually urges the scientist on is not some showy but worthless idea of being of service, but "a boundless, almost pathological thirst to penetrate the unknown, to uncover the secret." The prototype of the scientist, according to Mencken, is one of pure instinct, "not the liberator releasing slaves, the good Samaritan lifting up the fallen, but a dog sniffing tremendously at an infinite series of rat-holes."

According to Mahler,[11] it was absolutely irrepressible for her to see or look. One could call her a voyeur, she said. And yet, I suspect that, despite her pleasure in looking, Mahler was ambivalent about it. If you look carefully at the photograph on the cover of Paul Stepansky's *The Memoirs of Margaret S. Mahler*,[12] you can see that her eyes are not focused together, that she had what is called "a wandering eye," in which each eye goes off onto its own individual path. This quirk strongly suggests that, despite her comments to the contrary, Mahler was not totally without guilt about her voyeuristic tendencies.

Surely her dismal relationship with her mother contributed to the feelings of insecurity that plagued Mahler all her life. Speaking of a time when Mahler was already famous, Bluma Swerdloff said,[13] "We had a fortieth anniversary party at Columbia. When I arrived, she said, 'Please sit with me. Nobody will come and talk to me.' I didn't want to sit there, I wanted to smoke. In those days, everybody smoked. Of course two hundred people came and talked to her. The idea that nobody would talk to her was ridiculous."

Lotte Koehler agreed with Swerdloff's revelation about Mahler's lack of self esteem. Koehler said[14] Mahler was able to confirm others but she herself needed affirmation as well because insecurity and doubt lay hidden behind a facade of self-assurance, the foundations of which she had worked long and hard to secure. So, for example, this then eighty-year-old woman appeared for dinner in a sanatorium in a sleeveless, pleated black dress with a bright red belt. She explained that, old and in poor condition as she was, she could not otherwise look at herself in the mirror. "Mahler always felt unconfirmed as a woman."

That Margaret never completely resolved her Oedipus complex seems perfectly understandable today, when we have the work of Margaret Mahler herself to guide us. Her Oedipus Complex must have been contaminated by her early need for a mother. The favorite of her father, a graduate of the Vienna University School of Medicine and a main medical district officer, Margaret never had to compete with either her mother or her sister for his approval. What guilt it must have caused in the sensitive little girl! The guilt could only have been intensified by Margaret's belief throughout her childhood that her mother was a deeply unhappy woman, and that she herself was the cause of Eugenia's misery. Margaret lived all her life with the painful knowledge that the envy of her mother and sister prevented them from loving her.

Anni Bergman and Caroline Ellman[15] speak of the difficulty experienced by cases in which the little girl's primary love relationship is with her father, not her mother. Such a child has to separate from the same father with whom she had to fall in love, as she becomes an oedipal child. She must resolve both the separation-individuation and the oedipal conflicts with the same person, the father. "Rapprochement conflicts and oedipal conflicts may become entangled with each other," Bergman and Ellman say, "making it extremely difficult for the daughter to own her own life and to transfer the love that belongs to the father to another man."

An anecdote told by Louise Kaplan further suggests that Mahler never mastered the Oedipus complex. In this incident, Mahler symbolically removed her father from her mother's bed, and vice versa. The Kaplans were invited for a summer weekend at Mahler's country home. When it was time to go to sleep, Mahler took Donald into the upstairs guest bedroom, and said, "You will sleep here." Then she took Louise to her bedroom, next to the one that Mahler occupied and said, "You will sleep in this bedroom."

"'But Margaret,'" Louise she said protested, "'Don and I have been married a long time and are used to sleeping together.' ... Mahler answered, 'I may wake up in

Dr. Gustav Schoenberger, Margaret's father, in 1927. He was the love of Margaret's life.

the night and need something. You have to stay with me because Peggy isn't here.' It was then that I realized that Donald had been invited to be a guest and I was invited to take the place of Mahler's servant. I was put on this tiny bed which Peggy, her caretaker, used, and Donald went to the guest room. If people didn't get her orders straight Margaret would prod them with a cane. She used to prod Peggy with it. There was a cane in our relationship, too. She said, 'If I need you I'll bang the cane on the floor.' Every time I nearly fell asleep, I would hear the cane banging. At one point she woke me up and said, 'I need my back rubbed.' Then she woke me up again at 5 o'clock and said, 'You can get my breakfast.' I said, 'I'm sure Donald would like to join us for breakfast.' She said, 'Wake Donald! Oh no. He needs to get his rest.'"

Margaret's father, Dr. Gustav Schoenberger, was born in Fertoszent-miklos, a town near Sopron. Since his native language was Hungarian and his wife's was German, the children were forced to speak German with their

Margaret Schoenberger as an adolescent in 1915.

mother and Hungarian with their father, which may well have contributed to Mahler's difficulty with speaking English and her heavy laborious style of writing. Dr. Schoenberger was an exceptional man who was worthy of being the father of so illustrious a daughter. He was a prominent physician and the recipient of many government honors. A high ranking commissioner of health of the entire district and a general practitioner, he conducted most of his business at his residence, although he had a lovely office in the town hall. One can assume from his preference that he enjoyed being at home and near his loved ones.

He was the first president of the Jewish community of Sopron, and the head of the local hospital. Accepted in the leading society of Sopron as part of an exceptional group in Hungary, he was a high ranking member of the "elite" Jewish group of citizens. He built a magnificent old age home for Jews in Sopron almost singlehandedly, with government grants and matching government contributions. The building still stands, as a monument to the philanthropic doctor, as well as a home for the aged. A plaque is still there which says, "This is the home which was erected under the leadership of Dr. Gustav M. Shoenberger." The outstanding physician and humanitarian served as an ego ideal and role model for Margaret as long as she lived. She thought her wish to work with children perhaps was a compromise formation.[16] She hoped to be a physician like her father, but wanted to work with children as a testimonial to her femininity, to become "a baby doctor" as well as an analyst.

Nevertheless, when she developed problems with the opposite sex, she did not blame the father who insisted she remain single, or the mother who told Margaret she was ugly, but ascribed her difficulties to her lack of acceptance of a feminine role. She never really thought she was womanly or submissive enough, and, unsurprisingly in the light of her father's admonitions, always had to feel superior to men. When her beautiful younger sister entered adolescence surrounded by admirers, Margaret applied herself to reading about Einsteinian relativity. She absolutely denied that she was an attractive woman, and refrained from looking in mirrors until she reached her sixties. Margaret was sure no man would ever love her, and if perchance one did he was immediately devalued in her mind.

It was her mother's view of Margaret as an ugly woman rather than her father's kinder judgement that largely determined her wretched self image. Despite her profound love for Dr. Schoenberger, Margaret did not believe his voice was the controlling one in the family. When Lucy Freeman remarked[17] that she gathered Margaret's father was the dominant force in the family, Margaret denied it. She said, "Oh no, not in my family or in my life. Far from it. My mother was the dominant force. Only in influence, a constructive influence, was my father the force."

As we're known since Freud, a good joke is a voice from the unconscious. Like the typical Hungarian, Mahler enjoyed a play on words. Perhaps her favorite joke, as told to me by Dr. Leo Madow,[18] best illustrates her attitude toward men. Dr. Madow said, "A woman was walking down the street and met a soldier. She stopped him and said, 'Would you like to have a party?' He agreed and went up to her room with her. After it was over she said, 'How about some money?' He answered, 'A gentleman officer never takes money.'" We laughed, and Dr. Madow said, "I guess that tells a lot about Margaret Mahler's views about men."

High School in Budapest (1911–1916)

From the time she was very little, Margaret identified with her beloved physician father and wanted to be a doctor herself. Just as Mahler would defy the dogmas of psychoanalysis when she didn't believe in them (i.e., "Margaret couldn't hold back from giving advice [to her patients]. She wasn't nearly as classical as she thought she was"[19]), Dr. Schoenberger listened to his heart rather than to the mores of the times. Thus he had some very advanced ideas about child rearing for the early nineteen hundreds, when no middle schools were available for girls in Sopron. There was a lyceum, a real gymnasium, and three very good high schools in the town, but girls were not allowed to attend them. Margaret went up to the sixth grade in Sopron, where she received an education perhaps equivalent to that of American junior high schools. Her father had studied at the University of Vienna. Margaret wanted to follow in his footsteps and study in Vienna but it was more convenient for her to go to gymnasium in Budapest where she could stay with her Aunt Irma, her mother's sister. This aunt disliked her niece

Margaret Schoenberger in late adolescence, 1917.

intensely. Margaret suspected it was because her own mother didn't like her either and used to complain about her to Irma. Such things usually work two ways, and Margaret ended up disliking Aunt Irma as much as Irma disliked her. Nevertheless, Margaret felt she had no choice but to live with auntie. If she had not had a relative to stay with, Margaret suspected that her parents would not have let her leave home at so early an age. To begin the first step of the long voyage ahead, Margaret "bit the bullet" and agreed to stay with the despised aunt, for she always knew it was a temporary arrangement and that one day she would train in Vienna.

To Margaret's everlasting gratitude, Dr. Schoenberger allowed her to go to school in Budapest in order to be given a so-called "higher daughter" education in a higher daughter school (Hohere Tochter Schule) where she could round out her middle school education. She was only the second young girl from a "good" background in all of Sopron to go away to school.

It was crucial for her future development that Margaret's father encouraged her differentiation from his way of thinking and her path to individuation. Dr. Schoenberger gave the fourteen-year-old the choice of either going to Switzerland and finishing school or of sticking to her plan to switch to the gymnasium. He really was against her leaving home, because he felt it was not the right thing for "a nice little girl from a small Hungarian town" to go off into the world herself. Also, we can suspect that he wanted to keep the child of his heart close to his side. Nevertheless, he acquiesced to her wish. One must admire a parent who is able to rise above his own preferences and allow his child to develop along the lines of her own choice. It is a rare parent even today who can do that. Without Dr. Schoenberger's support of separation-individuation in his daughter's life, she might never have been able to develop the theory. Margaret said, "My father had such confidence in me that it seems almost ridiculous nowadays to say, but he felt that my judgment was completely competent, and neither he nor my mother were over-protective parents. I am very very grateful for that."[20]

A bit later in her life, he further demonstrated his remarkable emotional support of his daughter. As chief public officer of his district, Dr. Schoenberger frequently escorted extremely disturbed psychotics to the state hospital in neighboring Pressburg. He knew nothing about the differences between psychiatry and psychoanalysis, and was contemptuous of how little was done for the patients. Yet when Margaret told her father she was interested in psychoanalysis, he read Freud, even though he had been disparaging of psychiatry. Margaret appreciated his open-mindedness all her life. His confidence in his daughter helped her to become the person she needed to be. It is interesting that, with such a father, there is no evidence that Margaret had any need for adolescent rebelliousness.

Margaret prepared for the admissions examination to the Vaci Utca[21] high school in Budapest and enrolled there for her last two years. The young girl went in and out of her aunt's home in Budapest, as she couldn't live with her parents in Sopron and attend *Vaci Utca*. Margaret was lonely living in a house where she was unwanted and unloved. She said, "My parents remained in the small town. They would not come. I begged them to come and they didn't make it."[22] One can imagine how painful it was for the fourteen-year-old girl to be living away from home in an atmosphere where she breathed in hostility with the air. The situation was a confirmation of her lifelong feelings of rejection by her mother and a repetition of the worst trauma of her childhood.

With her undaunted way of overcoming adversity, Margaret found a surrogate home with her friend Alice on Nap Hegy (Sun Hill), one of the gentle, tree-laden hills of Buda. Budapest is a city of two parts, separated by the Danube. The Buda side is hilly and dotted with old churches, castles, ramparts, and elegant homes. The natural setting, with its combination of the hills and the river, was beautiful, and the stylish apartment houses and wide avenues lined with trees made for a pleasant environment. Margaret soon began to enjoy Budapest, known as "The Eastern European Paris." People often walked along the promenade by the Danube on summer evenings. With Margaret's love of nature, we can imagine her strolling with her friend along the gray stone river wall, delighted by the sound and smell of the silvery-green waters of the Danube. She must have loved the tall grasses, the red and yellow wildflowers on the river's banks, and the sweet smell of violets sold along the streets in the springtime by peasant woman hoping to earn enough to pay for their next meal. She would have loved, too, the acacias and lilacs which bloomed after the May showers, and the apricots, plums, chrysanthemums and lilacs budding on the hill. But most of all she loved being the best friend of Alice, who later on became the first wife of Michael Balint and the author of the remarkable book *The Psychology of the Nursery*. It was a wonderful experience for the girls to live together for a time while attending Vaci Utca. To add to Margaret's delight, Alice's mother was Vilma Kovacs,[23] a distinguished Hungarian analyst in analysis with Ferenczi. Alice frequently took the lonely Margaret home with her to Nap Hegy, where the kindhearted Kovacs treated her with compassion and love, almost as if she were their adopted child.

When the girls were about fifteen years old, an event took place which was to change Margaret's life forever, along with the history of developmental theory. Alice made off with her mother's copy of Ferenczi's newly published essay on Freud's psychoanalytic theory, the lectures that Ferenczi had delivered at Clark University in Worcester, Massachusetts, in 1909. The girls read the paper surreptitiously underneath a school desk. We can almost hear them giggling under the bench. Margaret saw in the article how analysis works and its therapeutic possibilities and realized immediately that she wanted to become a psychoanalyst. Then Alice found a more forbidden paper, Freud's Three Essays on the Theory of Sexuality, which the girls devoured with even greater avidity, and discovered for the first time the theory of infantile sexuality. Margaret, with her gift of insight, knew right away that the book was a great discovery. It left her with an unshakeable belief in the existence of the unconscious, a sophisticated conviction for a fifteen-year-old in provincial Hungary, or anywhere else, for that matter.

Mahler said later[24] that she was happy to have begun her analytic studies with the reading of Freud's original work. She believed that many people nowadays, especially young colleagues and candidates, learn about Freud through the inferences and elaborations of his followers. They not only want to save time, but somewhat defensively are more comfortable being further away from the source.

Psychoanalysis really began for Margaret in the living room of the Kovacs, who ran a kind of salon for psychoanalysts, where the majority were important lay analysts. The participants treated Margaret and Alice like grown-ups, and allowed them to take part in the adult conversations on many topics, including psychoanalysis. The atmosphere there was very different from that in Vienna, Margaret said, where it was "Leave the children out. This is for grown-ups."[25] At the salon, she met important Hungarian analysts like Therese Benedek, R.C. Bak, Imre Herman, and the great Sandor Ferenczi, who introduced the eager students to their thinking on the importance of the early mother-child relationship in the development of emotional health and illness. There she also found a broad cultural atmosphere, where people like Geza Roheim, the famous anthropologist, and Robert Bereny, the painter who became famous for his caricatures of the first and second generation of psychoanalysts, congregated. As Margaret said about the members of the salon, "They dwelt among the Titans." According to Mahler,[26] it was the Hungarian analysts who coined the expression "dual unity," the concept of two separate individuals functioning as one being. These ideas made a lot of sense to a girl who had experienced the lack of such a relationship with her mother, and were to become the bedrock of her life's work. Margaret said, "I am more and more aware that my Budapest time was by far the most important influence for my later professional life."[27]

News Items, 1919–1920[28]

The law of Numerus clausus was proposed in August 1919 by the Budapest University medical school, which originally targeted limiting the number of women at the university, which did not include religious or ethnical discrimination at that time. Later the dean of the theological school (Kmosk-Mihßly) proposed to extend the limitations on an ethnical basis because of the dominant number of Jews at the medical, legal and arts faculties. The law of Numerus clausus was passed in 1920.

News Items, 1919–1920

Hitler discharged from the army. Expanded his influence in the party. He formed a group of thugs he uses to quash disorder at party meetings and to break up rival party's meetings. The group later became the Sturmabteilung, or S.A., the brown-shirted storm troopers. In 1920 Hitler chose the swastika as the Nazi party emblem.

News Item, 1920

The Kapp Putsch took place in Weimar Germany in March 1920. Wolfgang Kapp was a right-wing journalist who opposed all that he believed Friedrich Ebert stood for, especially after what he considered the humiliation of the Treaty of Versailles. Those who fought for Kapp were future supporters of the fledgling Nazi Party. Ironically, the Erhardt Brigade put a swastika on their helmets to identify who they were.

News Items, 1919–1920

Admiral Miklós Horthy was made commander in chief of the Hungarian armed forces in 1919, and in 1920 was elected regent by the National Assembly. Horthy was head of a right wing, anti–Communist, often anti–Semitic counterrevolutionary government that controlled Hungary from 1920 through the end of World War II. Under Horthy's rule, Hungary became the first post–World War I nationalist dictatorship in Europe, ruthlessly suppressing all political opposition.

News Item, 1921

Hitler accepted as formal leader of the Nazi party, with full dictatorial powers.

2

Medical Training[1]

Margaret Becomes a Physician (1917–1922)

Although Margaret was attending the gymnasium in order to become a medical student, she was afraid to tell her father of her plans, because she thought he was against her becoming a doctor. To make matters worse, he particularly disliked psychiatry, which at that point did little more than institutionalize the unfortunate patients. As the health officer of Oedenberg, which at the time had no state hospital, he often had to take disturbed psychotic patients to Pressbourg, and despaired over the inability of psychiatry to help them get well. Nevertheless, like Lady Macbeth urging her husband to "screw his courage to the sticking place," [2] Margaret braced herself to tell Dr. Schoenberger her plans when she went home for the Easter holidays. To her surprise and delight, she found that the conflict was only in her own head, and that her father wasn't against her studying medicine at all. Once again, he supported her wish. He said wistfully, "For a girl it would be very nice to have a dainty specialty of medicine, for example ophthalmology, and not psychiatry. But darling, if that makes you happy, I am all with you." His reaction was liberating to his loving daughter and became another important milestone in her life. It is easy to understand why Mahler thought separation-individuation was so important. Although she was probably unaware of it at the time, Dr. Schoenberger's acceptance of her need for autonomy at this crossroads of her life started her on the road to becoming the great Margaret Mahler.

Analytical minds may wonder why Margaret believed her father was against her studying medicine when he was so supportive of all other aspects

of her life except marriage. Was it a projection of her own doubts? Was identification with her physician father forbidden in her mind, because medicine was a masculine profession? Was she afraid that as a physician she would
be competing with him and thereby instill his anger? Even worse, did she
sense on some unconscious level that she would surpass him, and, like Macbeth, be killing off the king? Or did the feminine part of her nature have a
foreboding that studying medicine would make it difficult to marry and
have children? We only know that she said, "These vicissitudes were interpolated by my own neurosis between my resolve to study medicine, and —
how would you say, and my self-imposed taboos."[3] For whatever reasons the
"vicissitudes were interpolated" by her neurosis, Margaret's conscious choice
was encouraged by her father and there was no turning back for either one.

Because of Margaret's fear of her father's disapproval, she first enrolled
in the university art department because she was interested in the arts, an
avocation that lasted all her life. She wanted to be a sculptor, but with her
ability to look facts in the face, she soon realized that she wasn't talented
enough. Another person might have been devastated by the recognition that
she lacked the ability to carry out her ambitions, but, characteristically, Margaret made the best of things and enrolled in a course at Budapest University on the esthetics of art. Unfortunately, or perhaps fortunately for
posterity, the faculty of the history of art and esthetics at the university was
not very good at that time and Margaret was bored to tears. So after a single semester she decided to put art aside in terms of a career and enjoy it as
a hobby, the evidence of which can be seen in her extensive collection of
sculptures of mothers and babies and the female body. Because she then felt
secure in the support of her father, she decided to go ahead and become a
physician.

Straightening her backbone again, the courageous young woman
marched into the office of the dean of admissions of the medical school and
declared her wish to matriculate. Despite the fact that she was a young Jewish woman, she must have impressed the dean with her intelligence, ambition, impressive record, and perhaps her ability to assert herself, for she was
immediately admitted to the school. She was even permitted to matriculate
in the middle of the school year, and became an official medical student.
Only a brave young woman could have presumed to undertake such a venture. Only the future Margaret Mahler could have succeeded at it.

After Margaret entered medical school, anti–Semitism spread alarm-
ingly in Hungary, a nation and a culture which had been for the most part
immensely hospitable to Jews and had inspired what was sometimes called
The Golden Age of Jews in Hungary.[4] Frank Hernadi,[5] an independent
Hungarian scholar, gives the following reasons for the rise of anti–Semitism

in 1920 and thereafter: "Jews were falsely blamed, in part, for the loss of the war, and were envied for their education and often for the resulting personal wealth in a ravaged nation. World War I was one of the most devastating losses for Hungary during its entire one thousand year long history: the country was carved up, so that it lost two thirds of its original territory, and with it, eleven million people, more than half of its population. The remaining area was devastated and burdened with immense war reparations for the Allies. The rise of extreme ethnic hatred and hysterical nationalism was the result of a nation going psychotic over its horrible loss. People searched for scapegoats, and whom to blame? In typical discriminatory manner, those who were 'different.'"

Anti-Semitism rose even more drastically under "The White Terror" in Hungary during Admiral Miklós Horthy's regime, when it became impossible for Jews to study in Hungary. Under Horthy's rule, Hungary became the first post–World War I nationalist dictatorship in Europe, ruthlessly suppressing all political opposition. When the numerous clausus, which limited the number of Jews who were permitted to study in universities, was passed, Margaret could no longer stay in Budapest, so she decided to matriculate at the University of Munich medical school. A change of schools was not so unusual in those days, as it was customary for medical students to move from one university to another in order to benefit from the expertise of well-known professors. Her sister, Suzannah, who played the harpsichord and piano, wanted to study with a certain teacher at the Odeon, and was happy to make the move. In addition, they wanted to see as much of the world as they could. So the Schoenberger sisters, Alice Balint, and several young people with whom Margaret had shared a flat went as a body to Munich. Acting as part of a group remained characteristic of Mahler all her life, as she rarely did anything alone.

Margaret had an unusual gift for choosing the most influential and greatest teachers. Professor Meinhard von Pfaundler, one of Germany's leading pediatricians of his times, was director of the Munich University Clinic. Margaret promptly applied for a position with him. To her great pleasure, she was appointed as an *co–Assistentin* at Pfaundler's Children's Clinic. The placement in pediatrics was perfect for the young medical student, since she could not train yet in psychoanalysis, although it always remained in the back of her mind. She also was hired as co–Assistentin by another prominent pediatrician, Dr. Rudolph von Degkwitz, and participated in his pioneer work in developing a serum to prevent measles, which was then a highly dangerous and contagious disease. The work was Margaret's first research activity. She became so enthusiastic about it that it became another landmark in her life. Thrilled with von Degkwitz and his scientific contributions, she made another monumental life decision that her future lay in research.

She spent her first clinical year with von Degkwitz, and did so well that she was appointed an assistant. But, as with millions of others, the horrors of Nazi history again interfered with her plans. After the Kapp Putsch (the Kapp Revolt) of 1920, which she never really understood and was not politically interested enough to investigate, anti–Semitism dramatically intensified. People from Eastern Europe were discriminated against, along with the Jews. Soon an ordnance was passed which forbade Jews from living in Munich proper, and Margaret and Susannah were greatly inconvenienced by a forced move to the suburb of Solln bei Munchen. The additional time required for Margaret to get to school and the clinic complicated her life even more.

One day in the boardinghouse where the students were eating lunch, they were stunned by a sudden break-in of police. The police, in an effort to browbeat them enough to make them leave even suburban Munich, put them in jail for two or three hours. Fortunately, authorities and other influential people arranged to have them released shortly after. Nevertheless, Margaret was shocked and petrified, and the terrifying memory came back to haunt her all her life. Never one to turn her back on reality, the incident confirmed beyond doubt the knowledge that she had to leave Munich.

By this time, Margaret was certain of what her next move would be. She had decided that she wanted to go to school in Jena. Unfortunately, her sister refused to leave Munich. Less able to look truth in the face than Margaret, Susannah denied that they were in danger. She insisted on continuing her harpsichord studies, even though shooting had already broken out around the Odeon Conservatory. Behind her refusal to leave Munich was the knowledge that, if Margaret left Munich, their parents, who considered Susannah too young and unreliable to stay there alone, would insist that she return home. Margaret, remembering her father's admonition to take care of Susannah, was intimidated for a while. But Dr. Schoenberger's belief in Margaret was beginning to show results, as she continued to make progress along the lines of separation-individuation. The miserable living situation in Munich, where the inflation rate was horrendous and supplies were in short supply, further motivated her to overrule her sister's objections and to leave Munich. This meant that Susannah had to go home to Sopron alone, as Margaret shook off her father's edict and looked after her own interests. But Margaret was truly individuating from her father and by this time was able to feel that Susannah was not her responsibility.

Unlike her easy gliding into the Munich medical school, burgeoning anti–Semitism made it extremely difficult for her to gain admission to medical school in Jena. There were already organized anti–Semitic student groups, the so-called ASTA (Allgemeine Studenter Ausschus) (General Students' Committee) who protested the admittance of Jews (including Margaret Schoenberger) to the university. She was in the courtyard of the Jena University when the president of ASTA announced in a speech that the eastern Jewish woman who was admitted to the Jena Medical School was the first in that Aryan institution. Friends standing with her asked who the woman was and Margaret had to say that she was that woman. This was not her first experience with anti–Semitism. She first gained knowledge of its existence when she was only four years old. Pogroms had threatened her maternal grandmother in Esterhaza, the birthplace of her father. As a result, the grandmother had come to live with the Schoenbergers and became Margaret's roommate, thus depriving the little girl of her privacy. A few years later, she experienced a personal attack by her elementary school classmates, who sent a note around the room which said, "Do not talk to Schoenberger, as the Jews crucifed Christ." Margaret was devastated, and cringed inwardly whenever she remembered the incident. Nevertheless, she had been through attacks before and survived. If she could help it, she was not about to let another deter her from getting what she wanted.

Once again Margaret's courageous efforts, although of a different nature to be sure, got her into a medical school. She appealed to the government of the Weimar Republic to admit her, and to anyone else she could think of who might help. One of her sponsors, Professor Peterfly, who like many others was impressed by the talents and determination of the young woman, helped her to see the father of psychoanalyst Peter Blos in Karlsruhe. The senior Blos was a highly influential doctor who fostered her acceptance to the medical school by the government of the Weimar Republic. In spite of the hostility of many faculty members and the pressure of one or two of the most prominent, Margaret Schoenberger became a student at the Medical School of Jena. She was graduated three years later and officially became a doctor of medicine, with a magna cum laude degree. There was no summa cum laude that year and only two magna cum laude. Despite her difficulties in being admitted into the University of Jena, Margaret Mahler was awarded one of them.

She almost didn't get her diploma. Dr. Abel, an anti–Semitic professor, decided that she hadn't had enough time to do her medical studies properly, as she had taken a laboratory technician's course at the same time she was attending medical school. He said that she couldn't possibly have met the requirements of a medical student and was not ready to write the dissertation required at that time. He didn't know Margaret Schoenberger. As usual, she was rescued by a father figure. Professor Jussuf Ibrahim and other people on her side prevailed, and Margaret became a physician.

The Clinics (1920–1922)

Dr. Ibrahim, the foremost child neurologist of the time and author of the important chapter on "Pediatric Neurology" in Emil Feer's major work, Pediatric Textbook, ran a clinic for children in Jena. It says a great deal about Margaret's drive to learn that four of her professors of pediatrics were contributors to the famous Pediatric Textbook With her instinct for knowing what was best for her, Mahler wanted to work with Ibrahim, whom she greatly admired, and where she would be a little closer to her deepest interest, psychoanalysis. If she couldn't study to be an analyst yet, she would do the next best thing and work with infants. Somewhere deep inside her she never doubted that one day she would become a psychoanalyst and the study of infants would serve her well.

At the University of Jena, Mahler enthusiastically became an assistant on the private ward of Ibrahim's Pediatric Clinic. Dr. Ibrahim hired Margaret even before she received her diploma as a physician. She worked on two of Ibrahim's projects at his private sanitarium, both dealing with sick infants. She was a special assistant in caring for the pilorus pilorus "spastic" [sic] infants[6] and also assisted with a second group of babies who fascinated her, the ruminating infant.[7] It perhaps is significant that Margaret, who suffered from intestinal problems of her own, was particularly interested in these babies.

Nevertheless, she was horrified at the physical treatment the ruminating infants received at Ibrahim's clinic. In an effort to force the children to keep their food down, their jawbones were locked into a position where they couldn't possibly have enjoyed eating. Even though the circumstances made it impossible for them to ruminate, they still brought up their food. Margaret felt that Ibrahim did better with the pre-oral spastic babies, whom he had fed with heavier food, which remains in the stomach longer than milk. Most of these children recovered, which Mahler attributed more to the excellent one-to-one nursing they received than to the maxilla placement. Despite their disagreement over the physical treatment of the ruminating infants, Margaret learned a great deal about the emotional side of infants' psychosomatic diseases, and Dr. Ibrahim proved to be a stimulating and inspiring teacher. She felt that of all her pediatric mentors, Ibrahim was most aware of the psyche of the child. All her life Maler felt she owed him a great deal, both for his teaching methods and his relationship with his little patients. It was a great experience for her to watch him play with them. He felt the human approach to small children was extremely important. An unmarried man, he would go to his private clinic on a Sunday, close the doors, and play with the children on the floor. Once, Margaret peeked through the keyhole and saw him riding the babies on his back, piggyback, and playing horsey with them. Children loved him, as they did Margaret Mahler at the Masters Children's Center many decades later.

Unfortunately, that is not the end of Ibrahim's history. Despite his fine work as a pediatrician and teacher, by the time he died in 1952 his reputation had been ruined. Until recently Ibrahim's name was attached to the clinic for child and adolescent medicine at the Friedrich-Schiller-Universität in Jena, the Kinderklinik Jussuf Ibrahim. An investigative commission, however, has concluded that Dr. Jussuf Ibrahim supported the euthanasia program of National Socialist Germany, and that from 1941 he took an active part in the killing of severely sick and handicapped children, defined by the Nazis as "unworthy life." As a result of the committee's findings, Ibrahim's name no longer is associated with the clinic. It is difficult to reconcile the image of the man who played horsey with babies with the Nazi who killed off sick children, but it becomes a bit easier when one recalls the locked jawbone apparatus in which he imprisoned them. Regardless, his downfall is another tragedy of the Holocaust. As Mahler felt that of all her pediatrician mentors, Ibrahim was most aware of the psyche of the child, let us hope that she never heard about the destruction of her idol. It would have broken her heart.

After Margaret finished medical school in Jena, she went to study in Heidelberg for two semesters. There she became quite sick. At the age of fourteen or fifteen, she had been struck down by an unsuccessful appendectomy. She suffered dreadfully with abdominal pain and symptoms which suggested a strangulation of the intestines. Later Mahler said that she was sure that her illness had psychological meaning, even though the surgery had been repaired very badly. Like the sword of Damocles, the constant threat hung over her head that she would have a new seizure and her abdomen would need to be cut wide open. One doesn't have to postulate castration anxiety to understand her terror.

The attacks of abdominal pain became increasingly severe, and Margaret, who was now twenty-four years old, was put on antispasmodic medication. This helped diminish the pain, but she experienced so many setbacks and difficulties that the surgeons and the internists called a meeting to decide on further treatment. One famous surgeon recommended that she have an exploratory operation. To alleviate the intolerable pain and its interference with her life, she decided to follow his recommendation, despite the fact that the internists disagreed with him. She was diagnosed with Heirshsprung disease, a congenital disorder of the colon rectum which is unable to relax and permit the passage of stool. For a while everyone feared that it would be necessary to cut out a piece of her colon, which before the age of antibiotics was a dangerous, life threatening operation.

Her father disliked the idea of the surgery, even though he had to give his consent. When Dr. Schoenberger was ambivalent about attending an event, he dragged his heels at attending it. As he would at Margaret's wedding much later in their lives, he arrived at the hospital too late to be of service. Margaret became more and more convinced that he had been late because he couldn't bear the thought of her being operated on with a possible colostomy. We can only imagine the fright experienced by the ailing young woman before she was carried into the operating room, as she anxiously awaited the father who never came.

Margaret was right; they did have to open up her abdomen. But surprisingly enough after the dramatic prologue to surgery it turned out that she was suffering only from severe adhesions. The surgeons removed them, and she recovered very quickly. It is interesting that in her interview with Dr. Swerdloff,[8] Mahler simply recited the physiological facts about her illness and surgery, without giving any psychological insight. It seems highly likely that the young girl was extremely homesick and longed to be with her parents.

After she got well, Mahler led an interesting life in Jena, the home of the Jena Glassworks and the Zeiss factory.[9] In this highly sophisticated atmosphere, Margaret took pleasure in attending the lectures of various evening schools and the many beautiful concerts. Even though Jena was characterized by strong Anti-Semitism, it was a university town and boasted many progressive students and faculty. Always one to take advantage of cultural benefits, Margaret enjoyed her stay in Jena. She also was very near to Weimar, where the Bauhaus of the famous architect Gropius[10] was situated, which, with her love of art, she enjoyed visiting.

From Jena she went to Heidelberg. Perhaps because "it takes one to know one," Margaret always was able to make friends with the cream of the literary and academic worlds. At Heidelberg she became a friend of the poet Friedrich Gundolf and Dr. Emil Lederer, an important professor of economics who often held open house. Many well known people, such as the philosopher Karl Jaspers, whose work on psychopathology fascinated Margaret, and Max Weber, the sociologist, came to the open houses. Other sociologists who attended included the Hungarian Nicholas Halasi. Margaret always felt welcome in the circle that met at Lederer's house. The discussions held by the group were deep and broad. The young Margaret voraciously read everything she could get her hands on that figured in their conversations, thus broadening her knowledge of the arts, the sciences, the humanities, and politics.

Margaret was good in groups, and enjoyed Lederer's open houses very much. They reminded her of the wonderful times she had at the home of the Kovacs in Budapest when she was a girl. As was becoming more and more evident, Margaret had a penchant for gathering loving fathers around her. Another friend she met at the Lederers who was unbelievably fatherly to her was the famous scientist Karl Mannheim. His wife, Julia Mannheim, was a Hungarian who later became a psychoanalyst in the clique who clustered around Anna Freud.

Margaret's parents were very eager to get her back home, but she was strongly individuating and didn't want to live with them any more. As a compromise, right after her graduation from Jena in 1922, she moved to Vienna. She had never really lived in Vienna before, but it was only forty minutes from Sopron, which was practically a suburb of Vienna. It was about one hour and a quarter by the little four cylinder Austin she drove to visit her parents. She applied right away for a residency at the university and worked there pending her nostrification[11] to gain her medical diploma and license for Vienna.

News Item, 1923

On November 8 1923, Hitler led an attempt to take over the local Bavarian government in Munich in a move known as the "Beer Hall Putsch." The coup was not successful, but he used the action to gain publicity for himself and his ideas. Hitler was arrested, charged with treason, and sentenced to five years in prison. During his incarceration, Hitler began writing *Mein Kampf.*

In between these years, there was a plebiscite for the population of Sopron. The people could choose to be either Hungarians or Austrians. Mahler got her Austrian papers around 1926, so that she also could apply for a license to practice in Vienna. By the end of 1923, she took her examinations in forensic medicine, which physicians who were trained in Germany had to pass in order to obtain an Austrian license. In similar vein, if a physician had an Austrian diploma and sought a license to practice in Germany, he or she had to take exams in skin and venereal diseases. That was the "nostrification" which validated a medical degree acquired outside the country. Margaret and the wife of Sigfried Bernfeld studied together and thoroughly coached each other until they could say the material backward and forward. We don't know about Mrs. Bernfeld, but Margaret, as usual, passed with flying colors.

At the time Margaret was taking a class to prepare for her nostrification, there was a famous criminal case of a crafty female murderer of children. Her name was Vukobrankovitch. She had been assigned to Professor

Haberda by the court. With her customary packed schedule, Margaret did not have time to follow the newspapers or gossip about the murder. There were twenty or twenty-five young men taking the whole gamut of medical school examinations, whereas she took only the nostrification in forensic medicine. To her surprise, Professor Haberda, who was teaching the class, turned to Margaret and her male colleagues and said, "Gentlemen, the Frau Dr. Schoenberger and Mrs. Vukobrankovitch have given me much more clever answers than you!" When she entered the von Pirquet Clinic the next day, everybody knew "the little Schoenberger" had been paired with Vuko-brankovitch, the murderess.

Margaret had always wanted to keep in contact with the psychoana-lytic movement, but was too busy before she passed her nostrification. Right after the exam she got herself an appointment as an aid to the brilliant physi-cian and researcher, Baron Clemens von Pirquet, which eventually was to lead her to the desired path of psychoanalysis.

At the clinic there was a kind of sub-clinic, or department, called *Heilpedagogik*, translated as remedial education. It was something between a child guidance clinic and child psychiatry, under the chairmanship of a Dr. Lazar. Margaret did not like what she saw in Dr. Lazar's department and thought it was contradictory to what she believed in. The remedial ped-agogic department was a mess. At that time there were no child guidance clinics. It was an inpatient child psychiatric ward, and, at the same time, its outpatient department was very busy. Mahler said,[12] "They dispensed the kind of child psychiatry that I would never, never want to see again, any-where! They just didn't know what to do with those kids." More boys than girls were brought for treatment, as they were taken there only when they were a disturbance to the family. As an example of the "treatment" advo-cated in the clinic, most of the boys had undescended testicles. The doc-tors performed an operation to pull them down. Mahler said, "You can imagine, all these children had a very great change of personality." She said that if she had been at a psychiatric institute, she would have spoken up, but it would have done no good at von Pirquet's clinic. That was one of the things that drove her to go back to Vienna to study psychoanalysis.

Although she disagreed vehemently with his psychological approach and felt she was exploited as a woman, Margaret enjoyed working with the highly esteemed and handsome Dr. von Pirquet. He had the profile of a movie star, a tall stature, strikingly bright blue eyes, and fine features that radiated charm and kindness. A gentleman, he dressed carefully, talked in simple language, and had a good sense of humor. In addition, he was a brilliant, famous man who spoke many languages and was known as a *Prachtmensch*, a Renaissance man. One could venture to say that she had a typical adolescent crush on the doctor. Many women besides Margaret were fascinated by him, but he remained faithful to his sick wife all his life.

They called Margaret's position Hilfarztin (doctor's helper). Even though she was an enormous help to the doctor, her rank was lower than an assistant's. Von Pirquet was a great anti-feminist, and never once had a female associate. He liked Margaret and was very generous in awarding her privileges like finding her interesting and closely related jobs, but he never gave her a full assistant's title. Although she claimed she was not a women's liberation person, she asked him "just as a sidelight" why she couldn't be officially an assistant.[13] He answered, "I will never have a woman as an assistant. I like you very much and you can stay here as long as you want to, but if one looks like you, then one marries and has children." I imagine his "explanation" didn't go over too well with Margaret Mahler. But there is no record that her famous temper came into action in response. Another incident occurred between Mahler and von Pirquet which smacks of anti-feminism. Mahler had just gotten her first pair of glasses. Von Pirquet said to her, "Would you do me a favor? Would you just put those eye glasses into your pocket? I can't look at you. It doesn't fit you." She had to look like his idea of a woman, no matter whether she could see well or not.

Despite his prejudice, he correlated a paper he was writing with one of her articles on the two peaks of the enlargement of the tonsils in childhood. She had visited all the kindergartens and schools of Vienna, and measured the size of the many hundred, perhaps even a couple of thousand, sets of tonsils. Then the two investigators, the new and the old, conceptualized their findings. He was very interested in statistics and the nutrition of infants. A man ahead of his times, he created the "nem" (the acronym of the nutritional equivalent of milk) system of nutrition, which was very close to the modern calory count.

It is interesting that a different account of Mahler's collaboration with von Pirquet is given in *Clemens Von Pirquet: His Life and Work*,[14] by Richard Wagner. Von Pirquet designed a chart called *Size of Tonsils in 5,670 Children*, using Mahler's statistics (p. 180). Yet no mention of her name is made either in the chart or the book. Even worse, Wagner states that von Pirquet "assigned to an *intern* the task of assessing the size of tonsils of a statistically significant number of normal children during each year of childhood." Von Pirquet was known as a generous man, but he certainly wasn't magnanimous in giving credit to Margaret Schoenberger, where it was due.

It was dismaying how much she liked von Pirquet as a person, unhappy as she was with his unpsychological approach. "I think I was a little bit in love with him," she admitted. "I adored Pirquet. But at the same time, I somewhere knew in my gut that what he did was absolutely wrong."[15]

Von Pirquet was a brilliant man, perhaps a genius, and Margaret was always fascinated with great intellects. He was an innovative and creative thinker. For example, he detected allergy in 1906 when no one else knew anything about it, and used the term for the first time to describe an "altered response" of his patients' bodies. He also originated a skin test for tuberculosis, and he and Schick discovered important facts about antitoxins, in regard to the time required for formation of antibodies. Johns Hopkins Hospital in Baltimore hired him as the first full professor of pediatrics when he was only thirty-five years old. Margaret was besotted with his research, which she found absolutely fascinating. She was always interested in one form of research or another, and the statistical approach in following a disease is a motif that runs through all her work Perhaps being human, she was as impressed by the fact that von Pirquet was a baron as by his good looks and charm. But still his treatment of babies gnawed at her. With her characteristic directness, Margaret talked about the distressing psychological situation to von Pirquet, but it was too far removed from his real interests for him to really hear her. Despite his intellectual brilliance, he wasn't able to see what was obvious to his young assistant, that infants need mothering if they are to survive. For example, she noted that those babies who were especially cared for, like the floor maid's baby, got better, while the "boxed" babies sickened even more and died. As a result, she was very unhappy at the clinic, especially after Béla Schick, the adjunct of the chief, von Pirquet, left for America. Schick was somebody who saw the whole child, whereas von Pirquet, despite his brilliance, saw only the organs from the somatic side. Margaret didn't learn very much about pediatrics, as she spent most of her time helping the chief with his endless statistics and diagrams. In contrast, she had learned a great deal from Schick. It was a lonely position she took on the needs of infants after Schick left. She knew the time was fast approaching when she wouldn't be able to work with von Pirquet any longer.

The baron himself must have been an unhappy person. He and his wife committed suicide together when he was only fifty-five years old. None of his colleagues had any idea he was contemplating killing himself. The verdict at the inquest was suicide by cyanide poisoning. The suicide was carefully premeditated, and carried out with cool deliberation and firm purpose, the action of a man who wished to end his life at his own convenience. Freud said[16] that every person wishes to die in his own way. Von Pirquet succeeded in it.

The curve of von Pirquet's creativity shows a sharp ascent in his youth, a long period of mature productivity, and a slow decline as he approached his fiftieth year. Like most geniuses, he had reached the apex of his creativity at the age of thirty. In seeking a motive, it seems clear that he had reached the end of his reserves and was unwilling to continue a life that no longer was of interest to him. Goethe gave the only explanation that makes any sense. He wrote,[17] "Every exceptional person has a certain mission he is called upon to fulfill. When he has accomplished it, he is no longer needed on earth." In the case of von Pirquet, being a baron, a brilliant, handsome man, and a famous innovator obviously were not enough to keep him alive as he plummeted the downhill spiral of his creativity.

Late in her life, Mahler received a copy of Wagner's book, where she first found out about the suicide. She had little comment to make about it, at least any that is recorded. If she knew why von Pirquet killed himself, at least to this writer's knowledge she never said so.

After she left the von Pirquet clinic, Mahler joined the staff of another institution in Vienna, the Moll Well Baby Clinic, the Mutter Beratungs Stelle (Mother Advice Center), where the thinking was much closer to her own. The institute, she said,[18] "had an avant-garde, really progressive policy, namely that a baby not only belongs to a mother, but that the mother or a mothering person must remain with a sick baby if the baby is to get well." Dr. Leopold Moll was one of the first physicians to understand how important it was to help the mother in order to heal the baby. His philosophy was like Anna Freud's, who said that, for babies, love is the mental vitamin. The love-starved infants died in droves at the von Pirquet clinic and elsewhere of severe alimentary disturbances that nobody sees anymore, like toxic diarrhea. People at the clinic had no idea that the infants might survive if their mothers attended them. In contrast to von Pirquet, who believed in keeping babies in glass cubicles so as not to get any bacteria inside the cases, the Moll hospital was architecturally connected to a baby-nurses' school. The young student nurses, who were known worldwide as the "Moll sisters," all loved babies. Each was assigned a sick infant. The nurses would be with "their" baby constantly. Every baby had a young mothering person all for himself or herself who was encouraged to walk the baby up and down, day and night, if necessary.

The results were dramatic. The diarrhea stopped. Children who would have died if they had been in any other hospital were brought out of their comatose, toxic condition. The babies seemed to thrive, and most of them got well, although many of them had been as sick as the von Pirquet babies. It was a completely different situation than in the von Pirquet clinic, where statistics did not look beyond the body. Mahler said,[19] "I learned there only what one shouldn't do in child psychiatry." Students at von Pirquet's weren't free to criticize anything about him or the clinic. But at Moll's they could speak their minds and be listened to. Margaret wanted to write a paper comparing her experiences at Pirquet's with those at the Moll Clinic, but she never did. Till the day she died, she continued to reproach herself that she had lacked the courage.

To help earn her keep, Margaret spent a pleasant summer with the Moll transports of children. Moll had a group of young patients who were at risk for tuberculosis whom he took to Italy. Margaret went with them as a physician, and earned enough to travel further to Florence, Venice, Ravenna, and so forth. One city she refrained from visiting at the time was Rome. She said she wanted to have enough leisure to really see it. She didn't get to the Eternal City until the late fifties, when she flew there from the United States, and presumably she had enough time to take it in to her heart's content.

As far as Margaret's pediatric mentors go, Professor Pfaundler had a long and successful career as a pediatrician. His only recorded catastrophe was the bombing of his house during the war. While little is known about the personal life of Moll, of Mahler's other mentors — von Pirquet, who committed suicide, Ibrahim, who became a Nazi, and von Degkwitz — it seems that the latter was the least traumatized. He had a lengthy, prosperous family and professional life. Married to Dr. Kleinschmidt, a child psychiatrist, their son also became a psychiatrist. Years later, the junior Dr. von Degkwitz wrote and asked Mahler for a copy of a paper she had published. She was happy to respond and to inform him of her past experiences with his father.

News Items, 1924–1929

Hitler was released from prison in December 1924 after serving only six months of his sentence. At that time, the Nazi Party and its associated newspapers were banned by the government and Hitler was forbidden to speak publicly. The support for National Socialism was waning throughout Germany. Nevertheless, Hitler managed to increased the party membership and develop the organization of the Nazi party throughout Germany. He also created the infamous SS (Schutzstaffel), which was initially intended to be Hitler's bodyguard.

3

Her Analysts

Helene Deutsch (1926–1927)

While she was working at the von Pirquet clinic, Margaret went into a training analysis. She had stayed in touch with her girlhood friend, Alice Kovacs, who by that time had married the analyst Michael Balint and was Alice Balint. Margaret knew she had to find an analyst and discussed finding one with Alice. A potential analysand had little choice in those days but to consult a friend who was in analysis or happened to know a practicing analyst. Now there are referrals by physicians, professional referral services, and recommendations by training societies, along with knowledgeable friends. Alice put Margaret in touch with her mother, Mrs. Vilma Kovacs, who was in a training analysis with the incomparable Sandor Ferenczi. She contacted him about Margaret. By this time, there was a whole flock of educators who were interested in psychoanalysis. Margaret joined them soon after she arrived in Vienna, where Willi Hoffer had gotten her involved in his new venture, a periodical, *The Zeitschrift fur Psychoanalytische Pedagogik*. Margaret assisted him with it, which gave her the opportunity to meet many colleagues who shared her interests. Margaret also went to see the great Paul Federn and asked him to analyze her, but he refused to take her on. She never understood why, but it is interesting that this woman who was anything but shy speculated that perhaps she had not been aggressive enough in her request.

Before Margaret made her selection of analyst, she happened to be a guest at the Kovacs' home. Sandor Ferenczi, whom she loved and admired, was also there. According to Mahler,[1] Dr. Ferenczi was a warm and brilliant person. He was informal, yet he also had great stature. He was not afraid of being relaxed about his position. He enjoyed talking with her and letting her free associate. She told him a story right away about how she as a child would watch over her father during his nap by going around with the fly swatter and swatting flies. The story delighted him. "Ferenczi sparkled," she said. "He had so many ideas. I think Ernest Jones did him a great disservice in his Freud biography, in that he really did not quite stick to the historic truth. That is not only my opinion about Jones. He was tremendously jealous."

In *A Biographical Sketch of Elizabeth Gero-Heymann*, Abby Adams-Silvan[2] augments Mahler's portrait of Ferenczi as an inspiration to students. "He was a good teacher," she says, quoting Gero-Heymann. "Very generous and just not at all narcissistic. We met at his house. He reached out, encouraged students who were hesitant to speak, and he seemed never to forget anything. He wrote down everything in his diaries, even what he had for dinner or what film he saw. He never wasted a minute. If a patient were late he would sit down and write in his diary, his book, or a paper. His book is still a classic. It will never be outdated."

Margaret talked with Ferenczi about her need for analysis, and he recommended that she go to a woman analyst. He felt she would have an easier time with a man, since she had a better relationship with her father than her mother, but would undergo a much deeper analysis with a woman. Margaret took his advice and selected Helene Deutsch for her analyst. It turned out to be a catastrophic decision.

In 1926, after undue pressure from her analyst, Ferenczi, Deutsch agreed to put Margaret on her waiting list for a training analysis. In her over-concern for her father, who was a physician on a fixed salary and still had a child he was putting through expensive training at the Academy of Music, Margaret told herself she could not afford the usual cost of analysis. When she found out through the grapevine that there were "deserving" applicants or candidates who got a training analysis for much less than the usual fee, she swallowed her pride and applied to Deutsch for a low-fee training analysis. Margaret had another feeling that induced her to ask for a reduced fee: It was arrogance. She knew that her father would have paid for the sessions, even if he had to take out a loan, but she felt she should not have to pay for her analysis like everybody else. Years of her father's affirmations of her superiority had convinced Margaret that she was an "exception" and should be treated like one. The feeling was strengthened by Ferenczi's opinion that she "deserved only the best," including a free training analysis. Such an attitude was not the best way to begin analytic treatment, especially with a narcissistic woman like Helene Deutsch.

After a very long time, during which Mahler was terrified that Deutsch had changed her mind about analyzing her, the long awaited call came through. It was not until 1926, *four years* after Margaret had applied for an analysis with her, that Deutsch informed Mahler they could begin their analytic work.

Unfortunately, the first session began with the analyst's comment, "I have taken you as my patient ninety percent for the sake of Dr. Ferenczi, and ten percent because you seem to be a nice human being." From that moment on Mahler said she did nothing in the analysis but try to prove to Deutsch that she was ninety percent a "nice human being." (Deutsch's statement was unconscionable, and unthinkable from a supposedly neutral analyst today.)

Deutsch was an exquisite lady. For a woman like Margaret who did not think of herself as attractive, Deutsch was an awesome role model. Margaret particularly admired her lovely eyes. She had come from Poland, and Margaret associated her with the Madonna of Czestochowa, the dazzling miracle-working protectress of the Polish people with mysterious healing powers. On an unconscious level, she no doubt hoped that Deutsch would utilize her omnipotence and resolve Margaret's problems with career, mother and men in one fell swoop. In adolescent fashion, she was full of admiration and awe for the stunning, famous analyst who was a direct analytic descendant of Freud, and she fantasied that she would become Deutsch's favorite child. Unfortunately, her feelings were not reciprocated. Margaret didn't make it with Deutsch any more than she did with her own mother. Hints of this began to seep through very soon in her analysis. In the first session, Deutch told Margaret that she had a "sticky libido." Margaret countered with a satiric dream in which she was stuck to a freshly painted toilet seat. On an unconscious level, her disappointment with the analyst had begun.

Deutsch was a good friend of the famous analyst, Sandor Rado. Once, during one of Margaret's sessions, Deutsch received a phone call from Berlin. It was Rado and of course it made a big impression on Margaret. It was in the middle of the hour, and Deutsch asked her patient to go out of the room, as she had a long distance call. Was this another indication of trouble brewing in Margaret's analysis? Margaret thought so. (Analysts today do not accept phone calls during sessions, and even if Deutsch had answered the phone, she could have told Rado that she was working and would return his call later.)

Deutsch seems to have had quite a conflict about Margaret's analysis. She also had quite a conflict with two of her other patients. She was writing one of her books at the time, and more often than not Mahler got a telephone call in the morning from Deutsch's chamber maid saying, "Dr.

Deutsch is very sorry but she cannot see you today; come next week."At the same time, Mahler knew that her close friend, Dr. Fanny von Hahn Kende, who had come from Budapest for analysis and therefore had less time than Margaret, was seen by Deutsch in every one of her assigned sessions. Fanny was somewhat older than Margaret and had a family. At the time, she was in the process of getting a divorce, and it was urgent for her to get through her analysis as quickly as possible. Margaret knew it would be very easy to rationalize why Fanny was considered first. Nevertheless she was terribly upset about the situation. It was too close to her childhood experience, when Suzannah was so obviously the preferred sibling. Margaret was painfully aware that Fanny was getting five or six hours of analysis a week, while she at most had three or four and was given extra long Christmas and Easter vacations. As the friends were together day and night, Margaret always was advised when Dr. van Kende had her sessions. The pain this caused her was too much like watching her sister be nursed. She was unable to talk with her friend without complaining about the terrible things Deutsch was doing to her. Mahler said,[3] "Fanny and I acted out quite crazily. She had two or three much younger sisters, to whom she was not only an older sister but a little mother, and she did the same thing with me." Fanny reported in her analytic hours about Margaret in detail, until the frustrated Deutch gave her an ultimatum: "Either give up the friendship with Margaret Schoenberger or leave the analysis!"

When Margaret heard of Deutsch's decree, she thought it sounded like what happened to Victor Tausk. She heard from von Hahn Kende a story Deutsch had told her. When she was in analysis with Freud, who didn't want to take Tausk into analysis, he finagled Dr. Deutsch to analyze him. Deutsch could not do anything in her analysis but talk about Tausk. Freud said to her, "Listen, this must stop! You are not analyzing yourself. All you do is talk about Dr. Tausk's analysis." Dr. Victor Tausk committed suicide, after Freud rejected him for analysis. The incident was glossed over by Freud and his followers, a tradition usually emulated by Mahler.

Nevertheless, she was terribly shocked by what had happened to Tausk, and identified with him herself. It is even possible she thought of suicide, considering the depths of her despair, which almost certainly revived the pain she felt at her mother's rejection. To make matters worse, although Margaret had to leave the treatment, von Hahn Kende was permitted to remain in analysis with Deutsch. It speaks well for Mahler's character that she and Fanny were able to remain good friends. They renewed their friendship when Fanny came to New York and Margaret, who loved Fanny dearly, saw her up to the time of her death.

Mahler had a crush on her beautiful analyst, a perfectly appropriate reaction in psychoanalysis known as "transference.[4]" She felt that her love for Deutsch was one of the things the analyst could not handle, or didn't want to handle. Deutsch was treated like an empress or a queen by the other members of the society, most of whom were in awe of her. Her regal bearing and aristocratic look made Margaret worship her all the more. Perhaps Deutsch sensed that someday Mahler would supercede her as the Empress of Psychoanalysis and was not happy about it. Be that as it may, after thirteen or fourteen months of analysis, Mahler was thrown out of treatment the very session she told Deutsch a dream that was clearly homosexual, in which Deutsch helped her pull up her panties as a child. She dreamed that she was in the bathroom and Deutsch was Margaret's nurse and put the little flap on her pajamas back up on her behind. Margaret was doing exactly what a patient in analysis is supposed to do; she brought in a dream and gave her associations to it. Nevertheless, at the end of the hour, Deutsch told Margaret that she'd better go to another analyst, a man. She confessed that she could not analyze her, and pointedly added that even the Professor met people whom he felt he couldn't analyze.

Again, what horrendous technique for a psychoanalyst! The patient in analysis is instructed to say whatever comes to mind, including (perhaps especially) all feelings for the analyst. The supposedly neutral analyst is then required to analyze the feelings as transference, the desires the patient had as a child for an authority figure like a parent or the nurse in Margaret's dream which are no longer appropriate for an adult. In Margaret's case, as a small girl she may well have wanted the nurse to pull up her panties, and in so doing have erotic physical contact with her. If properly analyzed, Margaret would have realized that while she had wanted the nurse to button her up, she had no real desire for Deutsch to do so, and that her wish was merely a childhood fantasy. This kind of resolution is a tremendously important step for the success of any analysis, and essential for every analyst to negotiate. One who has not resolved his or her transference to the training analyst cannot be objective about future patients, will find it difficult if not impossible to resolve their problems, and may even be a danger to them. Deutsch apparently was unaware of the basic tenets of psychoanalysis such as transference and the analyst's noncritical acceptance of the revelations of the patient, or at least ignored them. I suspect that her own analysis was incomplete, even though she was analyzed by the great Freud himself, and did not delve into such matters in depth. (Today an analyst who ignores transference would not be permitted to practice unsupervised, if at all, in a good psychoanalytic institute, and would probably be instructed to return for further personal analysis.)

Margaret's analysis ended in disaster, with Deutsch's announcement that her patient was unanalyzable. The reasons for terminating an analysis were not told the patient in those days, as they usually are now. The decision of the analyst was absolutely final. Deutsch just told Mahler that her analysis wasn't working out and she would have to go to someone else. In one day and out the next. Just like that, the analysis was over, with no regard for the intolerable pain and suffering Deutsch was putting her patient through. It was terrible analytic technique, as well as inhumane behavior. Mahler told Swedloff[5] that the termination was glorious politics, typical of Dr. Deutsch's personal style and her penchant for power politics. (In the U.S. today, particularly in the New York Psychoanalytic Institute, the case would go before the students' committee, who would carefully consider the evidence. They probably would seek another opinion by a senior analyst known to be both impartial and empathic. In that way the candidate would be given another chance to succeed with an analyst the committee believed could cope with the situation.)

Mahler also told Swerdloff that Deutsch frequently mentioned Freud in her analysis, and compared herself to him. In trying to explain Deutsch's rejection of her, Mahler said she had produced plenty of associations, but they were difficult to analyze because they were mostly resistance material. (But a well trained analyst analyzes resistances, which are involuntary and the patient's right, and does not discharge a person for having them.)

The important psychoanalyst Jenny Waelder-Hall in all likelihood gave the major explanation for Deutsch's rejection. Waelder-Hall said to Margaret, "Anybody who knew Helene would know that she is not able to analyze somebody without money." Margaret responded that Deutsch had resented her from the beginning, and told her right then that she was doing it for Ferenczi.

To Margaret's everlasting gratitude, Ferenczi stood up for her to Deutsch and repeated to Margaret what he had said to her former analyst. His remarks somewhat alleviated the pain Deutsch's rejection caused her, which, despite her disavowal, remained with her all her life. Mahler told Swerdloff,[6] "You know, for years I have stored what he said. For about the last twenty-five years I got over it,[7] but not before, because Ferenczi said to Deutsch when she visited him in Budapest, 'You did not do us any service, Dr. Deutsch. You did not do us any favor. If you felt that you could not do the job and still started, you did definite damage to Schoenberger.'"

A big hullabaloo among the Viennese psychoanalysts about the Schoenberger case followed, because Deutsch, who had been analyzed by Freud himself, had a great and powerful influence on the educational committee of the Vienna Psychoanalytic. If Deutsch found a patient unanalyzable, the rest of the society in all likelihood chugged along in her footsteps. Deutsch's cruel rejection of Margaret could have ruined her career. But, probably because of the influence of Ferenczi, Margaret was given a second chance and told to seek another analyst. She was informed that she must not choose her own analyst, but could go to any of three people they listed, Richard Sterba, Grete Bibring, and Margaret's friend, Willi Hoffer, whom she selected as her next analyst. Unfortunately, he was a Ph.D. and couldn't take her in analysis at that time because he was studying for his medical degree. She absolutely refused to go to the other two because they were selected by Helene Deutsch. She said,[8] "I was angry and unhappy enough that I would not do anything that Helene Deutsch told me."

Mahler reminisced that a candidate was very dependent in his career on what member of the hierarchy he was in analysis with. "Let's be quite frank and sincere about it," she said. "If I had been successful as an analysand of Mrs. Deutsch, my career would have flourished about ten or fifteen years earlier than it did."

Mahler suffered badly from the aftereffects of Deutsch's rejection for many years, even after she came to America. She talked about it to her friends until quite late in her life. Deutsch's rejection was particularly important because it was a repetition of the constant rebuffs Margaret had suffered at the hands of her mother, another instance of an unanalyzed transference. (At the very least, Deutsch should have kept Margaret in analysis until the problem was worked through. Deutsch should have shown Margaret that while she had only one mother whose love she desperately needed, there were many psychoanalysts, among whom Mahler could have had her pick. A mother's rejection can be life threatening: an analyst's rejection is not.) Mahler said that, in the beginning, she wanted to give vent to her very justified anger and get revenge or devalue Deutsch for setting her back professionally and personally. But fortunately for her reputation, she refrained from "acting out."

Stepansky[9] confirmed that Mahler never got over her bitterness about Deutsch's rejection. As late as her eighty-eighth year, Mahler was still furious about it, although Deutsch had only analyzed Mahler for fourteen months when she was twenty-nine years old. She carried the grudge for fifty-eight years!

Non-analysts may wonder why Deutsch's rejection had so strong an effect on Margaret. There are two major reasons, the personal and the professional. On a personal level, because Margaret had been rejected by her own mother, she experienced Deutch's dismissal as a repetition of the original trauma, and relived all the pain she felt during her childhood. Professionally, who one's analyst was provided (and still provides) an analytic pedigree. As previously mentioned, Deutsch had been analyzed by Freud.

A successful analysis with Deutsch would have qualified Margaret as a third generation Freudian, with all the respect and admiration such a position brings. As Kirsner wrote about the New York Psychoanalytic Admissions Committee,[10] it "made or broke careers. To be rejected rendered one a second class citizen while admission ... promised a prestigious and wealthy career." At that time (and perhaps, in some measure, even today) the issue of an analyst's competence was far less important in guaranteeing success than the renown of his or her analyst. Rejection by so famous an analyst as Deutsch could well have sounded Mahler's professional death knell. A training analysis was (and is) still the most important part of an analyst's training, considered of far greater importance than case supervision and seminars. Without an accepted analysis, Mahler was left with no standing at all in the analytic community.

Three quarters of a century later, analysts still ponder over Deutsch's rejection of Margaret. For example, Paul Roazen,[11] who wrote a biography of Helene Deutsch,[12] had a much more sympathetic attitude toward Deutsch's termination of Mahler's analysis. On reading the manuscript of this book, Roazen wrote Bond:[13] "Given how difficult so many people found Mahler to be, I wonder why you aren't a little more tolerant of how hard Helene might have found working with Mahler in analysis. Sudden terminations were not unusual in the 1920s, it would be anachronistic to think that even Freud then did not do such things."

In order to understand the impact that Dr. Deutsch had on the young Margaret Schoenberger, we should take a quick glance at Deutsch's own life. Helene Rosenbach Deutsch[14] was born in Przemysl, Poland, to Wilhelm and Regina Rosenbach on October 9th, 1884, thirteen years before the birth of Mahler. Like Mahler's father, Wilhelm was Jewish, middle class, and a professional man, in his case a lawyer. Helene was the youngest child of four, having two sisters and a brother. Deutsch hated her mother because the woman beat her regularly, as Helene was not a boy. Like Mahler, Deutsch was her father's favorite child, which didn't stop her mother from beating her. Perhaps Mahler's dismissal began here, with Deutsch's hatred of her mother.

Helene left school at the age of fourteen. Upon returning home, her mother had plans for her to marry and have children. Helene had another agenda. She ran away from home, refusing to return until her parents signed a paper allowing her to attend the university. At the age of sixteen, she began an affair with Herman Lieberman. It is said that she took on the lover to spite her mother. Lieberman was much older than Helene, was married, and had a child. Their affair lasted on and off until 1912 (for 28 years!), when she married Felix Deutsch.

In 1910, Deutsch left Lieberman to study in Munich. There she had her lover's baby aborted. As in Mahler's case, a book by Freud changed both Deutsch's career and her life. In 1916 she read *The Interpretation of Dreams*. She had wanted to study law, in identification with her father (again similar to Mahler) but after reading Freud's book, she became interested in psychoanalysis.

Shortly after she married Felix, Deutsch was graduated with a doctorate in medicine. Again like Mahler, Deutsch sought out and studied with the best professors in the field. She began her work in Vienna University's Psychiatric Clinic under the direction of Wagner-Jauregg. In 1914 she left the Vienna clinic to study under Emil Kraepelin in Munich. While Mahler never had children, Deutsch had difficulty in remaining pregnant. She had several miscarriages before finally having a successful pregnancy (her son, Martin) in 1916. It is interesting that although both of the Deutsches were busy analysts and writers, Felix did most of the "mothering" of the child. It seems that Mahler's first choice of analyst was no more maternal a woman than her own mother.

At that time, Deutsch began her work with Sigmund Freud, where she was accepted in his Wednesday night meetings. One of the first women to join Freud's Vienna Psychoanalytic Society, she became a member in 1918. As did Margaret, Deutsch managed to captivate her (male) professors, including Sigmund Freud, whose favorite she became. During her analysis with Freud, she felt she was falling in love with him. Deutsch was not entirely content with the analysis, however. She believed that Freud focused too much on her relationship with her father.

In 1924, about the time of Mahler's analysis, Deutsch began to look at women and sexuality closer. She felt that problems are caused in women from a conflict between narcissism and mother's love. These ideas reflect on Deutsch's own life, and again, are reminiscent of Mahler's difficulties.

Deutsch's book, *The Psychology of Women*, like most of her work, was heavily based on her own life. She said that girls' problems were caused by a lack of detachment from their mothers. Another reflection on her own life can be found in Deutsch's views of infertility in women. She felt that it was caused by either the woman's hatred of her own mother's sexuality or her feeling that she would be an incompetent mother.

Much to Deutsch's dismay, Freud did not recognize her work as an expansion of his theories. She blamed his lack of credit on his daughter Anna's jealousy of Deutsch. Some thought of Deutsch as an heir of sorts to Freud, possibly accounting for his daughter's envy. A jealous woman herself, however, it is not surprising that Deutsch explained her frustrations on the jealousy of another woman.[15] Perhaps there was room for only one queen bee in Deutsch's *Weltanschauung*, and that job was already filled.

In 1964 Deutsch's husband died. A widowed friend of mine once said, "The longer my husband is dead, the better he looks!" Such was the case of Helene Deutsch. As time went on, she looked back at her life with her husband and began to idolize him. She remembered all the help he had given her while she pursued her career, especially in taking care of their son. Mahler, like my widowed friend, also had a change of heart when her former husband died, and had their ashes buried together. During the war, Deutsch also left Vienna for the United States, where she was joined by her husband. And like Mahler, Deutsch lost all contact with her family after the Nazi invasion and became depressed.

How alike the two women were! If Mahler suffered from repressed homosexuality, it is quite possible that Deutsch, with a similar maternal history, had developed comparable repressions. As previously stated, Mahler herself felt that Deutsch could not handle her own homosexuality. If unable to face her own hidden sexual conflicts, she could not have dealt satisfactorily with Margaret's.

On March 29th, 1982, Helene Deutsch died at the age of 97. It's doubtful that Margaret Mahler mourned her very much.

Strangely enough, while scrolling through some material from Deutsch's books on the Internet, I came across the following excerpt, which, if it refers to Mahler, has nothing to do with homosexuality and changes everything we know about her analyst's rejection. In the book,[16] Deutsch writes of people who become paranoid as a defense against their own unconscious guilt.

She speaks of a patient of hers who was unable to pay her analytic fees. Instead of being grateful for the analyst's patience, the patient became extremely aggressive. She began searching through the past couple of years of analysis, "remembering slights from the analyst, ways the analyst had misunderstood her or mistreated her." Deutsch describes these as "a flood of minor incidents that had occurred during the analysis and which she was able to twist to suit her purposes." The patient maintained, for instance, that her analysis, and her whole future, had already been ruined by a telephone conversation which had curtailed her session by a few minutes ... and she insisted that Deutsch had done this because of her deep antipathy toward the patient. By casting the blame on her analyst, the patient was able to feel guiltless and, as a result, free from depression.

We have no proof, of course, that the patient referred to in the excerpt is Margaret, but it is unlikely that Deutsch treated two patients so similar in microscopic detail, from Margaret's free sessions, to her known paranoid thinking, to her objection to the phone call during her analytic hour, to her proclivity for being aggressive. If this is truly Margaret Schoenberger of whom Deutsch speaks, we are given insight "from the horse's mouth" as to why Deutsch thought she could not treat Mahler and why she ended the analysis. It is quite a different story than the one told by Mahler, and of great historical interest. (But if the patient Deutsch speaks of *is* Mahler, it was unconscionable of Deutsch to publish an account of identifiable material from the analysis of a patient who is herself an analyst and likely to read the book, and whose life and history are known to many colleagues.)

Upset as Margaret was by her failure with Deutsch, she would not allow the fiasco to stop her drive for professional advancement. After leaving the von Pirquet Clinic, she began to balance her practice of pediatrics and her training for psychoanalysis. First she needed to acquire an overall academic psychiatric background, and she worked as an extern at Steinhof, a state institution closely allied with the University Psychiatric Clinic headed by Wagner-Jauregg and later by Poetzl. Then she accepted a job as health and welfare physician in the public school system of Vienna, and later on became head of a well baby clinic.

News Item, 1929

The collapse of the Wall Street stock exchange in 1929 led to a world-wide recession which hit Germany especially hard. Millions were unemployed. These conditions were beneficial to Hitler in his Nazi campaign. Chancellor Bruening was unable to pass a new finance bill and was forced to ask President Hindenburg to dissolve the Reichstag and call for new elections. Hitler campaigned hard for the Nazi candidates, promising the public a way out of their current hardship. The results of the election made the Nazi Party the second largest party in the Reichstag. Hitler also began to win over the support of both the army and the large industrialists, who contributed financially to the Nazi Party.

August Aichhorn

Margaret's employment by the city was to bring about a revolutionary affair that would turn her world upside down. It brought her in contact with August Aichhorn, author of *Wayward Youth*,[17] the famous book on delinquency. Margaret was enchanted by his magnetic personality and immediately fell in love with him. Ignoring the recommendations of the Vienna Psychoanalytic Institute as well as Ferenczi's advice, she asked Aichhorn to become her analyst. He agreed. It wasn't a very objective, "kosher" arrangement, she said, because she knew she had been singled out as "the exception." As her analysis with Aichhorn developed, so did their relationship, and they became lovers as well as analyst and patient. Mahler told Stepansky[18] that her close to three-year analysis with Aichhorn was helpful in many respects, but was not even close to a classical analysis. She and Aichhorn had fallen deeply in love, and when they became lovers the classical relationship between analyst and analysand flew out the window. By taking Margaret under his wing and doing everything possible to have her restored to the good graces of the Viennese psychoanalytic establishment, Aichhorn intensified Margaret's image of herself as an exception that had been instilled in her by her father. She then saw herself as a kind of Cinderella, the love object of a beautiful prince (Aichhorn) who would win her the favor of a beautiful stepmother (Deutsch). Margaret's so-called analysis under Aichhorn simply recapitulated her oedipal situation. Not a very classical analysis, indeed, nor one designed to change her feeling of being an "exception." No wonder Mahler said in her seventies that she had never resolved her Oedipus complex!

Margaret found Aichhorn a stunning personality and an ingenious man. She thought he was the most striking character she had ever met. A colorful man, he made a great impression on everyone who saw him work. At the same time, he was an elusive person, which gave him a mysterious air. He had a deep understanding of both male and female delinquents, superior to that of any analyst before or, arguably, after him. His original technique of applied analysis enabled him to reach psychopaths no therapist had been able to treat before. To do so, he first made himself emotionally available to the wayward youths so they could identify with and bond with him. As a result, they grew to love him and became dependent on the relationship and what he thought of them.

He used their dependency to persuade them to discontinue the lifestyle they were leading. He insisted that they live a new kind of life, instead of the one chosen because of the frustrations and abuse they experienced in their earlier lives. In the second part of their treatment, he turned their psychopathy into a neurosis, and was able to analyze them. Aichhorn's work with delinquents was completely unique. He spoke their language, and somehow could make them open up with him and divulge all their secrets. They intuitively trusted him. He understood the unconscious motivations behind their behavior, and would confront them with such interpretations as "You did this because of that." And they believed him. The young people always knew he was on their side, no matter what they confessed to him. Margaret thought Aichhorn was a genius, and more of an artist than a psychoanalyst. She had other fine teachers, such as Grete Bibring, who thought highly of Margaret's talents and was very encouraging, Marianne Kris, Jenny

Waelder-Hall, Eduard Hitschmann, and Jeanne Lampel-de Groot. But she considered Aichhorn the major, shaping force in her professional development, and believed that her style with children was due in large part to watching him work with patients. She learned a great deal from him about children, work, and people, and felt that he was the greatest of her teachers. She always said that ninety-nine percent of what she learned in technique with children was from Aichhorn. She only had to observe him at work to identify with him as a therapist.

Perhaps because of her training with Aichhorn, Mahler regarded herself as much a developmental psychologist at large as an analyst. She said,[19] "I was very much interested in development, and I think that is why I became a better than average child analyst and a more than average interested psychoanalyst, also interested in research."

When Mahler first worked at the Psychiatric Institute in New York, she conducted a clinical conference as the chief consultant of the children's service. Jacob Arlow said that Mahler was able to speak to a child from the children's ward with the whole audience around. Well-known people such as Marian Kenworthy of the New York School of Social Work were horrified, and expressed shock and dismay that "this refugee psychiatrist let those poor children talk before a whole audience and answer questions."[20] Mahler said she had learned from Aichhorn how to make a child feel completely at ease and oblivious to the fact that anyone else was present. She did it by completely empathizing with the child.

Irving Sternschein also was impressed with Mahler's wonderful skill with children. He said,[21] "My first impression of Dr. Margaret Mahler and her understanding of young people occurred in the early 1950's at a conference dealing with emotionally disturbed adolescents at the Hawthorne-Cedar Knolls Residential Treatment Center. When she was called upon to discuss the case of a schizophrenic boy in his early teens who was a talented pianist, her sensitivity to him and common sense about this troubled youngster were striking: She counseled the residence staff to do all they could to foster the development of his musical prowess. She reasoned that this perceived skill would help others to tolerate his peculiarities and otherwise odd behavior. She also made the point that his mastery of complex music was not unlike the incredible memories of savants, which was made possible by a failure of repressive mechanisms. These individuals retain whatever they focused on to the exclusion of other items in their visual or auditory fields. Mahler regularly impressed other professionals with her ability to reach and communicate with very young, often mute, distressed children. It was as if they sensed that, unlike many other adults, she understood them."

Surprisingly enough, when Mahler was asked what kind of cases she

considered the most fun, she answered[22] that she liked nice neurotic children and borderline grownups. She believed that an analyst could take a pri-
mordial transference of a borderline patient and develop it into a mature
transference. Like her mentor Aichhorn, Mahler was able to get positive
results with "impossible" patients as few analysts could.

Aichhorn used unusual methods to add to his knowledge of delinquency. Mahler told Noshpitz[23] that Aichhorn went to group meetings of
youths who were plotting subversive group action, because he wanted to
know how their minds worked. He prided himself on being able to predict
certain things in the underworld, and did not tell the authorities about them.
Aichhorn was an original thinker of great creativity, and also very much a
man of Vienna. When everybody wanted him to come to the United States
or any other country, he refused, saying he could not be happy anywhere
else than Vienna. He was also tremendously generous to Margaret. He continually referred patients to her so that she could live more comfortably,
once again, of course, breaking the rule about analytic neutrality. It was during her analysis with him that she was able to move to a decent apartment
and buy a small car to make her pediatric house calls. Margaret gloried in
the love of her new "father."

Although Aichhorn was a regular partner of Freud's, he was very
ambivalent about the hierarchy in the Vienna Psychoanalytic Society, and
was always afraid of the academic circles. He was in the inner sanctum, as
far as Freud and Anna Freud were concerned. Aichhorn and the Schnitlz-
ers were Freud's weekly card playing partners. They had card parties and
card games one evening a week. Anna Freud had a very special affection for
Aichhorn and he for her. One of the reasons he took to Mahler, and he said
almost as much, was that she somehow reminded him of Anna Freud, especially her eyes, her profile, and her accent. He felt almost omnipotent in his
own field, and he really was all powerful. Nevertheless, he had suspicions
about the hierarchy, and seldom went to the society's meetings.

He asked Margaret not to say anything about her analysis with him,
and then told the Institute, "I have analyzed Margaret Schoenberger and
she is ready to be accepted." He allowed her to tell about it after a few
months. Six months later, he went before the committee and said dramatically, "Her analysis goes excellently. She will be a prominent analyst." One
can question at this date whether Aichhorn's incredible understanding of
delinquents didn't arise at least partially from his own tendencies in that
direction, as seen in his accepting Margaret Mahler as a lover while she was
in analysis with him, and his deception of the committee at the Vienna Psychoanalytical Institute.

There was no doubt in Margaret's mind that Aichhorn liked her very much, in fact far too much for an objective analysis. At the same time, she worked with him and he was very open about the fact that he admired her talent. She and Dr. Kurt Eissler were Aichhorn's favorite pupils.

By this time Margaret was an official student of the Vienna Psychoanalytical Institute. She was graduated during her analysis with Aichhorn, so the analysis with him was acceptable to them, even though analyst and patient knew better. But rules were never made for Margaret or Aichhorn. She wanted to be analyzed by him, as well as to assist him and attend his roaming "youth welfare guidance clinics," where he treated the wayward youths who inspired his famous book. He held guidance clinics in seventeen districts, in almost all the districts of the municipality of Vienna, and went from station to station. She traveled with him to the clinics, which were located in the schools themselves. It was important to her to accompany him, as she felt she learned more there than anywhere else. As a result, she would have to rework her Oedipus complex with a rejecting mother and a biased father with another analyst, but at the time the grandiose analyst and patient agreed they could surmount the difficulty. In a personal sense it must have been sheer heaven for the beginning psychoanalyst to travel around the country with her lover and mentor, a trip in which learning and loving demanded equal rights. Margaret had tremendous admiration for his work, and he for hers. She made great professional if not analytical strides.

As for her own analysis, Margaret and Aichhorn saw the light after a while and realized that a lover does not make the most dispassionate therapist. Both knew that what she needed was a good classical analysis.[24] She had been with August Aichhorn two and a half years when they decided she should leave him and be analyzed by Willi Hoffer. When she terminated her analysis with Aichhorn, neither one was satisfied with what had been accomplished. "I was unanalyzed," she said,[25] even though she believed that in many ways her treatment had been quite successful. She said, "I enjoyed my life ever so much more. When I went into analysis I had an unusually strict superego and was a very impulsive person. Very impulsive, you know. Accompanied by what goes very often with impulsiveness — depression. Severe depression." Her friend and erstwhile psychiatrist, Bernard Pacella, would not have agreed that Aichhorn "cured" Mahler's depressions, as Dr. Pacella had to hospitalize her late in life for a deep depression.[26] Judging by her frequent uncontrolled outbursts of rage with friends, colleagues, and employees, it doesn't look like Aichhorn made much of a dent in her impulsiveness, either.

After the analysis with Aichhorn and their affair ended they continued to correspond on and off until he died in 1949. She sent him food and clothing during the war when his home in Vienna was destroyed by two bombings and his son was badly injured in the military service. Aichhorn was very grateful for her help. Margaret Mahler never got over her love for Aichhorn. As late as July 27, 1948, a little over a year before he died when she was fifty-one years old, she wrote him a sentimental, loving letter on his birthday.[27]

Winchester, New Hampshire. July 27, 1948[28]

Dear Director,

Today, on the twenty-seventh of July, I inevitably think of you. If personal wishes possess the tiniest bit of magical strength, you will reach the age of one hundred and twenty in the full freshness and joy of life.

I lie here in the grass on a lonely farm in the center of mountains and remember the many beautiful experiences you made possible for me. The older and riper one becomes — and it is unfortunate how late I have ripened — the clearer one is about the value of personal experiences.

I remember from my analysis the trashy little rhyme that I was unable to get out of my head. It's called "Little Anneliese."

In the middle of the green meadow
Anneliese lies and views the clouds.
She dreams of giants and of dwarfs
and of chocolate mountains and of Santa Claus.

Twenty-three years later, you are still the giant, the symbol of the dearest Santa Claus of all children — at least for me. I have just now drunk two highballs (whiskeys and sodas) with my American friend, Marya Farnum, author of the book *Modern Women: The Lost Sex*[29] [sic] — a best seller — and I told her about the author of *Wayward Youth!*"[30] — August Aichhorn's book!

I know that many people would join me in our love for you on this day.[31] Since human beings are egocentric, however, I would like to say to you how lucky and proud I am today to have known you and been in your aura. May you live long, dear highly esteemed friend, and forgive this very stupid, primitive, sentimental but honest birthday greeting.

In affectionate memory

Your

Margit Mahler

In those days, there was very little systematic training of analytic candidates. There were a few structured courses, such as Edward Bibring's course on the ego and the id, Sterba's course on some papers of Freud, and Helene Deutsch's seminar on technique, all of which Margaret attended. Soon she was accepted in Anna Freud's seminar on child analysis.

Margaret was a candidate in the late twenties and early thirties, as women were becoming increasingly accepted in the field. She had as her contemporaries a number of well known female analysts such as Jenny Waelder, Marianne Kris, Edith Buxbaum, and Anny Katan. In her interview with Mahler,[32] Nancy Chodorow asked how she explained the large proportion of women involved in psychoanalysis and their centrality in the field. Mahler answered by free associating to the question, and came up with a number of responses that surprised even her. She said she thought it must have had something to do with Freud's tremendous admiration for his daughter, who was the apple of his eye, as well as for Marie Bonaparte, and his feeling for the magnetic Lou Andreas-Salome, and with the tremendous power of Helene Deutsch. And, certainly, his requited love for his mother. Freud cared for these women, Mahler said, in spite of his questionable theory about female development. Then an interesting association came into her mind. On Freud's seventy-fifth birthday, she said, Thomas Mann gave a lecture at a famous concert hall in Vienna. It was quickly oversold. Frau Professor said to Freud, "Don't you get any ideas into your head.... It is for Thomas Mann and not for you that it is sold out." This story suggested to Mahler that Freud's household was really a matriarchy. "There were three women in that household who were all that important," she said. "There was Frau Professor, and Aunt Matilda, and the daughter." Freud was used to having women in power. In his own home, in contrast to his analytic kingdom where he was absolute ruler, it appears that he was just another child.

In the early days of psychoanalysis, analysts were esteemed by how near to Freud their training was. The closer an analyst was to being part of Freud's original circle, the more highly thought of that person was. Helene Deutsch gained her power by the fact that she was analyzed by Sandor Ferenczi, who had been analyzed by Freud. According to Mahler, her women contemporaries "were a little bit an in-between generation, not quite the second generation, but older than the third, much older," hence they were quite valued. Mahler had hoped to gain some of their prestige by her analysis with Helene Deutsch, but, unfortunately, that was not to be.

Mary O'Neill Hawkins was a woman analyst from that period who remained Mahler's good friend until she died. Hawkins was a courageous Protestant American who was studying analysis in Vienna. She had regularly risked her life by helping Jewish analysts flee across the Austrian border, as well as smuggling money and official papers for them. One reason Margaret valued Hawkins so much was that she had been in Margaret's parents' house and was the only person in America who knew her parents and was still alive. "I love her," Mahler said.[33]

Margaret told a funny anecdote involving Hawkins in America. The two friends had gone to a concert at Tanglewood. Mahler said, "Koussevitzsky was my conductor-sweetheart. Mary said, 'But don't you notice that he looks so much like your father?'" Mahler was thrilled and said, "Nobody else in America would have known to make that comparison."

By this time, Mahler was in private practice, which she started in a furnished room. There was no waiting room, and the children and their parents had to wait in the anteroom. Despite the shabby office, she was surprised to find that she developed a nice practice, which, to her delight, included many of the children of her colleagues. For example, Dr. Beno Samet, the ranking internist who was Freud's doctor when Schur was unavailable, sent Mahler his dearly beloved only son for treatment.

Dr. Samet also sent her his twin nephews for analysis. While working with them, she experienced a remarkable incident about the emergence of the self. The boys were sixteen months old when Hans looked at himself in the mirror and said, "Eric." Then he said, "Eric? Eric, there. Hans here." Hans had become aware for the first time that he and his twin were separate people. Mahler said it is only once in a lifetime that one is present at such a moment.[34]

Under Aichhorn's tutelage, she founded her own psychoanalytically oriented well-baby clinic at the outpatient clinic of Professor Zappert. Aichhorn also insisted that Margaret learn the use of the Rorschach test as a diagnostic tool, in which the individual looking at the ink blots projects his or her ideas of what the blots look like. Since the "pictures" are merely blots of ink with no inherent meaning, what the subject "sees" indicates a great deal about his or her psyche. Margaret's skill in the area stood her in good stead in supplementing her income. It also led to her collaboration on a research project with Dr. Judith Silberpfennig (later Judith Kestenberg) on the significance of the Rorschach in the diagnosis of patients with organic brain damage,[35] a paper considered a classic by Rorschach experts. Nevertheless, despite considerable gains, she knew that her analysis was far from complete. She was particularly dissatisfied with her sexuality and her adjustment to men. To remedy what had been unanalyzed, Margaret began her analysis with Willi Hoffer.

News Items, 1933

January 30: Adolph Hitler appointed Chancellor of Germany by Hindenburg. Hitler is the leader of the National Socialist German Workers Party and commander of the SA, the Storm Troopers

January 30: Law enacted for sterilization of inferiors, implemented three weeks later.

February 27: The Reichstag Building is set on fire by secret order of Hitler's chief of propaganda, Joseph Goebbels, a major step toward Adolf Hitler gaining complete control over the destiny of Germany. The fire was almost certainly planned by the Nazis, Goebbels and Goering in particular. As a result, Hitler was given an excuse to have all the Communist deputies of the Reichstag arrested, and managed to obtain a decree from President

Hindenburg giving the Nazi goverment powers to detain anyone they thought was a threat to the nation. The presidential decree gave free rein to the Nazi government to suppress the free speech of its political opponents.

February 28: Hitler persuaded President Hindenburg to sign an "emergency" decree authorizing Hitler to suspend all civil rights, arrest (and execute) any suspicious person. A reign of terror ensued in which thousands were imprisoned. The non-Nazi press was outlawed.

March 20: The first Nazi concentration camp is opened at an old powder factory near Dachau. The camp is to be used to incarcerate thousands of political opponents of the regime.

April 1: Hitler declared a one-day boycott of Jewish businesses. Signs were posted all over Germany saying, "Do not buy from Jews."

April 7: All Jewish civil servants forced to retire. Jews were denied admission to the bar.

May 10: Under orders from Goebbels, Nazi gangs burned truckloads of Germany's top literary works written by Jews, including the works of Freud.

July 14: Laws for the prevention of Hereditary Disease mandated the sterilization of the mentally ill.

August 29: It is officially confirmed that the Nazis were sending Jews to concentration camps on a variety of trumped up charges.

October 14: Hitler withdrew from the League of Nations and the Versailles disarmament pact.

C. Willi Hoffer (1930–1936)

C. Willi Hoffer's style was not hampered by the requirements of the institute, because Margaret's membership already had been approved by the educational committee. The group that accepted her was heavily guarded, but nevertheless she heard that there had been one dissenting vote. It was that of Helene Deutsch, of course. Margaret had little choice of analyst in that small town, and only Hoffer could have analyzed her. He knew her work well. He knew her very well, as the two were already good friends, and she had been supervised by him during her analysis with Aichhorn. Margaret remained in analysis with Hoffer on and off until about 1935. When the Nazis came, she returned for another piece of analysis. All in all, it lasted for about four years.

At that time, there were only a handful of senior analytic students at the beginning of their treatment. Many of the canons of analysis had not been formulated yet, and this frequently caused major complications in the treatment of candidates. For example, there was no rigid rule as there is today about keeping the private life of the analyst a "blank screen." With Hoffer, there was nothing blank about the screen, as he sought and utilized Margaret's cooperation and collaboration in publishing the Zeitschrift fur Psychoanalytische Pedagogik periodical.

Despite these flaws in analytic technique, Margaret considered her analysis with Hoffer highly successful. As she said in her interview with Lucy Freeman,[36] "In the analysis with Hoffer there was analytic work done and my character structure changed, I think, as far as one can change. The degree of my adaptation and the degree of my sublimation changed for the better, and I was very satisfactorily rated."

Mahler may have believed that her analysis with Hoffer was a great success, but the major problem for which she entered analysis with Deutsch, her difficulties with men, was never resolved. Her marriage to Paul Mahler was a disaster, and to my knowledge, she never had a satisfactory personal relationship with any man. She always felt superior to the men who were interested in her and was abusive to them. According to Bluma Swerdloff,[37] after her divorce Mahler almost married a well-known European gentleman, but didn't because she felt that the man was an opportunist who only wanted to marry her because of her fame. Selma Kramer said, "Boy, was he lucky!" Selma was her best friend.

Ruth Lax also met Mahler's boyfriend. Lax said,[38] "During the many years of my friendship with Margaret Mahler, she had visited with my husband and me and we often went out to dinner together. On one such occasion, she came with her boyfriend. He acted towards her in an adoring way."

Anni Bergman had a similar story to tell:[39] "Margaret found a boyfriend who was wonderful and loved her dearly. She was happy for a short time and really blossomed. I never knew the whole story but he did something that enraged her and she ended the relationship. He was dying to get back together with her, but she told me she was never going to speak with him again."

Fortunately, Margaret did better on a professional level than she did on a romantic level. It was when she became the head of a well-baby clinic at the Mauthner-Markoff Hospital that Mahler was struck by the great insight that was to make psychoanalytic history and to change the course of countless lives to come. Once a week, she treated average mothers with their normal babies at the clinic. There she made the profound observation that these well babies were in a twilight state of existence. Although they were fully developed physically they had not really been *born psychologically*, in that they were not tuned in to the external world. Psychologically, the infants were still in the womb state. In the midst of her infantile psychosis studies at the Masters Children's Center much later, Mahler came to the conclusion that these infants were very similar to two psychotic latency children she had treated privately. In her child psychosis studies, Mahler observed that a symbiotic child psychosis occurs through arrest of the mother-infant relationship in the symbiotic stage of development. Through her observations of these children, and her parallel project with normal infants at the Masters Children's Center, she became more and more convinced of the *symbiotic origin of human existence,* that the emotional birth of the human child occurs *in duo* with the mother or not at all. Mahler's idea was similar to Winnicott's theory that without a mother there is no baby. Having in mind the pictures of similar states in these two widely divergent groups of children, she and Manuel Furer first spelled them out in 1968 in their book, *On Human Symbiosis and the Vicissitudes of Individuation: Infantile Psychosis.*[40]

News Item, 1933

The Enabling Act, placed before the Reichstag on March 23, 1933, allowed the powers of legislation to be taken away from the Reichstag and transferred to Hitler's cabinet for a period of four years. Dictatorial powers were legally conferred on Adolf Hitler. On July 14 Hitler passed a law dictating that the Nazi Party was the sole political party allowed in Germany. The Nazification of Germany was underway.

News Items, 1934–1936

June 30: In a huge blood purge of at least 1,000 "enemies," called "the Night of the Long Knives," Hitler orders the Gestapo to murder Ernst Roehm, leader of Germany's political left, and many others against whom the Nazi leaders had a score to settle.

July 13: Heinrich Himmler, a former chicken farmer and the chief of the SS, assumed command of all Nazi concentration camps. Himmler and his "black shirts" were made responsible for policing Germany.

August 2: President Hindenburg died. Hitler became the "Fuehrer and Reich Chancellor" and the title of president was abolished. He had totalitarian dictatorial power.

News Item, 1935

During the years following Hitler's consolidation of power he set about the "Nazification" of Germany and its release from the armament restrictions of the Versailles Treaty. Censorship was extreme and covered all aspects of life including the press, films, radio, books and even art. Trade unions were suppressed, churches were persecuted, and ministers who preached non–Nazi doctrine were frequently arrested by the Gestapo and carried off to concentration camps. All youth associations were abolished and re-formed in a single entity as the Hitler Youth organization. The Jewish population was increasingly persecuted and ostracized from society. Under the Nuremburg Laws of September 1935 Jews were no longer considered to be German citizens and therefore no longer had any legal rights. Jews were no longer allowed to hold public office, to work in the civil service, the media, farming, teaching, or the stock exchange, and eventually were barred from practicing law or medicine. Hostility towards Jews from other Germans was encouraged and even shops began to deny entry to Jews.

News Items, 1934

October 1934: Hitler broke the Versailles Treaty. He ordered the army to be trebled in size, from the 100,000 man Versailles Treaty limit, to 300,000 men. Admiral Raeder, the chief of the navy, began construction of warships far larger than the maximum size permitted by the Versailles Treaty. He secretly begans to build parts in foreign dockyards for the construction of submarines, also forbidden by the Treaty. Goering began training of air force pilots and the design of military aircraft. In March 1935 Hitler authorized Goering to reveal to a British official the existence of the Luftwaffe, the German air force. There was little reaction. A few days later, Hitler openly declared the introduction of military service and the creation of an army with approximately one half million men. This also brought no reaction from Britain and France. At the same time, Hitler announced that he had no intention of annexing Austria or re-militarising the Rhineland and will respect all the territorial clauses of the Versailles Treaty, and that he is prepared to mutually disarm the heaviest of weapons and limit the strength of the German Navy.

1934: Mental hospitals are encouraged to neglect mental patients. Funding is suspended.

News Items, 1935

May 21: Jews suspended form the Military.
July: Signs of *Juden Verboten* (No Jews allowed) became widespread.

July 30: Nazis intensified repression of Jews. Physical violence against Jewish citizens reached a new peak in Berlin's fashionable Kurfurstendamm.

September 6: Public sale of Jewish newspapers banned.

September 15: German Congress passed the first Nuremburg Laws, which redefined German Jews as noncitizens and banned Jews from political participation.

September 21: Under the Nuremberg Laws, Jewish doctors were forced to resign from private hospitals.

October 18: Marriage between healthy and ill people forbidden. Abortions of all Jewish fetuses up to the sixth month of pregnancy ordered.

News Items, 1936

March 7: Hitler sent German troops into the Rhineland, in violation of the treaties of Versailles and Locarno. Neither the French nor British moved to counter the flagrant breach of the Locarno Pact of 1925, which was designed to keep these areas west of the Rhine free from German military units. At the same time, Hitler publically preached his desire for peace throughout Europe and offered to negotiate new nonaggression pacts with several countries, including France and Belgium. He also began rapid construction of defensive fortifications along the French and Belgian frontiers. Meanwhile, Hitler's popularity within Germany was boosted, his position as leader strengthened and his control over the army generals secured.

May 10: Burning of books written by Jewish authors. Summer: The security that Hitler had gained for Germany from the military stronghold in the Rhineland meant less security for Austria and Czechoslovakia, whose safety required a swift response from France in the event of German aggression. This led the Austrian government to begin a course of appeasement of Hitler by, for example, giving Austrian Nazis influential positions within the government in return for a pledge from Hitler to confirm his recognition of Austrian sovereignty.

4

Marriage (1936–1953)

Margaret was very aware of her problems with men. As she told Helene Deutsch during their first interview, she realized that she always ran away from men just as the relationship was about to become serious. She attracted men whom she seemed to like, but she never was able to make a commitment. She had relationships with many outstanding people, including a professor and an associate professor. Many were seriously interested in her, but when Margaret went to Sopron her father always said, "You don't need that," or "What do you need this for?" At one point a professor from the clinic wanted to marry her. She considered it carefully, and told Dr. Schoenberger about the proposal. As one would anticipate, her father said, "What do you need him for? Your sister needs you." Margaret was shocked when she realized for the first time that Dr. Schoenberger was being very selfish,[1] and felt she had no recourse but to devalue her beloved father. Mahler believed that a girl needs a father who, without being seductive, accepts and enjoys her as a female. Margaret did not have that kind of father. Schoenberger, who was defensive rather than seductive, enjoyed her not as a female but "as a brain."

Whatever else one thinks of Dr. Schoenberger's wish to have his daughter remain single, one must say a word about the degree of individuation attained by the man. In Hungary, at that time, all "nice girls" married and had children. Those who didn't were considered an object of ridicule. The doctor was able to withstand the mores of the time whatever the social consequences, and have his beloved daughter stay unmarried. This must have been true of him in other aspects of his life, as well. He was a person with the courage of his convictions, right or wrong, and as such was a model for his daughter.

Margaret acceded to her father's wishes that she remain single, until 1936 when she was thirty-nine years old and in analysis with Willi Hoffer. At every major turning point in Margaret's life, it seems she needed a benevolent father figure to give her support to move ahead. As when her father gave his approval for her to enter medical school, she needed a benign father figure to give her permission to wed. She found that figure in Willi Hoffer. With his support, she married Dr. Paul Mahler, a chemist with a Ph.D.

"He had a classical education, a very wonderful classical education. He was much better educated and much more well rounded in his culture than I was," Margaret said.[2] "He was very Viennese. He was the only son and very attached to both his father and his mother."

Nevertheless, Paul Mahler was far from a successful man, and the marriage was in financial difficulties from the beginning. He was a junior partner of Viennese Cordial Factory, a family business that was doing badly and eventually caused him to go broke. Before the marriage he told Margaret that he felt obligated to invest as much money as his uncle, who was a wealthy man. His father had owned three houses in Vienna, and Paul, one of three children, was left a third of their worth. Paul put all his share into the business. The factory lost more and more money, until he and Margaret agreed that it would be better for him to resign his partnership and remain the factory manager on a fixed salary. While Margaret did well financially right away, Paul made very little money at all. This did not get the relationship off to an auspicious start. Nor did it improve during the course of the marriage. Paul's financial problems were to last the rest of his life.

Paul also made little contribution to the couple's social life. Margaret said,[3] "I knew many more people than my husband. I knew all these people before, and my husband was a real Viennese. He hardly got away from Vienna, maybe once or twice in his young life."

Characteristically, Dr. Schoenberger tried to discourage his daughter's marriage. When Paul came to Sopron to ask for Margaret's hand, the doctor warned him, "You must know what you are doing; she is not average." Margaret felt her father was really saying, "Watch out! She is not castrated, and may castrate you!" Dr. Schoenberger's ambivalence was demonstrated very clearly at the wedding. First, he arrived late to the celebration dinner. And secondly, even though he normally was a very generous man, he insisted in the middle of the wedding dinner that the Mahlers repay him for the cost of it. Although she was able to proceed with the marriage with the support of her analyst, her father's influence almost certainly contributed to Margaret's ambivalence toward Paul.

Unfortunately, Dr. Schonberger proved to be right about his son-in-law. Margaret soon learned that Paul had never really outgrown his ties to his parents, to the point where he was unable to seek employment outside of Vienna because it upset his father, who wept and said that Paul "could not do that" to him. Margaret felt that Paul was never really a husband to her, but in his unconscious a son who badly needed parenting himself. Thus he cast her in the role of mother, which left her frustrated and deeply deprived.

Nor did she believe that her marriage was a bona fide resolution to her psychological problems. She did not marry her father or anybody like her father, but a child who needed a parent himself. Her husband was not an emotionally generous man. He refused to be protective of Margaret, and while he was enormously proud of her, he made sure never to tell her about it. She knew because other people told her that he praised and spoke of her with great respect when she was not around, but in the couple's intimate life he was very close mouthed. He was already middle aged when they came to the States, and in the beginning got one inferior job after the other. Eventually he found a position with the Geigy Company that was appropriate in terms of his work, but unfortunately, as is typical with Swiss companies, he made very little money. On an unconscious level, at least, it appears that

Paul Mahler resting in front of a house while vacationing with Margaret in 1940.

Paul took every opportunity to frustrate his wife. While Margaret regretted that they didn't have children, Paul gave her such a hard time after they emigrated that she was glad they hadn't.

News Items, 1937–1938

January 1: Jewish doctors in Germany lost insurance under the Nuremberg Laws.

March 11–12: Germany invaded Austria. Hitler became the undisputed ruler of over seventy million people.

March 14: Hitler announced the "Anschluss," or annexation of Austria.

July 23: Effective in the new year, all Jews were ordered to carry a special identification card.

July 25: Jewish doctors forbidden to treat non–Jewish patients.

August 17: All Jewish boys required to insert "Israel" as their middle names; all Jewish girls required to take on the middle name of "Sara."

September 30: Jewish physicians lost their licenses to practice.

October 5: All Jewish passports and ration cards marked with a "J."

November 7: In Paris a teenaged Polish Jew, Herschel Grynszpan, assassinated Ernst von Rath, third secretary of the German Embassy. The teenager was attempting to avenge the mistreatment of his family in Poland.

November 9: Kristallnacht, the "Night of Broken Glass." Following the death of Ernst von Rath, and in retribution against Grynszpan's act, Goebbels instigated acts of violence against Jews throughout Berlin. More than ninety people were killed, store windows were broken and synagogues set on fire.

November 12: 26,000 Jews sent to concentration camps.

December 8: Jews could no longer attend German universities.

December 13: All Jewish owned businesses confiscated.

5

The Nazis (1919–1938)

Downplaying the horrors of the Nazi regime for her, Margaret said, "The Mahlers experienced plenty of suffering from the beginning of the Holocaust." As a Jew who lost many family members and dear friends in the Holocaust, who was banished from her homeland, and whose career was grossly interrupted, Margaret Mahler's life story is welded to history. She understood about living in daily terror, never knowing if she or her loved ones would survive another day. Every venture outside for Paul, every knock on the door for Margaret, every furtive glance from a stranger meant another panic attack to be endured. There was never a day, not a moment, when the Mahlers felt completely safe.

News Item, 1938

October 6: All Jewish passports and ration cards marked with a "J." The complicated lives of the Mahlers were made infinitely more difficult by the red tape the Nazis put them through. For example, they needed affidavits to leave Vienna, but had no idea how to get them, and met with one frustration after another in trying to have them issued. The financial situation was difficult for Margaret because her husband, now the manager of the factory named after his father, had no money in the bank. She had to pay the *Reichsfluchtsteuer*[1] from her own savings for the company's employees. Nobody was permitted to get away who did not pay the taxes for himself as well as for anyone who might mean a loss to the Nazi economy, which was ludicrous, of course, considering that the Nazis wanted to get rid of the

Jews. The Mahlers had to ransom their way out of Germany. They were allowed to take out only one and a half pounds apiece.

Margaret was luckier than most of her colleagues, insofar as anyone in her situation could be called lucky. Although Jewish physicians were forced to resign from private hospitals, and Jewish doctors lost their insurance and were not permitted to treat non–Jewish patients, Mahler had enough money to live on, and with the help of Aichhorn was accepted as an analyst for both children and adults. Nevertheless, with her usual unflinching acceptance of reality, she understood what the future held for them if they stayed in Vienna. She was much more aware than her husband of how they were marking time. When she wanted to get affidavits very early, long before the so-called Umbruch in which the Nazis took over, Paul said, "Oh, the Nazis are in their last gasp at the Sudeten, Germany." Margaret knew that wasn't true, but was powerless to act on her insight by getting affidavits from the Nazi machine.

The night before Schuschnig went to Berchtesgaden to meet Hitler, Beni Ferency, the outstanding Hungarian sculptor whose children were Mahler's patients, finished his beautiful sculpture of her.[2] There was not much time to celebrate its completion, however. Instead of having the general election that all of them expected, Hitler took over.

It was a terrible time for psychoanalysts, Christian as well as Jewish. Most analysts could no longer make enough money to survive. The famous child analyst Berta Bornstein came to Vienna in the thirties and almost starved. Although their relationship was later to change for the worse, at this time Mahler begged Aichhorn to refer the next available patient to Mrs. Bornstein, instead of sending them all to her. Bornstein came from Berlin where the Nazis had made it impossible to work, and even some famous analysts like Annie Reich and the Lowensteins felt forced by lack of income to move to Prague. By then, all the analysts had begun to leave Berlin.

Margaret pondered long and hard about how the Mahlers could leave Vienna without affidavits. Finally she came up with a solution. Among her analysands was the niece of Lady Leontine Sassoon, the widow of the viceroy of India. At Margaret's request, Lady Sassoon sent a letter to the Viennese Home Office of the British Embassy to the effect that Dr. Paul Mahler and his wife were herewith invited as her private guests pending arrangements to go to the United States. With that letter they went to the British Consulate. With great relief, instead of the three months' stay in England they asked for, they were given six months in Britain and allowed to prepay the passage from there to New York. They were permitted to pay it from their Austrian money, but no jewelry or anything else of value could be taken out of the country.

The Mahlers frantically got their affairs together in order to be able to leave. In doing so, Mahler had a rather tragicomic encounter with Mr. X, one of her patients who was a non–Jew employed in the Krupp factory, the great ammunition plant. He came and sat up and said what Mahler had been expecting him to say for some time, that he could not possibly come for analysis to her any longer, as he and many others in his position were being followed and investigated. Confirming her instinctual fears, he told her terrible stories of what happened to Jewish people and others the Nazis didn't approve of. He was afraid they would shadow him to Mahler's apartment and incarcerate her, along with many doctors, lawyers, and other professionals. The patient then helped Mahler solve a dilemma that long had puzzled her and Paul.

The mother of one of her former child patients and the first wife of the famous Hungarian sculptor, Ferency, had once asked Mahler if she wanted some baby clothes for the poor children in her well baby clinic. Mahler said fine. So the woman brought her a stack of baby clothes. To Mahler's astonishment, in between the layers of clothing she found a revolver. Although years had gone by, Mahler often thought of that revolver, and didn't know what to do with it, so she let it sit in piles of clothes. When she heard that the Hartmanns, the Bibrings, and the Maenchens had their apartments searched, she remembered the revolver, and knew the consequences if the Nazis discovered it. She and her husband used to go for long walks on Sunday. They decided to take the gun to the Vienna Woods and bury it there. They walked to the woods, and looked stealthily around. Then terrified that they were being observed, they turned around and brought the gun back home. Margaret said,[3] "We were so paranoid we could not get rid of the revolver even on our Sunday walk in the Vienna woods."

She then said to herself, "Mr. X works in an ammunition factory. He must have a firearms license." She told him that she had a revolver without a permit, and asked if he would take the gun. He accepted it, of course, and the revolver matter was solved. Incidentally, the patient was being treated by Mahler for *ejaculatio praecox*.[4] In telling the story, Mahler added, "I hope he got cured by somebody else."

News Items, 1938

March 11–12: Germany invaded Austria. Hitler now the undisputed ruler of over 70 million people.

March 14: Hitler announced the "Anschluss," or annexation, of Austria. Suzannah lived in Vienna much longer than her sister, Margaret. Like the proverbial ostrich, Suzannah, Paul and millions of other Jews refused to look the truth in the face. When Margaret emigrated to the United States, Suzannah remained where she was. Although her parents were in Sopron, she had a lover in Vienna; also the central headquarters of her profession was there. A harpsichordist, she felt she couldn't be successful anywhere else.

Strangely enough under the circumstances, Margaret found that she had grown psychologically. She was pleased to discover that she no longer believed she had to stay and protect Suzannah. As she often was with people she had been close to, Margaret was angry with her sister. One of the first things that came out in her analysis with Helene Deutsch was that Margaret had always asked too little from her father, so Margaret asked Dr. Schoenberger to help her get an apartment in Vienna. Margaret believed that Suzannah intervened and talked him out of it. After that, their relationship cooled down, never to fully recover. Suzannah still depended on her sister very much, and Margaret helped her until the last minute, but she was not a person who forgave easily. Nevertheless, she was relieved to hear that Suzannah was adopted by her good gentile friends, Professor Tokacs and his wife, who swore Suzannah was Mrs. Tokacs' sister and protected her from the Nazis. Because of her friends, Suzannah avoided the fate of so many others. "She escaped," Margaret said, "but with very great scars. She went back to Vienna but had great disappointments and upon her return she had a nervous breakdown."

To Margaret's despair, no communication was possible with her sister for a long time. Then, through much detective work and the assistance of a kind soldier, Margaret finally was able to discover where her sister was. Margaret then sent Suzannah lightweight clothing and other necessities. Mrs. Merta Blos, to whom Margaret felt eternally grateful, was also extremely helpful. Through Mrs. Blos's parents and relatives in Sweden, Margaret was able to get news about her parents occasionally, but as time went on it grew more and more difficult. After a while, it became impossible.

Because of the uncertain fate of her parents and sister, Margaret experienced the years between 1940 and 1946 as an endless nightmare. Nevertheless, she continued to feel considerable ambivalence toward Suzannah, who was making no effort to rescue the Schoenbergers.

News Items, 1939

May 3: Hungary was becoming increasingly anti–Semitic and adopted anti–Jewish laws for the deportation of 300,000 Jews.

September 1st: Germany invaded Poland.

October 12: Deportation of Austrian Jews to Poland began.

Shortly before the Mahlers left Vienna, Margaret saw her parents for the last time. The Hungarian government had allowed them a visa to visit Vienna for one day to say good-bye to her and then return home. The farewells were absolutely excruciating, as though they all sensed that they would never see each other again. Margaret, a woman of forty-one, sat on her mother's lap and cried like a baby, the infant she was never allowed to be.

It is interesting that the brutal Hungarian policy toward Jews relaxed enough to allow Margaret's parents to come say good-bye to her. A few talented Jewish artists and intellectuals were granted exemptions and permitted to remain in Hungary by a government aware of their tremendous contributions to the nation's culture.[5] Perhaps in a similar vein the authorization for Margaret's parents to visit her was given in recognition of the munificence of Dr. Schoenberger's contributions to the welfare of Sopron.

News Items, 1942

June 23: Opening of Auschwitz as a death camp.
September 23: First gassing experiments took place at Auschwitz
October 4: All Jews held in German concentration camps were ordered transported to Auschwitz.

News Items 1943

March 13: The Auschwitz death camp greatly enlarged.
April 21: Jews convicted of crimes were transported to extermination camps, principally Auschwitz. "Crimes" include traveling by public transportation, owning pets, having a hair cut in barber shops, owning a typewriter, electrical appliances, or any woolen clothing or furs.

News Items, 1944

March 19: German army occupied Hungary, 476,000 Jews moved to Auschwitz to be gassed, as the Russian army approached. Seventy percent of Hungarian Jews eventually were murdered.
July 24: The Nazis recorded their largest single total of executions — 46,000 Jews were gassed and burned in one day at Auschwitz.

Margaret's parents remained in Hungary, although her mother desperately wanted to emigrate and come after Margaret. Margaret was terribly distraught about her parents for years, and didn't know if they were dead or alive. In a letter to Pista[6] dated March 25, 1945, Margaret wrote:

> If I only would know that my father died peacefully in his home environment, I would accept this as the most easy departure for him from a world full of horrors. You would oblige me, therefore if you could find out through... the former Hungarian Consul Anton Ullein Revitsky of Sopron, whose parents were personal friends of my parents, when they last heard from my mother and whether there are any possibilities to find out about her. It would comfort me immensely if I knew when my father died and under what circumstances — you may imagine how important it would be for us to know. If only I knew how to proceed.
>
> Please, try to find out these things, With deep gratefulness,
>
> Margaret S. Mahler

Margaret found out later that her father had died a month before Hungary was taken over by the Nazis. Much as she grieved for him, she was happy that he had escaped the catastrophic news. Margaret's mother was another matter. She was taken to Auschwitz and murdered. Margaret learned about it from her friend Beni Ferency, the sculptor, who wrote her a beautiful letter in which he first talked about pleasant things and then gently told her about her mother's death. Seven tons of human hair, 348,000 men's suits, and 836,225 women's coats were all found at the Auschwitz concentration camp, the deathbed for 10,000 people daily.[7] Eugenia Wiener Schoenberger was among them. The news catapulted Margaret into a deep depression. She went for therapy to Dr. Edith Jacobson, who helped her recover, for which Margaret was very grateful.

Mahler never got over her grief for her mother. Joan Jackson said,[8] "Once when she was in a wheelchair I had to take her to Rockefeller Center to get a passport. There was a form I had to read to her. We didn't put in the dates. The guy at the desk asked, 'When did your parents die?' She screamed, 'Die? She didn't die. They were murdered by the Nazis!' She screamed it at the top of her lungs. I was so embarrassed. He just blanched. I guess he didn't hold it against her, because she did get her passport."

A dear friend of Mahler's, Harold Blum, spoke of personal discussions he had with Margaret, in which she spoke of her deepest feelings about her mother. He said, "We had a private conversation about her mother, who was murdered at Auschwitz. Mahler told me this as if she were revealing a dark secret. She said she would never forgive or forget her mother's murder, and had a memorial put up for her in the Hungarian cemetery which said, 'She died a martyr of the holocaust.'"

Mrs. Schoenberger was sent messages by the burgomaster, the mayor of the town, to please go over the border with her husband's nurse. She couldn't do it. She was always a good, obedient citizen, and she couldn't believe she would be dragged away or harmed. Hungary had always been hospitable to her and the Jews, and she couldn't acknowledge that it had changed. Her denial cost her her life.

The Anschluss of 1938, in which Germany annexed Austria, was only the culmination of Austria's political disintegration. The capitulation of Austria to Germany by Chancellor Kurt Schuschnigg rang the death knell to any independence Austria had left. By March 1938, when Hitler occupied the country, practically the entire psychoanalytic community had left for England or America. Never one to avoid facing reality, terrifying as it might be, Margaret understood quite early that the rise of Nazism in the thirties, the resulting series of putsches, and the assassination of Chancellor Dollfuss in 1934 meant that she and Paul would have to leave the country. Aichhorn, who was not a Jew, somehow managed to get reliable information about the Nazi plans, and may well have saved Paul's life. He called one morning and said,[9] "Don't you let Paul out, because the police station in your district has a quota of I don't know how many Jews to be rounded up." Margaret had to fight with Paul to keep him at home, as he thought his absence would let down the old uncle with whom he managed the factory.

Events inside her practice were also a cause for anxiety. One patient felt he had to terminate his analysis, as he was only partly Jewish, and was afraid for her life. She knew she would be unable to continue her practice much longer in the deteriorating political atmosphere, and events both inside and outside of her office convinced her that they had to emigrate right away.

It was unusual for a person to believe the unspeakable horrors that actually were in the offing. Even the Holocaust writer Christabel Bielenberg, who hailed from a politically involved family, acknowledged it was strange that she hadn't spoken out earlier in Hitler's Germany. "It's true we didn't protest soon enough about Hitler," she told an interviewer.[10] "We just didn't know what had hit us. You read about horrors in the newspapers, but you don't really wake up to them until they touch you personally." Many Jews, including some in Margaret's family, were in a state of denial about the atrocities that were going on. In January 1937, Margaret approached her husband's uncle, who lived in the Sudeten part of Germany, about the need to leave Austria. He made light of the situation, saying that the Nazis were only "whistling in the dark." Oddly enough, the Sudetenland was the first part of Austria to be annexed by Hitler.

Hitler's movements in 1937 and 1938 justified Mahler's alarm. In later years she would speak of the panic that seized many Jewish intellectuals when the Germans moved into Austria. She said the analysts, while certainly concerned, were less panicked by the Anschluss than other professionals. She said they behaved in a most "analyzed" fashion, working together most efficiently to see that every Jewish psychoanalyst was relocated. She was very proud of them and her profession.

Besides her mother, Margaret suffered the loss of many other family members to the Holocaust. A boy cousin a year older than Margaret of whom she was particularly fond was killed by the Nazis. Another cousin, Lily Mohacsi, married a Hungarian writer. When he was taken prisoner by the Nazis, Lily was either killed by them or committed suicide. A third cousin, Sandor, was torn apart by police dogs on the streets of Sopron. A great niece with her husband and two children had committed suicide the night before they were to be deported. Worst of all, the Nazis practically annihilated the entire Jewish community of Sopron.[11] Before being occupied by the Nazis, the town had boasted a population of 1,856 Jews. Two months later, 1,470 of these people had been deported to concentration camps, 40 were arrested, 286 were conscripted for forced labor, 55 were infirm elderly, and five were declared "honorary citizens" and allowed to remain.

It was Mahler's genius that, despite the terrible misfortunes she had endured from birth on, she was able to transcend her losses and become one of the great psychoanalytic researchers and teachers of the times. Alfred Kazin[12] speaks of "those historical tragedies in which the rejected of history find their souls again, in which the epics of the race are reborn." Margaret Mahler, thrust out of her homeland only to discover the depths of her selfhood in the flourishing atmosphere of America, epitomizes such a historical catastrophe. As a Jew, she made an important contribution to the rebirth of her race, even though the fatalities she suffered in the Holocaust were indelibly imprinted on her soul. Her complicated relationships with people and her rages, inconsistencies, and paranoid thinking surely were augmented by her tragic history. Does anyone ever really get over so many losses in so short a time? Mother, father, cousins, nieces, friends, her homeland, all gone forever. The bleeding stops, time heals over the surface, and injuries become invisible to the casual eye, but surely the deeper wounds fester for life, their fragile scar tissue split asunder by inconsequential events.

6

London (1938)

The Mahlers finally managed to get to London in May 1938 and stayed there until October. They were not guests of Lady Sassoon as she had written in the letter sponsoring them, but of the British Psychoanalytic Society, who were extremely generous to them, so long as they would not be relocating to Britain. They lived in a boardinghouse in Greencroft Gardens, which was owned and operated by Hedwig Abraham, the widow of the famous German analyst Karl Abraham. Their room and board were paid by the British Psychoanalytic Society.

While Mahler was living in Greencroft Gardens she was touched to receive a beautiful present from her mother. It was the last present she was ever to get from her. Mrs. Schoenberger owned a lovely pair of diamond earrings, which she had made into a set of identical rings, one for Margaret and one for Suzannah. It seems it took the Nazis to bring about Margaret's equal status with Suzannah in the eyes of her mother.

The Mahlers desperately needed to find a country where the two of them could go. It was a question of what country, if any, would admit them, and how many practicing analysts were already there. The British analysts wanted to help, but they also had to look after their own interests. If too many analysts were congregated in one area, none of them could earn a decent living. At one point it looked like the Mahlers would be assigned to South Africa, which utterly bewildered them, as they didn't know a soul in all of Africa or even what language was spoken there. Did the natives speak an African tongue, Margaret wondered? If so, how could she possibly practice her profession? Who would they talk to? With her digestive problems, would they be able to eat African food? Fortunately for their state of mind,

Grete Bibring came to their rescue and spoke vociferously against sending them to Africa. The analysts then called a conference to discuss the Mahler situation at the Freuds' house. Anna Freud and many internationally influential people like the Bibrings, Kris and Hartmann were there to make the decision. The choice was finally narrowed down to Great Britain and the United States. Margaret didn't want to go to America: It was so far away from her family, and she was intimidated by the idea. She said later,[1] "Only the Nazis could have sent me there." Nevertheless, she preferred to come to America, rather than remain where she was. She said the British were very nice to them, but the analysts picked only those people to remain whom they could use. Margaret Mahler was not one of them. They must have been afraid she would give them too much competition.

While they waited for an assignment, Margaret's days and some of her husband's were spent at the Woburn House, where they worked at rescuing people from the Viennese Holocaust. Margaret helped to liberate her husband's family and brought them to London. Characteristically, she also tried to earn her living, as she did not wish to depend solely on the generosity of the British Psychoanalytic Society. Besides treating some of the analysts' children, she gave Rorschach ink blot tests. As she was extremely gifted at interpreting pathology from such responses, she also taught Rorschach technique. She found the work very absorbing, and always remembered it with great warmth and gratitude. One of her little patients was the son of a German colleague. The child refused to understand or speak his native language in England, as he was very defensive about being German. Margaret, with her broken English, had great difficulty in communicating. When the child saw her grappling with the language, he taught her to speak it. We don't know if Mahler cured the boy or not, but he "cured" her. "He was my first competent English language teacher," she said.[2]

Some patients were sent to her in London by colleagues. Happily, she was able to reciprocate by making referrals to them. There were at least three of her former patients in London who had followed her from Vienna, one of whom was the niece of Lady Sassoon, who had helped them leave Vienna. Mahler continued her patients' treatment through the courtesy of a colleague in her Greencroft Gardens office, and Mahler was able to earn a very respectable income. In contrast to Margaret, who wasn't totally dependent on the good will of the British Psychoanalytic Society, there was nothing her husband found to do to earn money in London. He passed his time at Woburn House studying the Rorschach Test and English.

The couple was invited to the homes of a number of former Viennese colleagues, such as the Krisses and The Bibrings. The Hartmanns were not in London at that time. When certain analysts questioned whether the renowned Dr. Hartmann was Jewish, Margaret said he did not emphasize either his Jewishness or non–Jewishness, but that his love for his wife spoke for itself. What he actually told Margaret was that a tiny percentage of him was Jewish, so small that it doesn't matter. Margaret loved him and Robert Bok, who took care of Dora Hartmann after Heinz died, up to the time of Dora's death.

Jones was extremely generous when it became a fact that the Mahlers were sailing to America. He probably was happy to see Margaret go. He invited her to his Harley Street Office and demanded of her, "Dr. Mahler, how much money do you have to disembark with in the United States?" She answered, "Maybe ten or fifteen pounds." He said, "Dr. Mahler, you cannot disembark in the United States with that little money!" She said, "Our passage on the *Queen Mary* is paid for, and in the United States, my cousin, who has money in Switzerland, will keep us going." The cousin who had funds in Switzerland had promised to send them some. Jones said, "You cannot disembark in the United States with only fifteen pounds, and you will accept two thousand five hundred dollars. You will accept it as a loan from the British Psychoanalytic Society and you will not disembark without it." He said, "Not that you need it for living, but it will look very, very bad if you arrive in the United States without...." He meant that one does not come as a proletarian to the United States with no money.

A postscript to this story[3] occurred many years later in Philadelphia at a large celebration of Jones's seventy-sixth birthday and the publication of his book on Freud. He and Mahler were sitting on the dais, when she told how Jones insisted on lending her money to enter the United States. Jones said he didn't remember it at all. Mahler smiled and said, "Jones always was a gentleman."

Mahler always remained sympathetic to other European refugees. She sent money to her surviving European relatives all her life. She was also very gentle with certain European colleagues. For example, Henri Parens said,[4] "She knew I was very hurt, and had come here alone when I was thirteen. She didn't want to hurt me. She respected my thinking. For example when I wrote my aggression book I sent it to Mahler and asked if she would go over it. I still have the copy she edited."

Sometimes, the European connection formed the basis of a lasting friendship. Dr. Ernst Abelin was a friend of Mahler's from the time of he was employed at the Masters Children's Center in the mid sixties to the end of her life. According to him, they became friends because they had a European background in common. She would come to their summer home several times a summer, and bring nice presents for the children. Abelin enjoyed cooking European food for her.

Ava Bry Penman,[5] the daughter of Mahler's friend Thea Bry, in discussing the family's relationship with Mahler, spoke of a certain bond between people that went through the war: "Mahler had suffered tremendously and my parents understood this and accepted her; she had a place at our dining room table as was true of many immigrants who survived the war."

A third analyst, Dr. Raquel Berman,[6] who now lives and practices in Mexico City, Mexico, also became friends with Mahler because of their common European background. Berman said, "Margaret was of Austrian-Hungarian background. I was born in Poland, and came to Mexico in 1940, so we had something in common. One afternoon on an impulse I called her and asked if I could come up. She said yes, which was quite unusual, for she always insisted that people make an appointment with her."

Margaret Mahler, like millions of other Europeans, was deeply wounded by the war, and her creativity was cruelly curtailed by the Nazis who forced her to leave the country of her birth. Nevertheless, her emigration to the United States set off the flood of creativity that culminated in her work on symbiosis and separation-individuation. Her colleague, Dr. James Anthony, once asked her,[7] "If you had stayed in Europe, is it possible that you would have created as much?" Mahler, who agreed with Ernst Kris's belief in the stressful background of creativity, answered, "Whether or not the work I produced since my arrival in the USA deserves the epithet 'creative,' I firmly believe I would not have produced it either in quality or in scope had I remained in Vienna. The stressful process of emigration was probably the most powerful factor that prompted me to put into form, to integrate, to fully express and communicate to others the rich and varied experiences I had gained in my formative years and during the first part of my maturity in Europe."

In addition to the stress of losing family, home, and country, and emigrating to a strange country, Mahler arrived in the United States as a Jewish woman with little money or knowledge of the language. But with her enormous stores of energy and drive to succeed, she gradually found new sources of creativity in her adopted country, with its broad horizons, fresh opportunities for original work, new theories to research, and creative colleagues who offered support for her work.

7

America (1938–1985)

The Mahlers set sail for America in October 1938, on the *Queen Mary*. We can imagine the overpowering emotions felt by the forty-one-year-old Mahler, as the great ship slipped away from the homeland which had cast her out, and relentlessly carried her toward the great unknown. Surely she was relieved at escaping the constant threat to their lives, and felt anguish and grief for her lost homeland and the parents, sister, and many friends she might never see again. But she undoubtedly was panicked at the thought of being thrown into an unknown land where she didn't speak the language and might not be able to work. At the same time, how exhilarated the curious Margaret must felt at the idea of a whole new country and way of life to explore! And finally, if she dared, she would have overflowed with hope for the beginning of a beautiful new life. In all likelihood, her mind was flooded with questions, as the mighty ship made its way across the widening miles. Would she be able to make a living, when she didn't speak the language? Would psychoanalysis be practiced in America as it was in Europe? She had heard rumors to the contrary. If not, would she be considered "old hat," and relegated to the realms of charity? She would kill herself first. Would Paul be able to find a job? Would they have enough money for food? For rent? Where would they live? Would their old friends accept them, as they did in Europe? Would Americans snobbishly reject the "greenhorns" as less than equals? More to the point, would *she* like the brash, money-hungry Americans cultured Europeans disparaged? Knowing Margaret Mahler, we can visualize her spending much of the ordinarily peaceful ocean oasis working through these feelings. Then, as the ship approached the harbor, we can picture the eager Margaret leaning over the rails of the *Queen Mary* hungering for the first sight of what she hoped would be the Land of the Free.

When the Mahlers arrived in America on October 18, they were met at the dock by several colleagues, including Margaret's old friend, Berta Bornstein (who remained a friend until they got into difficulties later on). Berta helped the Mahlers get set up temporarily at the Hotel Paris on West End Avenue. Overcome by homesickness and grief, Mahler soon found a way to handle her anguish. She threw all her efforts into helping her European relatives get visas and sending them food and clothing and obtaining affidavits enabling her European colleagues to come to the United States. As Mahler said to Swerdloff,[1] "The pain of separation, of unbridgeable distance from loved ones, from everything that had been safe and familiar, was at first warded off by increased activity on behalf of those who were left behind."

Margaret was further befriended by a woman she greatly admired, Margaret Ribble, with whom she had studied at the Vienna Psychoanalytic Institute. The Mahlers enjoyed their first American summer vacation in Ribble's comfortable Provincetown house. Mahler and her hostess spent much of the summer discussing Ribble's work, which preceded her groundbreaking book, *The Rights of Infants*.[2] Mahler was thrilled with Ribble's concepts, as they corroborated her own conclusions at von Pirquet's clinic on the importance of mothering to the very life of the infant. Perhaps Mahler felt that Ribble's work made up a bit for her own failure to write up the contrast between von Pirquet's treatment of babies and that which followed at the Moll Clinic.

Dr. and Mrs. Leo Stone were also very generous to the Mahlers. Mrs. Stone alleviated Margaret's fright at being unable to speak the language, as she helped her to learn English. Soon Mahler was spending all her time preparing for the English examination and the state boards. The state board examination turned out to be a triumph for Margaret, who was one of only five percent of refugee physicians who passed the exam and received a New York State license in medicine and surgery. But in 1939 when she took the examination in English required of all foreigners before they are permitted to take the State Board examinations in medicine, she found to her despair that she had failed. Margaret Mahler simply did not flunk exams! She was totally embarrassed by her defeat and considered it a catastrophe, the only examination of her life she ever flunked, besides her first driving test in Hungary. (The scar of that driving test failure remained with Mahler all her life, as she invariably added to any mention of the test, "I later got to be an excellent driver.") Mahler had difficulty all her life with English, and always retained a strong Hungarian accent. As late as 1977, in the film she made on separation-individuation,[3] she pronounced "book" as "boook." She never learned to enunciate w's, saying "ve" for "we," "vun" for "one," and "acquvir-ing" for "acquiring." Mahler was not alone in making such errors. For many adult immigrants such as Mahler, certain letters are difficult to pronounce correctly; in particular, they find the letter *w* impossible to say. When path-ways in the brain to form certain letters are not developed in childhood, the individual forever loses the capacity to speak those letters correctly.

Mahler told a little anecdote about the difficulties she had with her accent.[4] It seems she never could satisfy anyone, no matter what their nation-ality, about her speech. When she first came to New York, she was asked to discuss a paper that was given at the American Hungarian Medical associ-ation. She worked very hard on it, as she was eager to make a good impres-sion on her new countrymen. To her dismay, when she finished her comments, her female colleagues approached her and said, "What an awful Viennese accent you have!"

Her Research Begins (1940)

After Mahler passed the State Board examination she received her med-ical license for New York State in the beginning of 1940, and began to work as a psychoanalyst. She then wrote and presented her highly original paper, Pseudoimbecility: A Magic Cap of Invisibility. This paper marked the begin-ning of Mahler's exciting research career. The major idea of the paper was that certain children pretend to be "dumb" in order to mask their knowl-edge of sex. One of the discussants was Dr. David Levy, whom Margaret liked and respected very much. He was extremely critical in his comments, which upset Margaret greatly, but he later wrote her that on rereading the paper he had become convinced that her theory was correct. Despite Dr. Levy's initial reproaches, Mahler was elated to find that the paper had turned out exceedingly well, and marked her formal acceptance into the New York Psychoanalytic Society. *The Psychoanalytic Quarterly* requested a copy of the lecture and subsequently published it. Her American career had begun with a bang. Dr. Margaret S. Mahler was on a roll!

It helped that she became friends with Dr. Benjamin Spock, who had been analyzed by the great Bert Lewin. Dr. Spock had much in common with Mahler, the most important being that both were pediatricians and psy-choanalysts. Mahler looked up to him as a mentor, although he actually was six years younger than she. Probably Spock's greatest contribution to the practice of pediatrics was to incorporate Freudian insights into his child rearing philosophy. Freud's views about infancy came from his clinical work with adults. He never dealt directly with children and rarely offered advice on their upbringing." Psychoanalysts couldn't give positive, practical advice about the right method or the right age for weaning," Spock said.[5] He was the first to figure out practical methods for raising children that utilized Freud's theories. His conclusions changed the child rearing practices of America, and in all likelihood, the course of history. Since there were few, if any, physicians who were trained in both pediatrics and psychoanalysis at that time, it is easy to see why Spock appreciated Margaret Mahler. He referred to Mahler her first child patients and introduced her to Caroline Zachary, head of the Bureau of Child Guidance. Mahler gave several lectures at Zachary's institute, and met many other famous people there, who also began to send her patients. Spock's fame no doubt contributed to Mahler's extremely successful lifelong practice, and she was always very grateful to him. One boy he sent her for analysis when the child was five years old grew up to live in Massachusetts, and remained in contact with her for decades. When he got married Mahler sent him a telegram. He showed it to all the wedding guests, telling them, "This is a telegram from my child analyst."

Margaret's roll continued, as her lifelong dream of doing extensive psychiatric research seemed about to come true. When she gave the pseudoimbecility paper in January 1941, she was immediately invited to head the outpatient department in the children's services of the New York Psychiatric Institute. At the outbreak of the war, Dr. Nolan Lewis, Chairman of the Columbia University Psychiatry Department, told Mahler that Dr. Reginald Lurie, the grant recipient of the Masonic Scottish Rights Funds, had been called into the service. Under circumstances that happen more often in fantasy than reality, Dr. Lewis offered Lurie's research money to Margaret Mahler for any project of her choosing.

She had been working in the children's outpatient department of Mount Sinai Hospital, where she treated a fascinating case of multiple tics, the Gilles de la Tourette disease. The child's pseudonym was Teddy. When she became head of the outpatient department of the Psychiatric Institute, she asked to take Teddy with her. Mahler and Leo Rangell wrote up the case quite extensively in *The Psychiatric Quarterly*.[6]

When the Scottish Rights Fund became available to her, Mahler couldn't have been more delighted. She decided that she would like to compare the case with others of comparable diagnosis. The project marked the beginning of her tic studies, and was her first extensive research design since the tonsil investigations with von Pirquet. The study resulted in about half a dozen papers in the literature by Mahler and her coworkers, Sam Ritvo, Irma Dross, Jean Luke and W. Daltroff. A number of the papers are still considered classics.

As often happens when one's deepest wishes come true, she relished the work immeasurably and opted to continue it. Mahler and Dr. Luke did a follow up study of the children diagnosed with the Gilles de la Tourette syndrome who had been treated at the New York Psychiatric Institute for the last ten to fifteen years. The results showed that a number of the tic patients developed a psychosis, whether or not they kept their tic symptoms. The highly innovative material was published in *The Journal of Nervous and Mental Disease*,[7] and brought her to the attention of many of her illustrious colleagues as a researcher to be watched.

Working night and day, Mahler was going strong in achieving her deepest desires. The study aroused her interest in another original project, the role of disorders of motility. Freud had singled out the mastery of motility as one of the main functions of the normal adult ego. Mahler formulated a new theory that the steady bombardment of the tiqueur's ego by involuntary tics weakened it to the point where it was incapable of coping with the difficult tasks of adolescence and of handling its dramatic changes and pressures.

With her intense investment in the project, Mahler soon realized that there was a gold mine of case material in the Psychiatric Institute. So after she and her coworkers had completed their study of tiqueurs and written up their findings, they zestfully began to investigate other psychoses in children. Mahler, chief resident John Ross, and Zeira deFries researched the symptoms of some schizophrenic-like and psychotic children and gave a paper on their results at the American Orthopsychiatric Association.

As was her usual wont, Mahler passionately threw herself into the study, and it is no surprise that she produced a conscientious and unique paper. Nevertheless, she was overwhelmed to find that her discussant was Dr. Leo Kanner, the great psychiatric expert on infantile autism. When Mahler arrived at the meeting to present her paper, Dr. William Langford[8] greeted her at the front door with, "Margaret, I hear that you have written a classic paper." "Oh?" she exclaimed. He said with excitement, "Do you know who your discussant is?" She didn't. He said, "It is Kanner, and Kanner himself told me that." The paper turned out to be tremendously important in the history of psychiatry, as it was the first dynamic approach in the literature to the symptomatology of childhood schizophrenia.

This was not the first time Mahler had seen psychotic elements in her youthful patients. She had treated two psychotic children years before in Vienna, and realized that they were neither neurotic nor organic. As was typical of Margaret Mahler, she held on to her convictions even though she was alone in her thinking. The idea that children could be psychotic had not yet permeated the thinking of any other practitioner in Europe or the

United States, in spite of Kanner's work on early infantile autism and Loretta Bender's school for psychotic children at Bellevue Psychiatric Hospital in New York City. Although Mahler's conclusions are more acceptable these days, there originally was great emotional resistance against accepting the concept of infantile psychosis, even by Anna Freud. Perhaps the idea of little children being "crazy," like Freud's theory of infantile sexuality, is just too painful for many of us to bear. But Margaret Mahler was an expert at facing harsh truths. With the encouragement of Kanner, the ever inventive Mahler expanded her work on infantile psychoses to include the psychoanalytic point of view. Thus began the famous project which was to change the course of psychoanalytic history.

Meanwhile, Dr. Milton Rosenbaum had asked her to join the faculty of the Albert Einstein College of Medicine, even before they were ready to take on patients. She accepted his offer, when she still was nominally an associate in psychiatry at Columbia University, and worked as consultant of children's services of the New York State Psychiatric Institute. Mahler was particularly pleased that Dr. Manuel Furer, whose mind functioned much like hers, became associated in the early 1950s with Albert Einstein.

Dr. Furer told me something about his early association with Mahler.

> If one just remembers the negative aspects of her personality one might easily appear antagonistic. The appearance she gave I perhaps understood differently from the others because she confided in me about her feelings of guilt. I first met Dr. Mahler when she was my interviewer for the New York Psychoanalytic Institute in 1954. During the course of the interview, as one might expect, I became somewhat anxious. In Margaret's characteristic way, she noticed and said, "You're anxious. Stop it!" I stopped. It was abrupt, but she meant to be helpful. That was her way to get on with things.
>
> The next time I met Dr. Mahler she was teaching in the Department of Psychiatry at Albert Einstein, at the Jacoby hospital. I had opened the Inpatient Psychiatry Service for children at that hospital and was still in charge of it. She approached me to be a coinvestigator in a grant application to the National Institute of Mental Health to investigate mental illness in preschool age children via a treatment program that she called Symbiotic Child Psychosis. She was both courageous and innovative, because at that time most psychiatrists did not believe psychosis existed in childhood, with the exception of my first teacher, the clinical researcher Dr. Loretta Bender.
>
> We applied for the grant with the help of Dr. Mort Reiser, who was then chairmen of the Department of Psychiatry at Yale University College of Medicine, in writing the application.

In my interview with Reiser,[9] he said, "It was a mutually respectful relationship. I had very high regard for her as a researcher and investigator, and she had a lot of respect for me as someone who knew about both psychoanalysis and psychiatric research. I was able to tease out the cutting edge thoughts and ideas that she had, and to help her 'translate' them into the language of experimental science. Margaret, Manny Fuhrer, and I met at my place in a series of meetings. We discussed her theories and what she wanted to do. I helped her write the application in a way that would ensure that her ideas would be clear to a NIMH 'study section.' In the process I came to know a lot about the way she thought."

Furer spoke of an unheard of twist of events concerning the grant they had been so successful in being awarded, although maybe it was not so strange to anyone who knew Margaret Mahler well.

Mahler was Hungarian and believed she did not express herself well in English. This was not true. Nevertheless, feeling that way, she often asked others to help edit what she wrote, including the grant application. We did obtain the grant and started the study at Jacoby Hospital. After a while we were called in by the then chairman of the department at Einstein, Dr. Milton Rosenbaum. I was on the faculty.

Dr. Rosenbaum said to Mahler, "Now that you have an appointment here, you will have to give a certain amount of hours to the department." Mahler said, "No, I got the grant, and that is what I want to do. I'm not going to do anything else." He said, "Then you can't be here anymore and will have to return the grant." She said, "All right, I won't be here anymore." He was filled with horror at the idea of anybody turning back a grant, and said, "Then you must send back the money." She said, "OK, I'll send it back." We hadn't hired many people yet, so returning the money was no big deal. Everything more or less had to be Mahler's way, especially when her ideas were at stake.

Subsequently, with similar determination, she looked high and dry for another institution to administer the grant. Through a friend she found out that the alumni association of Miss Masters School in Dobbs Ferry owned two adjoining townhouses on Horatio Street in Manhattan. We asked the National Institute of Mental Health for the grant to be returned and they immediately reinstated it. Given Mahler's reputation no review was requested, they simply returned the grant.

A number of publications by Dr. Mahler and myself, as well as by each of us independently, emerged from the study, describing in particular our method of treatment. This involved the mother in a crucial manner that was different from treatment in other places that excluded the mother.

Dr. Mahler also wanted to write a book about what she called infantile psychosis. The book consisted mostly of revisions of her previously published papers, with only minor additions from our recent work. After some discussion we decided on a compromise in which I was not the coauthor but a collaborator. In her introduction she indicated which chapters included my input.

Many people viewed Dr. Mahler as a demanding, unfeeling, and even mean person. This was a one-sided view. There were many times when she came to me to say she had hurt someone's feelings, particularly those who worked under her, and asked me to help her find a way to redress the impact of her words. In many instances we decided that the teaching she could do to further the education of these individuals and to foster their careers was the best way to deal with this problem. She felt good about that.

I want to emphasize that behind this behavior (as I've already indicated) was the determination and devotion to her work and ideas and her efforts to get people to advance them. This was expressed in an abrupt manner, i.e., "You get this done!" But in my view, Dr. Mahler, who was separated from her husband and widowed, was a very lonely person. That was hard for her to admit, so instead she appeared to be demanding and critical of those who she felt hadn't done as much for her as they should, which at times included me. On the other hand she was generous and careful to give respect to others. In an offhand comment I had given the name of "emotional refueling" to the behavior of toddlers who walked away from their mothers, only to turn around, look back and exchange smiles. Whenever it came up she always insisted that it was my description and my language.

After about seven years of the grant when the Masters Children's Center became a New York City clinic, Mahler decided she no longer would participate in the observations of psychotic children. Instead she would get a separate grant for the study of normal development by the observations of mothers and toddlers. I believe that because of her loneliness she found this gratifying, although one must always keep in mind that dedication to her ideas was the most important factor in her decision. The developmental schema that arose out of this study became established in the field of child development.

The last period of our connection was through my daughter, Dr. Jessica Furer. Dr. Mahler had known my children because of the visits we had made to her weekend house in Brookfield, Connecticut. She wrote a letter of recommendation for Jessica's application to the Albert Einstein College of Medicine. After Jessica was a student there, Mahler invited her to dinner several times a year, partly to follow her progress and partly to get to know more about the experience of women in medical school. She was always an educator.

They became friends, and Jessica visited Mahler when she was dying in New York Hospital, where Jessica was a fellow in cardiology. Before Dr. Mahler died at the hospital, she told a number of her friends that Jessica had been a great comfort to her. Toward the end Mahler gave me a large photo of herself.

At the time I was a student at the New York Psychoanalytic Institute, Dr. Mahler gave a course. I don't remember what it was. Subsequently it was no longer taught. I have no knowledge of why. But characteristic of her as a determined educator devoted not only to her ideas but to psychoanalysis she connected with an institute in Philadelphia which had very few teachers and training analysts, certainly none of her stature. For many years she was their only qualifying professor. There she created what she called "piggy-back supervision," as advanced students would sit in on her supervision to learn how to supervise. Singlehandedly, by going to Philadelphia and having the students come to her New York apartment, she created a strong institute that educated a number of analysts such as Henri Parens and Cal Settlage, who have since become important contributors to psychoanalysis. I know that they are all extremely grateful to her. It is another indication of her determination and devotion to psychoanalysis that she took this on.

Mahler found this research stage of her career fascinating. It was what she had been waiting for all her adult life, and exactly what she wanted to be doing. She and Furer were confident that they had discovered the ideal way to investigate the symbiotic nature of mankind. A nursery school setting did not do the job, as they had found out at Albert Einstein, but they were certain the therapeutic nursery project would work. So they applied for the grant to the National Institute of Mental Health, whose attitude at the time was sympathetic to psychoanalysis and to analysts who wanted to work on developmental issues.

Mahler knew full well that she was unable to answer questions like

"What do you expect to find?" and "What methods will you use?" Ruminating over such issues held up her grant application for at least ten years. Mahler said,[10] "I thought to myself that if I could know what I would find, along with the methods, I wouldn't be interested in doing the research." So she sought the help of Dr. Mort Reiser in writing the application.

When Mahler refused the grant money rather than "give a certain amount of hours to the department" at Albert Einstein, fortunately Sybil Escalona had come to work at the hospital, and Margaret sought her help in formulating their refusal. Sybil, an inveterate grant writer, understood the situation well and helped the researchers draft a letter to the National Institute of Mental Health. The letter graciously explained that although Mahler and Furer appreciated the Institute's generosity, they could not accept the grant at present, as neither they nor the hospital were ready to do the research. Margaret thought ruefully that she would never see another penny from the NIMH.

What an exceptional person Margaret Mahler was! Her integrity was beyond compare. I doubt if many people before or after have turned down "the stuff dreams are made of" because the quality of the reality fell slightly short of the dream. Surely she deserved what happened next in her story, which reads like a fairy tale.

Mary Crowley, an editor of the *Psychoanalytic Quarterly*, and a graduate of Miss Masters School, was the friend who told Mahler about the two buildings on Horatio Street. "Mahler offered to take the buildings off the hands, of the alumni saying, 'We'll make them the administrator and get the grant back.' So we opened the Masters Children's Center and soon started a project at the Center." Mahler enthusiastically explained[11] that they had first experimented with a few young psychotic children in a special nursery at Einstein. She then expanded on her first exciting success on the topic of symbiotic psychosis. She said they gave a report on their observations at a

Margaret Mahler, approximately 70, was working at the Masters Children Center when this photograph was taken around 1967.

lecture in a Pan-American meeting on Psychiatry, and in 1960 published a paper called "Observations on Research Regarding the Symbiotic Syndrome of Infantile Psychosis."[12] In the article, the researchers explained why a one-to-one relationship and the participation of the mother is an essential element in the therapy of a psychotic symbiotic child. Mahler added that they required the mother to sit in on the therapy for at least one third of the treatment. It made her part of the therapeutic process, in that she identified with the therapist and learned how to become a parent with whom the child could develop a normal symbiotic relationship. Mahler could help the psychotic children pick up their development, and at the same time vicariously heal her own infantile relationship with her mother. The Repetition Compulsion was at work again for Margaret Mahler, who was able to bring about a healthier ending to the child's (and her own) early trauma.

Symbiosis in human beings was first mentioned in Mahler's 1945 paper on the tic syndrome in children.[13] In a footnote of the orthopsychiatry paper which quoted the article by Mahler, Ross, and deFries, she said that one type of child psychosis originates in the second half of the first and in the second year of life. A second kind originates later in infancy. By then Mahler was already convinced that psychological and biological birth are two different events[14] which take place at separate times in the infant's life. She said that the idea was deep down in her engrams, in her memory traces, ever since she was a pediatrician at the head of the large well-baby clinic in Vienna in the early 1930s. She saw that normal babies brought to the clinic by their mothers were in "a twilight state of existence," unaware of existing outside the symbiotic orbit they occupied with their mothers. Margaret Mahler held on to her idea for almost thirty years, when it was brought to fruition at the Masters Children's Center.

8

Divorce (1953)

While Margaret's career was advancing in giant steps, Paul remained as needy financially as he was emotionally. Margaret knew he was not her equal, and she dominated the relationship. In no way did Paul exude the forcefulness of his charismatic wife. Her friend and colleague, Samuel Ritvo, said of Paul,[1] "I was invited to parties at her apartment and met her husband. He was a very well-mannered, gentle man, with a neat appearance in a European way. He was fairly quiet. Everyone was quiet in Margaret Mahler's presence." Ritvo's image of Paul Mahler as an unassuming man is corroborated by Swerdloff,[2] who said, "I have a vision of her husband walking behind her and carrying her suitcase filled with papers."

Mahler shouldered all the burdens of the marriage herself, including management of their household and most of the financial support. Already highly successful, while her husband had jobs far below his level of competency, she did everything possible to find adequate work for him, contacting friends and colleagues to hire him for Rorschach testing and inquiring about available jobs. She also tried to bolster his self-respect. Mahler told me that when she and her husband ate out at a restaurant, she would slip money to him under the table, to keep him from feeling humiliated when she paid the bill.[3] She resented, too, that he was a typical European man who refused to help with housekeeping duties, unlike many American husbands today who do their share of work around the house. But most painful to her was his wish to sleep as far away from her as possible.

In 1951 Dr. Mahler was enraged enough at her husband's passive aggression to consult Arthur Bondi, of Hoffman, Bondi, Buchwald, & Hoffman, about a divorce. A number of letters between the lawyer and his client clarify the subsequent sequence of events. The Mahlers had a little addition built on to the back of their Brookfield property. Margaret wrote Mr. Bondi that her husband usually slept there.[4] "He always wished to sleep as far away from me as possible," she complained. Finding it impossible to live with him any longer after seventeen years of marriage, she wanted a divorce.

Difficulties between the two had existed long before their divorce, in a realistic as well as a psychological sense. They really weren't even friends. The couple had little in common, except a love of music. Paul was an award-winning bridge player, while his wife had no interest whatever in games. Her competition took place in the real world. She was a nature lover, whereas Paul simply was not a country person. Their differences extended to taking care of their garden. She loved gardening; he did not, so she did all the work in it. He did not want to buy a summer house; she did, so she bought the property in Brookfield, Connecticut. He was resentful about the purchase, because Margaret had made the decision on her own and paid for it herself.

It is my suspicion, however, that Mahler would have put up with her husband's passive aggression if only he had let her inside of himself. In a

Margaret and Paul Mahler in approximately 1950— still together but apart.

Paul Mahler in 1940.

pathetic letter dated July 27, 1951,[5] Margaret wrote to Paul complaining
about his locked closet. In the letter, she told Paul that she was very distressed that he locked his closet, and that even their longtime cook, Rebecca,
commented adversely about him keeping it locked. Margaret informed him
that she was tempted to retaliate by locking her own closet, but would not
do so because he then would not have the benefit of an air conditioned
room. She added that she did not believe in a married couple having such
precious strictly private and secret possessions, and that she herself did not
mistrust people that way. It seems feasible that Margaret was symbolically
complaining about the withholding aspects of Paul's personality that kept
her "locked out," and that she was pleading to be let inside. Their sleeping
arrangements suggest that this speculation is correct.

By October 23, 1951, the couple ostensibly had decided to live apart,
or at least Margaret had decided they would live apart. She wrote her husband a letter,[6] followed by a nasty memorandum which suggests that her
resentment of him was rapidly growing. Unlike her usual custom, she
addressed him coldly as "Paul," and requested that he send her the chest of

drawers which belonged to her dining room set right away. She enclosed sixty dollars, so that he could replace the chest with one of his choosing. She concluded the letter with a warning that if his earnings did not show a rapid and "substantial upward trend," it would be necessary for him to make drastic professional changes in order to assume responsibility for his life in the future.

By October 29, 1951, Margaret, who was laid up with a cracked rib, was even more disgusted with her husband's inability or unwillingness to support himself and do his share of work around their homes. She sent him a bitter and vindictive memorandum[7] written in the third person, which hints that by this time they were not even talking to each other. She wrote that because of her cracked rib, she could not take the risk of driving to Brookfield that weekend. Therefore, she had asked to have the draining of the two water systems postponed. She wrote sarcastically:

Mr. Mahler will have to take the train back to NYC if the inconvenience of having to put up without running water for a day is unacceptable to him — or else put up with this and drive back with Dr. S. on Sunday. Never mind the dog, he will stay in my house and I will be back from Philadelphia Saturday evening and will take care of him.

I am amazed that after so much market research Mr. Mahler ended up by not only using up the $60.00 I paid him for giving me back the chest of drawers (which he has used all the years, but which I preferred to get back because it is a piece of my set of furniture), but bought himself one for $71.00. People with much more means than Mr. Mahler and I get themselves beautiful and good pieces of such furniture second hand or at auctions, particularly when they unfortunately have so much time for bargain-hunting as Mr. Mahler has. But I know it is useless and hopeless to argue with Mr. Mahler's views and ways — if he has to have a hard wood chest.

[Mahler continued raging at her husband's inability or unwillingness to make a living.] As to Mr. Mahler's letter, I only wish him to understand that it is my sincere opinion that it is no use to go on with his illusion of being a psychologist who can earn a living with testing. Nobody can help him there beyond an occasional test. I certainly cannot!! Analysts have very little use for Rorschach testing, anyway, as he well knows by now.

A distant relative of mine arrived here from Shanghai via Belgium one month ago. Within one week she got herself a job as a payroll clerk in a factory. She is living with an old couple (paying $8.00 a week for her room); the man is over seventy, gets old age pensions, but still took a job for $50 a month plus board in a hospital. He is not supposed to earn more than $50 a month; still he wishes to help his wife.

There is plenty of opportunity to work in New York City or in Newark or elsewhere in the U.S. if one is not choosy and does less strenuous running around for jobs, aimlessly, to reassure one's conscience and punish oneself in a conspicuous fashion, instead of really having made up one's own mind that one wants to take a job. What for was the bookkeeping course? Assistant clerkship or assistant-bookkeeping job even with very little earning, I believe, would be the most convenient, least tiresome, and perhaps available job for Mr. Mahler, but he would have to give up his vanity (not his pride, to be sure,) and come down to earth.

Mr. Mahler should not have turned down the Children's Village job if he wanted to work in the field of tutoring or psychology. Nobody can succeed here — he knows it — without provable American experience in any field.

The relationship between the Mahlers continued to deteriorate. On November 7, 1951, Margaret was even more furious with Paul. They had separated unofficially by then, with Margaret living at the stately El Dorado on Central Park West and Paul at their country house in Brookfield, Connecticut. In this letter, she was incensed that he took no responsibility for

Margaret and her beloved dogs at their country home in Brookfield, Connecticut in approximately 1950.

their beloved dog, Peppy, to say nothing of the fact that he took no responsibility for his wife. Illustrating her bitter dissatisfaction,[8] she wrote:

> Paul: I decided that I cannot take care of or pay for Peppy's care on weekends. Therefore I expect and *demand* that you take the dog *every* (not only when I am in Philadelphia) weekend. I shall insist that you take this ridiculously small responsibility without incurring any, even the smallest, expenses to me. It is a trifle compared to my responsibilities and burdens all week long. Furthermore, I do not wish to hear any repercussions, either directly or indirectly, about it if you feel that it is inconvenient for you to have the dog on weekends. You — by God — have been having enough free time, convenience and weekend leisure for years all week and all weekends! You will have to wake up and realize that you are supposed to be an adult "man."

On May 22, 1952, Dr. Mahler received a letter from her lawyer, Mr. Arthur Bondi[9] in which he advised her that he had finally succeeded in having a lengthy telephone conversation with her recalcitrant husband. As per Margaret's wish, the lawyer requested that Paul transfer his share of the Brookfield property to her. Paul asked what he would receive for it. The lawyer indignantly responded that Margaret had purchased the property alone, and he saw no reason to regard it as co-ownership. Paul countered with the comment that he had worked on the property, and therefore would not consent to the transfer of ownership. He insisted on meeting personally with Margaret, and would not discuss any further propositions before the meeting took place.

Mr. Bondi suggested such a meeting to Margaret, in order to "discuss further steps which may have to be taken in order to induce Mr. Mahler to comply with your request." Margaret answered that a meeting would be very difficult to arrange, as she worked from 9:00 A.M. to 8:00 P.M. practically every day, and then went to Philadelphia on Fridays for the weekend to teach.

On the same day, she wrote a letter to Mr. Bondi[10] telling him that she had left his office calmer and more confident than she had been. She said she believed that Mr. Mahler would be willing to bargain about Brookfield, and that the lawyer could go up to the sum of six thousand dollars to buy out Paul's co-ownership of the property. Margaret also felt that Paul would insist on his "rights" to use the room adjacent to the garage, in which "he always wished to sleep, as I mentioned to you, as far away from me as possible."

That the couple had a sexual problem was confirmed in my interview with Margaret's close friend, Dr. Bernard Pacella, who said,[11] "If she had a problem she would call me in to talk about things. She told me about her husband and a sexual problem. She never wanted to talk about it very much, but the relationship with her husband became a distant one."

It seems that Paul greatly objected to being forced to leave the apartment. On May 23, Margaret informed Mr. Bondi[12] that Dr. Marynia Farnham, a mutual friend of both Mahlers, told her that Paul had "carried on like a lunatic" after receiving the letter from his wife's lawyer. He ranted and raved that he had been thrown out of the apartment by Margaret and therefore had the right to get money and everything else from her. When he was told by Dr. Farnham that he had no right to a single penny, he maintained that he could make Margaret appear impossible, how "she did this, that and the other thing," how she behaved, and so forth.

> Margaret continued: In short, he wishes to resort to blackmail! He knows full well that he did not do a darn thing and did not earn for at least seven years out of the fourteen years we were together. Out of the six or seven years he earned less than perhaps a tenth or twelfth of my earnings. He and his friends coaxed me to open the joint account from which he paid out and *I paid in* to build him up, with the view that he finally get himself an occupation, the studies and books of which I myself paid for.
>
> As to the forcible removal from the apartment, I told you that life and work became impossible there. I proposed in writing several times that unless Mr. Mahler can get himself out from the present apartment by the time I came back from my vacation in Europe, he should stay there, but if so I will have to take another apartment which would mean a much higher rent — in that case he not only would have to pay the high rent (from his point of view high) of the 350 Central Park West apartment (the rent was $445.84), but I would not be able to help him financially. That was, I am sure, finally the reason that he moved out.
>
> Please, Mr. Bondi, whereas at first you may be conciliatory, if he intends with his accusations and blackmail tactics to attack or smear me, tell him that he should just go ahead. My integrity will withstand anything he wishes to do.
>
> Because he wants to be buried in the Danbury Jewish Cemetery, I will not make myself poorer and even less secure for my old age than I already am, and mostly due to his personality and his miswirtschaft (mismanagement) of my money and my life. He never gave me one constructive alternative advice, but only criticized the way I spent my money (nothing extra, I assure you). I am really through with my patience and the ingratitude for all my generosity. He knows full well that all the time he was a Zimmerherr (a lodger) who was waited upon and did not have to pay one penny for it.

Margaret had already made up her mind to seek a separation agreement. When Paul asked that he be allowed as part of the settlement to use the small addition to the house where he usually slept, Margaret denied the request on May 27, 1952, reminding Mr. Bondi once more that Paul always liked to sleep as far away from her as possible.[13]

Despite the difficulties Paul was making by dragging his feet, it seems that progress in reaching an agreement was being made. On May 29, Mr. Bondi received another letter from Margaret[14] in which she said that Paul had been advised by his attorney that if he took a job and left the apartment at 350 Central Park West before her return from Europe without a second coronary attack to him, and to avoid further aggravation to her, she

A corner of Mahler's living room on Central Park West in the lovely apartment where Mahler lived and worked much of her life. (Courtesy Trude Fleishman)

would contribute $300 a month to his living expenses. She also repeated that she had told a mutual friend that unless Mr. Mahler left the apartment before her return, he could keep it and pay the rent for it himself. She added, "In this case I shall move, but under no circumstances will I resume work in a place where he obviously makes me unable to follow my profession to the best of my ability, because of the outlay of the apartment and the aggravations and interferences that he had been causing."

Mr. Bondi received an answer on June 2 from Mr. Mahler[15] to his letter of May 26. Paul complained that his interests in the property of Brookfield were not being taken into consideration. He added that in the years he was working, he had made small contributions to the maintenance of the property "in accordance with my abilities." Therefore, should the property be sold, he believed he should receive twenty percent of the net price. He added that in consideration of the state of his health and curtailed earning powers, Dr. Mahler should provide him with funds to make up the difference between his earnings and $300 per month.

In discussing the letter from Dr. Mahler with Bondi in October or November of 1951, Paul defended himself against her accusations. He wrote Bondi that his wife had insisted he take responsibility for his own support. According to Paul, he was seeking a job at that very time and obtained one in mid November, which he still had. In addition he said he had done everything possible to increase his income by doing psychological testing. As a result, since that time Dr. Margaret S. Mahler had had to make much smaller contributions to his support. He stressed that the above facts proved his willingness to burden Dr. Margaret S. Mahler as little as possible with his support, and therefore believed that his proposals were fair and reasonable.

Mr. Bondi received another letter from Mr. Mahler on June 12,[16] in which the effect was quite different from the previous one. The new letter was bitter and angry. In it, Mr. Mahler admonished the attorney that there was no point in meeting with him or in continuing "this fruitless exchange." He said he found Mr. Bondi's manner of communicating with him highly objectionable. He now believed that Dr. Margaret S. Mahler was not giving any consideration to their long association, or showing understanding of the grave difficulties under which he must work with his poor health. Nor does she take into account his feelings in any way. Since he feels powerless to oppose her wishes, he has no choice but to accept them."

It seems that Margaret was not the only person Paul could provoke into anger. Mr. Bondi responded testily to Mr. Mahler's letter on June 23:[17] "Your remark that my client does not consider your situation does a grave injustice to her and, as the facts show, is not tenable." He added that Dr. Mahler had waited a long time before requesting a meeting, in order to give Mr. Mahler time to build up his professional activities and to gain a sense of proportion about the separation.

Bondi further stated that he objected strenuously to the fact that Mahler refused to meet with him. He informed Paul that his refusal to discuss the situation made it practically impossible to come to a mutually desirable settlement. Such matters, he continued, cannot be resolved by correspondence going back and forth. An agreement as such cannot be one-sided but must be based on mutual understanding and give and take.

Bondi continued with the warning that should Mahler continue to refuse to accept Dr. Mahler's legal rights as a married woman, she would be forced to bring action against him in court. That she had not done so before, he added righteously, was due solely to her consideration for Mahler and her desire to save him legal costs, aggravation, and agitation. Bondi urged that Mahler reconsider the situation and thus prevent them from having to resort to that most undesirable measure, an action against him.

Mr. Bondi's threat to take him to court seems to have shocked Paul out of his heel dragging tactics and into action. The separation agreement was signed in July, 1952.[18] It stipulated that the couple had separated as a result of their arguments and lack of agreement. Paul was to have no rights to the property in Brookfield, Connecticut, as Margaret had paid for the property and its upkeep. Margaret Mahler would pay for her husband's support up to $5000. Each month he had to submit a statement of his income for that month. If he earned less than $300, Margaret Mahler was to pay him the difference between the income he submitted and $300. Paul made some minor protest about ownership of the property, saying that he had done work about the place, but Mr. Bondi answered[19] that Paul had absolutely no right to demand any part of the property, as Margaret had paid for and kept up its support. Evidently, Paul agreed to the divorce, as long as his wife sent him a monthly stipend.

It seems that Margaret, too, was dragging her heels about getting a divorce. Perhaps she continued to hope that the actuality of getting a divorce would shock Paul into behaving as a proper husband. On July 26, 1952, however, Paul got a bit of covert revenge when he wrote Margaret,[20] that under the arrangements of their separation agreement her financial obligations to him would cease if the agreement did not result in a divorce by November 1, 1953. The agreement stipulated that she would continue to make such payments if she had not made any efforts to obtain the divorce

Gravesite of the Mahlers where the mingled ashes of Margaret and Paul rest.

and that she would be entitled to stop payments if her efforts to obtain such decree failed for reason of his nonappearance.

Paul seems to have complied with the attorney's instructions, and the divorce was able to proceed. Many letters passed between the couple after the divorce, but they were cold letters and spoke almost entirely about his income and arrangements for the dog.

Paul died on March 15, 1956, and was cremated on March 18 of that year. Margaret Mahler was his sole beneficiary and received $4,014.54 in insurance payments. She bought an engraved bronze urn for his ashes, for which she paid $85.

Strangely enough for a woman who had divorced her husband in a bitter rage, when Paul died Margaret conserved his ashes and had them interred with hers in Sopron, next to the graves of her parents. I suspect that by doing so, Mahler finally achieved what she had wanted from Paul all along, a symbiotic state of complete unity. At long last, they were "one" and Paul no longer was able to frustrate her. Mahler's final statement on their relationship brings home what a sad story their union was. It seems that it wasn't for lack of love that she divorced him, but out of futility and disappointment. Mahler never remarried, or, to my knowledge, had another serious love affair, although she said to many people that she always "kept her eyes open" looking for one.

A remark made to me by Harold Blum[21] suggests how poignantly Mahler continued to wish for a man of her own. Blum said, "Once, when we were dancing together at her 80th birthday, she said she wished that she had had more fun when she was younger. I guess she meant with a young, attractive man." It appears Paul Mahler had never been that man.

But maybe that is not the whole story of the relationship between the Mahlers. I woke up this morning with a surprising dream in which Margaret said to me, "The years I mothered Paul were the best years of my life." Maybe. Perhaps that is why she had their ashes buried together. In which case it is good that she now rests with him for eternity.

9

The Philadelphia Story[1]

In 1950, when the Mahler's marriage had already begun to turn sour, Dr. LeRoy M.A. Maeder invited Margaret Mahler to be chairman of the child analysis curriculum for the Philadelphia Psychoanalytic Institute. There Margaret Mahler was to design and carry through one of the great programs in child analysis in analytic history. This chapter will attempt to record how and why Mahler originated the program, of what it consisted, her remarkable technique of teaching, how she overcame the rejection of her colleagues (with the exception of Anna Freud), and her eventual elevation to legendary stature by the international community of psychoanalysts.

Rejection by Colleagues (1940)

The New York Psychoanalytic Institute, where Mahler was teaching at the time, abounded in power struggles. According to Douglas Kirsner,[2] "For the four decades following World War II the New York Psychoanalytic Institute was controlled by a small inner group. This group felt they possessed special knowledge and acted as an anointed elite." Margaret Mahler was never accepted as a member of this ruling circle, because of what she called the "ambivalent if not double-edged reception of the European psychoanalysts by the New York Psychoanalyst leaders." To Mahler, the refugee from Nazi Europe, the Society seemed a repetition of the closed community in Vienna, where she had been unable to work creatively. She said,[3] "If one is passed over, as I was in Vienna, then one cannot create. To create, after all, is to believe that what one says will count." Mahler said later[4] that she was so awed by Anna Freud and Dr. Deutsch that she needed the atmosphere of America to be able to come out with her ideas.

Unfortunately, coming to the United States did not mean that Mahler automatically received the admiration of her colleagues. In fact, she reexperienced the rejection of her mother at the hands of no less a personage than Anna Freud. One of the great disappointments of Mahler's life was that Freud's daughter never accepted her as an equal. Anna Freud was an extremely important person to Margaret Mahler, but unfortunately her affections were not reciprocated. It was Anna Freud who unknowingly had precipitated Margaret's application to the Vienna Institute. When she worked at the von Pirquet clinic, the entire staff of the remedial pedagogic department had been invited to one of Miss Freud's lectures. Mahler was so dazzled by Anna Freud that she was inspired to apply to the Vienna Institute. But try as Mahler would, Miss Freud never paid any attention to her. Mahler was a member of her continuous case seminar. She said very little there, and if she did make a remark Anna Freud was never interested. Nevertheless, Mahler greatly admired Miss Freud, whom she had for a while as a supervisor. "But when I think about it, I am appalled," Mahler said,[5] "because I would give my material, I would be deadly afraid that she will interrupt me and ask questions, I finished and I was out." Mahler said that she was never comfortable with Anna Freud, and Anna Freud was never comfortable with her. "But then," she added,[6] "Anna Freud did not feel comfortable with most people." There were certain analysts she listened to very carefully, but Margaret Mahler was not among them.

Nor did Anna Freud think highly of Mahler's books and papers. Anna Freud and her followers were concerned only with what takes place within the mind, and did not consider Mahler's research on the behavior of infants the proper domain of psychoanalysis. Mahler, who did not take well to rejection, wooed Anna Freud, and sent her many small gifts and papers over the years, one of which was a pencil on a string. There is no indication that Miss Freud sent any presents to Mahler in return.

Mahler never gave up trying to woo Anna Freud. In 1966, when Mahler was sixty-nine years old, she was still trying to win Miss Freud's approval. At that time, Mahler told me[7] that she was going to deliver a paper at the Menninger Clinic. "I am going to give my paper there because Anna Freud will be there," she said. "I don't have to go to Kansas to deliver a paper." Poor Margit, doomed to repeat the rejection of her mother even with the great Anna Freud, who was no use at all in helping Margaret Mahler overcome the sad effects of the Repetition Compulsion![8]

The late Jacob Arlow was a witness to the pain Anna Freud's rejection caused Mahler. He said,[9] "I was not involved directly in the child analysis wars in the New York Psychoanalytic Institute, but I realized there was a disrespect for Margaret. There was a split between Mahler and Berta Bornstein, who had the support of such important people as Marianna Kris. For the longest time, as far as I can recall, the voice of Mahler was not heard much in child analysis discussions in New York. The rejection moved her to put down teaching rules in Philadelphia for child analysis. She was a no-nonsense lady, and said things straight, as she thought them. As a result I'm sure she experienced many painful moments at the meetings of the New York Institute and elsewhere. This was equally true of Anna Freud, when she gave some seminars in New York, and Mahler was repeatedly rebuffed with the things she had to say. There was a time when Anna Freud appeared at the New York Institute with the faculty. I can still see a picture of Margaret on the first row, first seat to the right, and have a feeling that some kind of rebuff was administered to her at that time. Anna Freud used to have a biennial or annual reading at the Freud Center in London, where a select group of people was invited to attend and participate. I do not recall if there was any interchange between her and Margaret, but not a whiff of reference to Margaret Mahler was made. I remember being in the library where the meetings were held and looking for Mahler's books. I don't recall coming across more than one."

Karen Berberian, Selma Kramer's daughter and a child psychologist, corroborated Anna Freud's snubbing of Mahler. Berberian said, "For reasons I never fully understood, Margaret's followers viewed Anna Freud as the enemy, because she apparently did not approve of changing psychoanalytic theory based on the data that Margaret was collecting."

Mahler confided in Fred Pine[10] about a particular distress. He said, "Mahler was quite disturbed about Anna Freud's work in 1965 about normality and pathology in childhood, which seemed to present Mahler's work in a non-understanding way. She was very troubled by that."

Anna Freud finally made one complimentary remark about Mahler's contributions that Margaret knew of. She was told by several people that Miss Freud said that the only two people who did not stop investigating beyond the obvious were René Spitz and Margaret Mahler. Mahler said to Swerdloff[11] that Anna Freud's students in Hampstead had used her concepts in many of their important papers. "I think they are the best papers that have come out of there," Mahler added defensively. Anna Freud's begrudging praise was of some consolation to Mahler, but it was too little and too late to make up for all the years of rejection.

Dissension at the New York Psychoanalytic Society

Besides her difficulties with the Viennese Psychoanalytic Association and Anna Freud, Mahler ran into complications at the New York Psychoanalytic Society. It is difficult to communicate the quality of the strife and dissension that permeated the society for many decades, in which an authoritarian clique ruled as tightly as the Catholic Church over its constituency. According to Kirsner,[12] such conflicts are endemic to psychoanalytic institutes. He speaks of the early New York Psychoanalytic Society as "an arrogant ruling clique who behaved as though they had a channel to the truth." Such splits and dissensions have been characteristic of the psychoanalytic community since the time of Freud himself. Could it be that these great analysts, like Mahler herself, never fully resolved the difficulties of the rapprochement subphase of separation-individuation, in which the toddler learns to integrate feelings of love and hate?

Unsurprisingly in that atmosphere, the New York Psychoanalytic Institute was wracked by quarrels and conflicts about the chairmanship of the child analysis program. Like many of the "unanointed" Society members, Mahler was at odds with the program. A split characterized by great animosity developed between Mahler and her former friend, Berta Bornstein, who had the support of such important people as Marianna Kris. It is still very difficult to get members to divulge the cause of the dissension, as they remain loyal to the institute even at this late date. For example, when asked about the division, an analyst who did not wish to be identified said, "A lot of things were going on at that time, which I am not at liberty to talk about. It was a long time ago and it is best to forget about the whole thing. Mahler represented a group of people who worked with children who were not given much credit. Berta Bornstein was a clinician, and did very different things with children. She simply taught how to treat children. It was very early in Mahler's career and there was no real understanding of what she was doing."

The analyst continued, "The New York Psychoanalytic Society had a philosophy that if you worked outside of analysis you weren't an analyst and were blackballed. Margaret was blackballed, and she never got over it. When she had written a number of papers, she was permitted to teach there one year, and then replaced. She was not happy about it."

When asked about the dissension, Manny Furer said[13] he was not around at the time of the split, but to his knowledge, people were asked to give certain courses, and there was no such thing as an instructor being fired. He also said that, knowing Margaret, she wouldn't stick around to be fired. She was a proud woman, and at the first indication of any conflict, she would have turned on her heels and left.

The best explanation of what really happened between the two women was given by Mahler herself, in a taped interview with Peter Neubauer and Selma Kramer.[14] According to Mahler, the main cause of her leaving the Institute was the derisive character of her former friend, Berta Bornstein.

Surprisingly enough for a person who seemed so competitive, Mahler said that Anna Freud had told her that she had to learn to compete. "To stay in New York would have been to compete," Mahler said. "I wanted to get away from so many people. The students there were very bad. There was no chance with Berta for anybody else. She destroyed everybody, even the students. As soon as somebody came out with something new she destroyed it." Mahler, then, left the New York Psychoanalytic Institute for Philadelphia to escape competition with the vitriolic Berta Bornstein. For, despite her own fierceness, it appears that when it came to criticism of herself, Margaret Mahler was a vulnerable woman who was unwilling to face Bornstein's ferocious attacks. The split permanently ruined the friendship between the women, along with Mahler's New York teaching career. As a result, she had to think about shifting her teaching activities elsewhere.

To make matters worse, Mahler felt the society was using her as a pawn to get Dr. David Levy removed from the Continuous Case Seminar and replaced by Bornstein. Mahler, who had been conducting the seminar for a year, was not reappointed. Bornstein, who, unlike Mahler, was fearless in the face of competition, was assigned to the position, which she held on to until shortly before her death. Mahler admired David Levy very much, and thought he was a creative thinker and excellent experimental researcher. She always regretted that she had been the innocent person who had caused him to resign not only from the New York Psychoanalytic Society but from the American Psychoanalytic Association. Margaret Mahler didn't take well to being treated like a "rejected country cousin." She found the situation especially difficult, being, as she put it, " the exceptional child of my father, with all its positive and negative aspects." Since she felt she no longer could work at the New York Psychoanalytic Society, she required another place to apply her teaching skills and was badly in need of a teaching institute when she received the Philadelphia offer. At the time, it seemed like a total defeat for Mahler.

The Philadelphia Institute

In respect to getting along with each other, the Philadelphia analysts were no different than their prestigious colleagues. Shortly before Mahler began teaching in Philadelphia, the institute was experiencing difficulties similar to those of the New York Psychoanalytic Society. A long-brewing split had occurred at the society which involved Pearson, the famous Temple University Medical School professor, Spurgeon English, and Maeder. The problem, again, was a power struggle between personalities. Pearson and

English had worked together and coauthored many books and articles, but found themselves becoming increasingly inimical. Pearson, who was much more orthodox than Maeder, joined the new group. Maeder was on English's side of the split, while Robert Waelder was in both schools. The training analysts were unable to see eye to eye, and each taught his or her own version of psychoanalysis. It was very confusing to the students, who were the real victims of the dispute. Mahler, who dreamed of training a network of highly trained child analysts, despaired of a state of affairs in which gifted potential child analysts were shortchanged in their education. She was badly tempted to remedy the situation, but cringed at the idea of entering into another professional brawl. Mahler consulted Phyllis Greenacre about her dilemma. Greenacre advised Mahler not to leave her alma mater or she would regret it. Many of her other colleagues cautioned her in similar fashion and said that running a training program in another city already permeated with dissent would not work. But Margaret Mahler was not a person who listened to advice, unless it was what she wanted to hear. So she went to Philadelphia tongue in cheek to attempt a new professional life.

In the first years she found it a very lonely position, especially because she had so few co-educators. In the still of the night she must have wondered if the New York analysts were correct in their assessment of her Philadelphia venture. But she refused to waste her time bickering and fighting. She knew she needed a fresh start as a teacher and was determined to get it, even if she had to create it herself. She had no doubt she was an excellent educator and took a calculated risk, even though it meant undergoing the hardship of traveling to Philadelphia every second weekend. It turned out to be a serendipitous choice that established her as a great teacher of analysis and was a move she never regretted.

All of this took place in the fifties. During that period the aging Mahler was incredibly busy. For ten years she was the chairman of the child analytic training program in Philadelphia, and commuted to train the child analysis candidates every other weekend from Friday afternoon until Sunday night or Monday morning. On Friday evenings at 7 o'clock, she conducted a continuous case seminar on child analysis which would go on until midnight or later, and on Saturday mornings she supervised the individual candidates. Then she ran an advanced seminar in which one candidate presented a continuing case of analytic material of what had transpired during the sessions of a child patient that week. The material consisted of what the child said or did, and how the young analyst responded. The presenter would send the notes to Margaret during the week and she studied them on the train coming to Philadelphia.

In addition to the tremendous amount of work involved in her Philadelphia teaching, Mahler had a practice in New York, and was also doing some teaching there and conducting research. It is probably just as well that the Mahler marriage was disintegrating. It is difficult to see where she would have had room in her busy life for a committed relationship. "That is more than a woman can do!" she groaned, in a rare lapse of her perfectionistic standards. Nevertheless, the move turned out to be one of the most gratifying experiences of her lifetime and led to what she considered her most lasting contribution.

"I don't think this is any subjective evaluation of it — that most of that group are now the leading child analysts in America," she said proudly in 1980.[15] "There is Cal Settlage in San Francisco, there is the present chairman who also was the previous chairman, and Selma Kramer, the present chairman of the Child Analysis committee and the Committee of the American, and other fine child analysts such as James Delano, Stewart Finch, and Saul Harris. There are people in Ann Arbor, there are people in Pittsburgh, etc."

After working from Friday afternoon through early Monday morning in Philadelphia, Mahler returned to New York to resume her practice and research duties. This horrendous schedule continued throughout the fifties and into the sixties, until the demands of her workload and perhaps her health necessitated that the candidates travel to New York to see her, rather than the reverse.

What besides her need to prove herself to her rejecting mother motivated Margaret Mahler to exhaust herself in the child analysis training program of the Philadelphia Institute for over a decade? Surely it was more than a wish: It was more like a craving, possibly related to the instinctual drive to have children. Or perhaps we can postulate a new instinct, the need to teach, akin to Freud's epistemological instinct, the need to know. There is no exact word in English to describe the urgency of Margaret's need, at least that I know of. There is, however, a Japanese word, ongaeshi, which means the act or compulsion to pass on knowledge. The word ongaeshi accurately describes Margaret Mahler's crusade to train the student child analysts of Philadelphia.

Despite her herculean efforts to teach the students, Mahler the perfectionist was dissatisfied with her initial results. She believed a much larger staff was required to train the students satisfactorily. She told the American Psychoanalytic Association that she needed another child analytic teacher, but they couldn't get anyone else who was willing to undertake the bimonthly trip to Philadelphia. Mahler said,[16] "I was very much aware of— I don't like today, and I didn't like at that point — incest, psychoanalytic incest, that the students should not be exposed to another teacher." To remedy the situation, she put her ingenious creativity to work and initiated a regular supervisory seminar in which senior candidates guided the new students. The student's first case was supervised by Mahler, but the second case was overseen by a senior candidate, who, in turn, was supervised by Mahler herself. She dubbed this system a "piggyback" supervision. The three participants would meet and discuss the supervision. Mahler would stay in the background and observe how the supervisors monitored the candidate. This would give her a bird's eye view of what everyone was doing. Kramer felt that the method of sitting there and seeing how the work was proceeding was infinitely superior to the usual "control" case in which the candidate tells the supervisor how he or she supervises. Years after Mahler originated this system of teaching, it was adopted by the American Psychoanalytic Association.

A few candidates objected to others being present at their supervision sessions, while most did not. For as the years passed the group had become very close and developed trust in each other and in Mahler, and were aware of the talents and foibles of their colleagues. Another reason for "sitting in" on someone else's supervisory session was a practical one. When people traveled from Philadelphia to New York, the train schedules did not exactly meet the beginning or end of the supervisory sessions. So with the permission of the supervisee, the candidates would quietly slip into the room and learn from Mahler's supervision, thus adding to the knowledge they gained during their own sessions.

The first meeting in Philadelphia was held at the home of Earl Loomis, one of the candidates of the Philadelphia Institute, who already had some experience in treating children in New York. Other members of that first group were Sandy Ford, Katherine Buckner, and Stuart Finch, who were second year candidates because they had taken some previous training with Pearson. Selma Kramer, a first year student, was permitted to attend the meetings, provided she took second year courses concurrently with the first year.

Mahler tried to stay out of analytic politics for two years, until a situation occurred which hit her where she lived. Unable to restrain herself any longer, she expounded to Pearson about the poor level of two analytic students. She felt they were not bona fide psychoanalytic candidates but were in the program only to get as much out of it as they could and to be able to drop names. Apparently her diatribe worked, as one no longer sees their names anywhere in the literature. The next year, when Calvin Settlage joined the group of candidates and Kramer was elected president of the society, the quality of students was more to Mahler's liking. "It was an entirely different ball game," she said at a meeting of several candidates. "Selma impressed me as an outstanding clinician, and Cal as a very talented theoretician. If I threw out some problems or gave some reaction to the material, they picked it up and it was a very rich experience." Selma Kramer added, "We had an *esprits de corps*." After that, Mahler and Maeder carefully screened the candidacies. One applicant, Dr. John S..., was "bumped" from the group. Mahler said, "He came up to New York, and knew nothing and was argumentative and we felt he was interfering."

The second year, Kramer was chosen to present a case in the Continuous Case Seminar. She brought in the material, and Mahler pointed out certain trends in it. She asked for elaboration and the clinician's reaction, and then the group took over and asked questions. The Continuous Case Seminar was open to many people, including a few from the Association. Perhaps twenty individuals attended. They were a heterogeneous group, including people from many professions. One was a surgeon who was interested in psychoanalysis, others were eligible social workers and psychologists. Although Mahler didn't mind their presence, it put some of the candidates under a good deal of pressure. For example, Selma Kramer said, "M_____ S_____ was there from the association. She would sit there with her beady little eyes and wait for somebody to make a mistake. Then she would jump." Mahler said the students from the association were like siblings who went from one parent to the other, who each wanted to appear the better parent.

As if this wasn't enough for one weekend, Mahler presided on Saturdays over an Advanced Technique Seminar, which only candidates in training were allowed to attend. It was not a continuous case seminar, but a much smaller group who provided material that had been sent to Mahler during the week. She would pick out somebody and ask that person to present such and such from their case. After a while, the candidates got together and formulated certain concepts like dealing with the masturbation conflict or a particular defense. She also would refer the candidates to literature, such as basic analytic concepts. The Saturday meetings were really a combination of lectures and presentations. On Friday nights, the presenter was the only one who gave case material, but on Saturday, each person would have individual supervision. The sessions would start in the morning and continue until late at night, or even until Sunday. They were a kind of tutorial, with only two people there, Mahler and the presenter. She kept up that schedule for approximately six years, until Kramer and Settlage were able to take over the supervision. They realized that they couldn't expect Mahler to continue indefinitely with that kind of work load. So at first they changed Mahler's Philadelphia visits to once a month, and once a month the candidates would come to New York. Later, all the meetings were held in Mahler's apartment or her Brookfield house.

Mahler, with her penchant for innovation, singlehandedly tried to remedy the lack of sufficient teachers. In addition to her piggyback supervision, she introduced the group to a practice she called reporting. She would assign one candidate to be the reporter to summarize what happened in each seminar. The person would be asked to point out the "red thread" of the case which had been discussed, such as special theoretical issues or specific problems in technique like how to deal with resistance. These reports would be read at the beginning of each session, so there was a continuity between what had gone on before and how it fit into the next hour of the case. The candidate who did the reporting had to condense pages of notes, and doing so gave the reporter a real feeling for what had gone on in that session.

Mahler was generous with the candidates in other ways besides her time. When they came to her home in New York, she fed them delicious European food along with the supervision. She also was generous to the candidates in a way that Helene Deutsch had not been. Selma Kramer recalled that Mahler had given her and Cal Settlage each a book for Christmas which was engraved, "To the Sorcerer's Apprentice." Mahler repeated the story to them that when she was in analysis with Deustch she had a dream of the Sorcerer's Apprentice in which she could not stop the water from coming and coming and coming; she could not stop the flood. She went on to explain that Deutsch was furious because she, Mahler, had the audacity to see herself as the apprentice of the sorcerer, and, what was equally forbidden, to think of analysis as magical. Mahler was not about to replicate Deutsch's behavior with her own students. The Repetition Compulsion was at work again, but this time it had a better ending.

Mahler said to her students that the more subjective an analyst's influence is, the worse it is from the analytic point of view. Kramer agreed and told of a person coming into the child analysis program in Philadelphia at which she was teaching. He gave her what was meant as a compliment: "I thought you were going to be another Margaret Mahler, that is, you were going to mouth everything that she said, but you know, I find that you learned something and you're doing it in your own way." Kramer recalled that Margaret had given her the worst time ever when she told Kramer something one week and she used it the next week, when it didn't apply at all. Mahler exclaimed, "Good heavens!"

Kramer confessed that indeed she had inadvertently used Margaret's words, and that Margaret really had laid her low. She told a Hungarian folk tale about a foolish young man who brought a cow somewhere and was told that he should have led the creature by a rope. The next week the man was sent for butter, and instead of carrying it he dragged it by a rope. Mahler taught her disciples not to imitate but to think analytically. She encouraged each candidate to do and say things their own way within the realm of good technique, and taught them that no two analysts should work in exactly the same way.

In corroboration of that philosophy, Kramer said that Mahler herself worked differently from other analysts. Kramer spoke of attending Pearson's psychiatric clinic at Temple University during her residency. He never saw parents, and had a social worker see them only once to take the child's history. According to Kramer, Pearson thought parents so low that "he wouldn't even spit on them." He believed they were terrible creatures who caused all the child's problems. Mahler had a very different attitude and referred her students to an article by Dorothy Burlingham on what she called "the informative alliance." It gave a sense of people working together, and was very different from what Kramer had learned at Temple. Pearson thought that parents were "abysmally bad." Mahler, on the other hand, instructed her students that it was in the interest of the child for the analyst to support the parents. When she needed to make a referral to a child analyst in New York, Mahler found it difficult to do, because although the analyst was otherwise excellent, she knew the mother would have a dreadful time with him. Kramer said that Mahler had taught them that the parent-child relationship is a living relationship, in contrast to the analysis which would end some day. She stressed that the analyst should not overestimate his or her importance to the child. Mahler added that if the young patient goes into a rage against the parent, and the analyst says, "Yes, yes, you are right, this was awful," the next hour the child would have a resistance. He might turn against the analyst because he felt so guilty. What the analyst should say in such a case would be something like, "Well, you see it that way now." Kramer added, "Or at least, let the child know he's ambivalent, he's angry but he still loves."

In an interview with Nancy Chodorow,[17] Mahler despaired of those analysts who did not give any credit to mothering, or recognize what mothering really means in terms of basic pleasure. She already had emphasized her philosophy on the subject as early as in her first book, *On Human Symbiosis and the Vicissitudes of Individuation*,[18] and was pleased that it continued to bring in almost as much in royalties as her more famous book, *The Psychological Birth of the Human Infant*.[19] Mahler was very aware of the part mothers play in human development because of her experiences with her own mother. "I had a very hard time with my mother. I came at a time she certainly didn't bargain for it," she said.[20] "And yet as I grew older, or I became more mature, my understanding of my father diminished and my understanding of my mother grew in leaps and bounds. I still did not solve that mystery, but I am one of the very few child analysts who never fell into this ubiquitous shortcoming of child analysts to be very strict with the mother. I always see the mother's side of it. I was tremendously interested in the mother/child relationship from the beginning, and wanted to know how much the adaptation of the child is a result of good endowment, because I certainly had to adapt to an awful lot."

Joyce Edward[21] spoke of Mahler's support of the much maligned parents of autistic children. Edward said:

> I, who was then serving as a social worker in a school for autistic children, learned of her ideas on childhood schizophrenia through her writings and through a course I took with Rubin Blanck. At the time when Mahler was studying this pathology, the prevailing view was that autism was caused by failures on the part of the parents. A major figure proposing this was Leo Kanner. I cannot recall whether he used the term "refrigerator" parents in describing these mothers and fathers, but it was a frequently used term. Such a view of course added to the agony that parents of these children faced, and I found that it did not seem to apply to the mothers and fathers I was working with. While there were a few parents whose own pathology might have contributed to their offspring's difficulties, in the main I found that the mothers and fathers of the children in our program were not cold or withdrawn. They were well connected with their other children and seem to be able to help promote their development. Whatever anxiety and depression they manifest seemed to me to be primarily the result of the difficulties they faced in dealing with their very troubled and very difficult to raise autistic children.
>
> When I discovered Mahler's writings, it was at a time when the psychiatrist and psychologist on our clinical team were convinced that it was the pathology of the parents that led to childhood autism, and I was something of a lone voice when I questioned that parental failures were the cause of this severe disorder.
>
> As you know, Mahler concluded that childhood autism, with some exceptions, is the result of some innate deficit in a child, which prevents them from taking advantage of the nurturing their parents seek to provide.

On another note, Chodorow asked Mahler,[22] "What ways of thinking or qualities of yours do you believe have been important to the contributions you've made as a psychoanalyst?"

Mahler, who neglected to mention her pressing need to make her mother and Anna Freud love her, answered, "Tremendous curiosity ... Not being afraid of what one finds out.... Very much self-esteem.... Unfortunately, it was the opposite of it as far as my femaleness is concerned, which made my life very one-sided."

Chodorow, the famous feminist, asked, "Do you think there are ways that you were influenced by the fact that you are a woman?"

"I had a fabulous career as a teacher," Mahler responded. "I think because I was a woman, my Philadelphia students, who are now all over the United States, must have had some transference, some special transference to me as a mother.... Clinically, I am much less pre-oedipal than my pupils. I am not making such a big thing out of the pre-oedipal. For example, a certain institute which is very ego oriented thinks that because Mahler found those, those ... what are they called? subphases? they can cure it. I took the wind out of their sails in that I told them that we can go back only so far, and that if there is a structural deficiency, you cannot undo it."

Incidentally, this statement of Mahler's took the wind out of my sails, too, along with those of the "ego-oriented institute," as I had tried many times with only varying degrees of success to correct structural deficiencies.

Long before the Mahler Symposiums became a yearly event, the Philadelphia Psychoanalytic Institute had annual seminars. Mahler would come down for one weekend a month and there would be programs for the child analyst candidates.

Mahler often stayed at Kramer's house for the weekend. She first came right after Kramer's son Jimmy was born in 1953 and continued to visit as long as she was able to travel. Kramer was extremely attentive to Mahler and did everything she could to assure her comfort. According to Cal Settlage,[23] "Kramer had a mothering attitude toward Mahler, and it was something to be envied." Every year on the night before the annual Mahler symposium, Selma Kramer would give a party honoring Mahler. The following is a description by Selma's daughter, Karen Berberian, of those parties.[24]

> The party was held on the Friday night before the symposium on Saturday. My mother came up with the idea of the party as a way of making sure that the out-of-town speakers arrived in advance. Until the very end, when my parents were too old and too sick, the party was at their house. They had a tent put up in the backyard, and people were free to roam the first floor of the house, including the living room, dining room, her office, the enclosed back porch, the back patio and the tent. The party was always catered. The food was very good, usually salmon, beef, salad, asparagus, wine, appetizers, something like that. It was served as a buffet in the dining room. My mother always needed something from me at the last minute, usually snack tables and the salted mixed nuts.
>
> All the local discussants were there, as were her favorite students. I imagine other people were invited because they were officers of the Philadelphia Psychoanalytic Society. She invited some people who were less important in the local psychoanalytic hierarchy — social workers and psychologists — because they were her friends. Her good friends Harold and Mildred Parker, both musicians, were always present. My husband, John, attended at first, but not always. I was almost always there.
>
> Margaret would sit on the sofa like a queen, and people would come up to her and pay their respects. Sometimes John was the only person who remembered to bring her some food. He was probably the only person who was not under her spell. Therefore he could think clearly and remember that she needed to eat.
>
> My mother greeted the guests at the front door and saw that people were introduced to each other. My father, the eternal engineer, was in charge of making things work, like seeing that the tent was ordered and installed correctly and that the bar functioned. He always hired the same person to tend bar, a police officer who moonlighted as a bartender. My father paid everyone at the end of the evening and tipped the servers. I think there was funding for the party, at first from the Medical College of Pennsylvania, later from Jefferson. The party was over by 11 P.M., as everyone had to get up early the next morning to attend the symposium. I do not

remember toasts, speeches, music, or entertainment. Everyone was dressed up. Most of the analysts were nice to my father, John, and me, but they also spent a lot of time trying to impress each other.

Mahler came to Philadelphia from 1950 to 1956, and the candidates came to New York from 1956 until 1961. Some analysts continued indefinitely to come to her in New York for individual supervision. A few even came to the house in Brookfield. The supervision didn't exactly end; it petered out as Cal Settlage and Selma Kramer became full supervisors in child analysis and took over Mahler's teaching duties. During the last years of coming to New York, they started a continuous case seminar in Philadelphia, to form the basis for a later program of their own. Individuation was Mahler's lifetime goal, whether for herself or those fortunate enough to be taught by her. She regularly rose above the clash of wills that destroys many an analytic community and accomplished what she had set out to do in Philadelphia; she had taught her students to get along without her.

The rejected child also had proven herself worthy of her mother's (and Anna Freud's) love. Margaret Mahler had overcome mighty odds and, rightfully, felt proud of herself. At least for a little while, she had conquered the Repetition Compulsion.[25]

10

The Masters Children's Center

The Great Research Begins (1956)

When asked once if she was a good analyst, Mahler answered, "I don't know if I am a good analyst, but I know that I am a fine teacher of child analysis." Mahler's opinion of herself as a fine teacher is corroborated by Raquel Berman, along with many others, who said,[1] "I was in one of her collective supervisions. McDevitt and others were there. I was very impressed. *She supervised with the precision of a surgeon.*" But magnificent as Mahler's accomplishments as a teacher of child analysis were, there was another aspect of her genius that clamored equally to be lived out, that of the researcher. How that facet of her personality developed and its incredible results will be the focus of this chapter.

In 1956, the Masters board at 75 Horatio Street had received as a heritage from an alumnus of the Masters finishing school two lovely Greenwich Village buildings, which were fully equipped to be nursery schools. The board was in a quandary as to what to do with them. Then an educator named Mrs. Margaret Freed told them that Drs. Mahler and Furer had a project which could fit very well into the buildings. The board immediately invited the researchers to make Masters Children's Center their professional home.

Convinced that the usual nursery approach was not the right method with very sick, psychotic children, Mahler and Furer spent the first year and a half diligently working out their plans for a therapeutic nursery and trying to get on their feet financially. In 1959, with Mahler's customary "chutzpah,"[2] they reapplied to the National Institute for Mental Health to reinstate the grant to investigate the natural history of symbiotic child psychoses. To their amazement, the entire grant was reestablished. Masters Children's Center was unknown to the NIMH, but because of Margaret's fame, no doubt, the grant was awarded to the researchers.

Along with the NIMH grant, Mahler gained the support of the Schlumberger people from Houston, who were vastly wealthy and owned an oil services company. "They were enormously successful and their stock was an important matter with the Masters Children's Center, as well as the Mahler Foundation," according to Irving Sternschein, an American Psychoanalytic Association colleague of Mahler and treasurer of the Mahler Foundation.[3] "Mahler got to dominate the Schlumbergers, who had a wonderful collection of art. They were very supportive financially of the Mahler Foundation, giving them stocks that increased in value. The MacArthur Foundation in Chicago was also helpful. She always had good relationships with people of that ilk. They got to rely on her, and were very interested in what she was doing with children. The Foundation was set up based on their compassion. They funded separation-individuation, supporting the administrating arm of that research."

The Separation-Individuation Process (1959–1975)

Mahler had long had intuitive feelings about the roots of symbiotic child psychoses. Beginning with her insights at the well-baby clinic at the Mauthner-Markhoff Hospital in Vienna, she felt that infants were born psychologically unfinished. As Henri Poincare said many years ago, "It is through intuition that we discover, but through science that we prove." Margaret Mahler was now ready to put her "hunches" to a scientific test and demonstrate to the world that they were fact.

Soon after Mahler and Furer began their tripartite research at the Masters Children's Center, Mahler increasingly wondered why so many infants emerged from the first three years of life with a firm sense of their identity, while a small minority remained locked into the boundaries of their mother's psyche, unable to develop personalities of their own. For years she had been haunted by her observation that normal infants and symbiotic psychotic children shared the common trait of twilight existence. Despite tremendous differences between the two groups, Mahler could not put the similarity out of her mind. To put the investigative "itch" to rest, she and Emanuel Furer began a pilot study entitled "How do normal children attain their first sense of entity and identity?" which Mahler described as[4] "the earliest awareness of a sense of being ... not a sense of *who* I am, but *that* I am." In their study, the researchers compared a group of normal babies and their mothers with the severely disturbed children in the psychosis project.

At first the investigators believed that psychological birth, unlike its physical predecessor, takes place in the second year of life, but there was absolutely no data on that period in the late fifties. At the time, they were working with neighborhood mothers and their children from the age of eleven months on. To their astonishment, they discovered that infants nearing their second year were well along in the psychological birth process. Mahler called it separation-individuation. The new findings meant, of course, that the study would require younger subjects than they had anticipated. From about the third year of the research, therefore, they had to find mothers and their babies practically from birth on. The mothers at the center, however, turned out to be very helpful and brought their second and third children to participate in the research. By the time these infants reached the age of eleven months, Mahler was delighted to confirmed that they already were differentiated from their mothers. As a result, Mahler concluded that emerging from the twilight state she called symbiosis is a normal development at eleven months of age.

A symbiotic union is necessary for the survival of the human infant, who, unlike the young of other animal species, is born unprepared for living on its own and exists in a state of absolute, prolonged dependency. The process of "growing up" implies a gradual outgrowing of the normal state of symbiosis, of "oneness" with the mother. As one wise analyst put it, every step the child takes is a step away from mother. This process is much slower in the emotional and psychological spheres than in the physical. Going from lap-babyhood to toddlerhood requires gradual steps of a separation-individuation process. It thus encompasses a lifelong mourning process, for every new move toward independent functioning brings with it the threat of object loss.[5]

With this philosophy in mind, Mahler went on to formulate two main tracks of development: separation and individuation. The latter coincides with the evolution of ego functions such as perception, memory, and reality testing, which require the emotional availability of the mother for optimal unfolding. Separation, on the other hand, concerns differentiation from the mother and "issues involved in the child's dawning awareness of his being a separate person from his mother — the movement from unknowing symbiotic union, through awareness of separateness, to a sense of self and to object relatedness to the mother."[6] Separation is mainly served by motility. As the infant develops the ability to move away from mother on their own volition, they becomes more and more aware that they are a person separate from her.

There are numerous ways the separation-individuation process can fail, or partially fail. For example, the two parts to the process, individuation and separation, may not develop concurrently, and one autonomous function may make for difficulties when it develops far ahead of the rest of the personality. In this regard, Mahler spoke of late walkers, who seemed farther advanced in their thinking than their more ambulatory peers, and of early walkers, who were not aware that they were separate from their mothers. These children wandered much further away from "home base" than was safe for them, and were unable to control their impulses.

She gave as an example[7] the case of Jay, who walked precociously at ten and a half months. Unfortunately, his body schema and spatial orientation were still in a stage of symbiotic fusion and confusion. The normal infant of twelve to fourteen months, who is gradually separating and individuating, cautiously rises from all fours to take their first unaided steps. They reassure themselves that support is within reach, and knows they can sink to their haunches should they deem it necessary. Jay, because of his lagging reality testing, was unable to perform these security measures. He appeared reckless, impetuous, and disoriented, and frequently got himself into dangerous situations. He climbed onto high places, he fell, he disregarded obstacles in his path and bumped into them. Nor did Jay learn from experience, for he continued to suffer hard falls for the next eighteen months. His mother, for reasons Mahler did not wish to go into at the time, was unable to be of any help. Fortunately, Jay showed an early pleasure in the use of words, and was able to communicate with her on that level. But there was a serious discrepancy in the rate of growth and quality of his lines of development. Mahler felt the crucial deficiency was in his disturbed body image, which robbed him of his identity. Jay later attained a borderline adjustment with schizoid features, and Mahler correctly foresaw that he would need to develop a "false self," whereby the individual presents a false image or a mask of himself to the world, in order to function in his social environment.

On the basis of her observations, Mahler was able to postulate four consistently occurring stages in the separation-individuation process.[8] Symbiosis, at its peak of four or five months, is followed by *after symbiosis*, the first step of the separation-individuation process. It overlaps with *the subphase of differentiation*, and lasts from five or six months of age to nine to eleven months. Mahler describes this period as *hatching*. Newborns have been born physically, she writes, but like unhatched chickens, have not yet come out of their shell. During this period, the infant gradually takes over the functions of locomotion — creeping, standing, etc.,— and becomes less dependant on his mother. The child also progresses in hand, mouth and eye coordination, and finds obvious pleasure in the use of his or her body, in objects, and in going after goals other than mother. Above all, the baby is fascinated by both his own and his mother's body. Mahler gives six to seven months as "the peak of the child's hair-pulling, face-patting, manual, tactile and visual exploration of the mother's mouth, nose, face,"[9] as well as the feel of parts of her body and "the discovery of a brooch, eyeglasses or a pendant" which he zealously learns are attached to but not a part of her. This behavior helps the infant distinguish between his own body and his mother's. In this subphase, the baby becomes interested in looking beyond the immediate surroundings by straining away from his mother's body, the first indication of breaking out of his passive lap-babyhood. All infants like to move away and stay just a bit of a distance away from mother, and as soon as they are able, slide down from the mother's lap. But they like to play it safe by remaining as close to her as possible, preferably playing at her feet.

The normal child now begins what Mahler calls "comparative scanning," or "checking back to mother."[10] He seems to compare mother's features with the unknown, and to familiarize himself further with "what *is* mother; what feels, tastes, smells, looks like, and has the 'clang' of mother." Like a tennis player following the ball, the baby is learning to discriminate between mother and non-mother.

In children whose symbiotic period has been less than optimal, acute stranger anxiety may make its appearance at this time. The better the symbiotic relationship between infant and mother has been, as discernible through the "checking back" pattern, the less acute will be the stranger anxiety experienced by the child.

"The differentiation phase," Mahler says, "slowly glides into the practicing phrase."[11] The second subphase, the practicing period, usually begins when the toddler moves away from mother. Three developments contribute to the child's first steps into awareness of separation and individuation, body differentiation from the mother, the establishment of a specific relationship with her, and the child's autonomous functioning in close physical proximity to her.[12] This phase may begin any time after the tenth month. The subphase is divided into an early and late period. At about seven months, the infant climbs down from his mother's lap and starts to crawl away from mother. Intoxicated with his or her explorations, he creeps farther and farther away from her. As my late husband, Rudy Bond, said on observing our son Zane exuberantly making his first self-guided tour of the living room, "To him, it is like us going to Paris." Anna Freud, in her developmental lines, calls the baby's investigations "from the mother to the toy." The optimal psychological space between mother and child during this stage of development allows the practicing infant to inspect his or her exciting new world at some physical distance from the mother. She continues to be needed as a home base, however, to fulfill the baby's demand for emotional refueling through physical contact. One frequently sees "seven-to-ten-month-olds crawling or rapidly paddling to the mother, righting themselves on her leg, touching her in other ways, or just leaning against her."[13] Even such brief contact allows the depleted toddler to perk up and resume his or her explorations, along with pleasure in functioning.

The energy spurred by the new relationship with mother and the child's new achievements seem to spill over from an all-encompassing interest in her onto inanimate objects, such as a blanket, toy, diaper, or bottle. Nevertheless, despite the fascination with his or her new interests, the baby's primary involvement remains with mother.

Mahler states,[14] "The mother's renunciation of possession of the body of the infant boy or girl at this point in the toddler's development is the *sine qua non* requirement for normal separation-individuation." Such a relinquishment, she continues, is necessary in promoting the infant's autonomous growth and is the first prerequisite for the development of the child's self-esteem. She wryly adds, however, that most mothers are not happy about the development and find the concession deplorable.

Mahler gives the history of Mark,[15] a toddler who was unable to establish an optimal distance from his mother during the practicing period with disastrous results. She was ambivalent about Mark as soon as he ceased to be her symbiotic child. She either avoided body contact with him or interrupted his autonomous activities to pick him up and hug him. Of course, the interventions were for her needs, not his. As a result, the child was unable to function at a distance from her.

The late practicing phase is characterized by what is arguably the single greatest achievement of humankind, the ability to walk upright. *It brings about the end of the "hatching process" or the psychological birth of a human being.* During the practicing period, the child develops a compulsive interest in exercising motor skills and exploring the world. The young investigator begins to venture farther and farther away from mother's feet, and is so absorbed in activity that he or she seems unaware of her for long periods of time. Mahler calls this interlude "the love affair with the world," and says the toddlers behave as if they are drunk with their newfound abilities. According to Pine,[16] at this point locomotion appears to be an end in itself, and it is only later that the child begins to use it for aims such as avoiding or initiating separation from the mother. During this period, children do not require sustained coddling or body closeness, but seem to take the mother's psychic availability for granted. They are satisfied by toddling up to her from time to time for "emotional refueling," the term originated by Emanuel Furer to indicate the need of toddlers to return to their mothers now and then for renewal of their bonds. According to Anni Bergman,[17] emotional refueling seems to give the spent infant renewed energy for exploration. Nevertheless, not all of the toddler's excursions take place within mother's realm. Mahler's favorite question[18] was to ask all young fathers and mothers how the first steps took place. In ninety percent of cases, she says, the child walks away from mother or the mother is out of the house. Nature, Mahler continues, has built into the infant not only the potential for clinging but also the means to become autonomous and to part from mother.

Mood changes are prevalent at this time. The child who is elated by his or her explorations suddenly becomes "low-keyed,"[19] on becoming aware that mother has left the room. At these times, the toddler slows down, shows diminished interest in the surroundings, and regresses to the inwardly focused gaze of the symbiotic period. According to Mahler, this low-keyedness is suggestive of a miniature depression.

Not only does the child have to adjust to the inevitable separation brought about by the maturation of motility, but the mother, too, must accept the fact that her beloved lap-baby can move away from her at will. This marks a developmental step that produces many conflicts in the mother, sometimes bringing about a mourning reaction. Certain mothers who regard their child as part of their bodies find this a particularly painful period. Some mothers cannot accept the relentless demands of the child, while others cannot face his or her increasing independence. Every step they take is a step away from mother. And every step they take changes the mother-child relationship. One cannot expect mothers to be totally happy about the toll. According to Professor Martin Bergmann,[20] symbiosis is the basis of all ecstasy. And who among us wholeheartedly renounces ecstasy?

In a lecture on separation-individuation, Anni Bergman[21] spoke of the great influence the reactions of the mother bring to the child's development According to her, there are important individual differences in the way each mother's sensitivity affects the quality of her child's attachment, resulting in great variations in mother/infant relationships. At the same time the child is seeking a new image of their mother, the mother has to change too, as the pair search for a new way of being together.

The toddler now begins to vocalize syllables, grunts, and gestures, the number and quality of which also differ notably among infants. Little by little, the child begins to exude syllables expressing such diverse emotions as love, fright, surprise, joy, anger, alarm, pain and suffering. This primitive prattle provides the basic elements out of which symbolic language eventually is formed. If the mother remains quietly accessible and shares the toddler's adventures on an emotional level, communication in syllables and gestures subsides and words gradually become primary.

According to Mahler,[22] "normal separation-individuation makes it possible for the baby to function separately in the presence of the mother, who continually confronts the child with threats of object loss minor enough for him to handle. Mahler frequently stated that she considered the normal separation-individuation process to be the first essential prerequisite for the development of a sense of identity, which she defines as "the cohesive cathexis of our securely individuated and differentiated self image.[23] In contrast to cases of traumatic separation, the normal process of individuation takes place at a time when the child is developmentally ready for and takes pleasure in independent functioning. Such progress requires the libidinal presence of the mother. As Fred Pine states,[24] "A child, in the second year of life, busily at play and seeming to be absorbed with inanimate objects and with his own motor activities and vocalizations, may immediately lose all pleasure in these activities when the mother leaves the room.... Pleasures are not sustained autonomously but require the general organizing presence of the mother." According to Mahler, one can best assess the normality of the individuation process by observing the quality of the baby's wooing behavior with his or her mother. A toddler who is desperate to claim mother's response or one who displays a complete lack of interest in her attention is a deeply troubled child.

Mahler traces the unfolding of the normal process of separation-individuation to the first two years of life, at which time the infant "hatches" from the symbiotic membrane. She compares this subphase of individuation to a second birth experience.

The third and most important subphase, *the rapprochement subphase*, takes place at around fourteen to twenty-two months.[25] In contrast to the child's behavior in the practicing period when mother was used as a "home base" to be turned to in times of need, at around fifteen months she turns into a person with whom the toddler wants to share the expansion of his world. He demonstrates this chiefly by lugging back numerous objects from his explorations and dumping them in her lap. The articles as such were important, but the need to share them with mother was primary.

Throughout the practicing subphase, the child's new achievements have delighted the entire world, particularly their adoring mother. The admiration heightens the baby's self love, and contributes greatly to the practicing infant's feelings of grandeur. At sixteen to eighteen months, however, the infant pays a price. As they becomes more and more conscious of mother's absence from the room, the child's interest in the surroundings diminish, activities slow down, and attention appears to turn inward. They have become more and more aware of being a separate person, and a little one at that. It is a terrifying insight that causes the toddler to deflate like a punctured tire. The relative indifference to mother's presence abates as the child gradually accepts a subordinate position and gives up the delusion of their omnipotence.

From about eighteen months on, infants enjoy exercising their autonomy, and resent being reminded of their helplessness. According to Mahler,[26] "the period of rapprochement was thus characterized by a sometimes rapid alternation of the desire to reject mother, and to cling to her with coercive, determined tenacity in words and acts." The desire to be "separate, grand, and omnipotent often conflicted with the desire to have mother magically fulfill all one's wishes — without the need to recognize that help was actually coming from the outside." This is the characteristic ambivalence of the eighteen to twenty-two-month-old child. As awareness of separation grows, the toddler compensates for the loss by insisting on sharing every new experience and skill with mother. For this reason, Mahler calls the period rapprochement.

The subphase is ushered in with the appearance of the word "no." Here both mother and baby are open to experiencing one of the great disappointments in life. The toddler seems to need to share every new acquisition of skill, and experiences pleasure in functioning to the degree that they have succeeded in capturing mother's interest. But mother, who believed that her infant no longer needed her as much, may now be preoccupied with a new baby, or has returned to work and is no longer available on a full time basis. As Thomas Wolf aptly phrased it, "You Can't Go Home Again." The toddler is disappointed, bewildered, furious, and unable to forgive mother. How they succeed in negotiating the phase and the manner in which the mother responds to the crisis may well determine the infant's future character. The degree of emotional health the child will attain is greatly dependent on the success of the rapprochement subphase, when the normal child learns to delay gratification, to tolerate separation, and to integrate conflicting feelings of love and hate. The *rapprochement subphase* is at the crossroads of development. When it is executed successfully, the fortunate toddler goes on to develop object constancy.

According to Anni Bergman,[27] favored toys help the toddlers of this period to cope with their problems, such as mother or body parts (feces) disappearing, being in control, and feeling both strong and powerful and being a helpless baby who is cared for in all respects. Bergman believes that the most helpful toys for the rapprochement toddler include puzzles, blocks for building towers, balls for throwing and retrieving, nesting cubes and other toys which make things go away and return, and dolls and teddy bears. Which toy is the favorite of a particular child depends on the extent of his or her development of skills as well as the manner in which conflicts over

separation-individuation are experienced. Books are a particularly important means of helping the growing toddler master the rapprochement phase.
Bergman states that books allow the child to create the stories of his activities, his emerging self, and his life, as he grows to understand the world
around him by its reflection in stories. Sometimes the stories are directly
concerned with life as he knows it, such as books about animals and babies.
Bergman gives the example of Peter, a boy who was particularly interested
in building tunnels with blocks and making trains disappear into and reap-
pear out of the tunnel. Bergman thought the play was Peter's way of coping with his mother's appearances and disappearances.

Children differ so greatly in the speed with which they move from one
developmental step to the next and in points of fixation along the way that
it is sometimes difficult to distinguish the pathological from what is simply
delayed progress. For example, Virginia Woolf did not speak until she was
three years old, when she began to talk in paragraphs.[28] According to Mahler,
"It is very important that the mother not be too anxious if the child is a late
walker or speaker, unless he is very deviant. She must be aware very early
of what the norms are, in order to tell what are dangerous." Potential danger signals during this phase are severe sleep disturbances, excessive separation anxiety, constant shadowing of the mother, or continual darting away
with the aim of provoking the mother to chase after the toddler. Hilary, the
child discussed in chapter twelve, is an example of a child who characteristically darted away from her mother. Attention should be paid to such symptoms, with a possible referral to psychotherapy for mother and child.

In an interview with Mahler, Milton Senn[29] asked how her observations and new perceptions of development influenced her treatment of psychotic infants and older children with emotional problems. Mahler answered
that indeed *rapprochement* greatly influences the technique she and other
child analysts use. Many analysts consider that everything begins with the
Oedipal phase, and that one cannot treat anything in the pre–Oedipal period
with psychoanalytic technique. Other analysts, however, believe the eight-
een-month to three-year level is almost as important for mental health as
the Oedipal. Mahler herself maintained that *while the Oedipal constellation
forms the core of normal development, the Oedipus conflict is shaped and formed
by what went on in the rapprochement subphase.*

If all goes well, the toddler slowly realizes that he is dependent on
mother, that they are not the same person, and that, like it or not, she and
father have their own interests which frequently exclude him. Battling and
dragging his heels all the way, the child gradually accepts that he is not the
center of the universe, and that he must give up the delusion of his own
grandeur. This is the *rapprochement crisis,* the struggle between mother and

child that one sees on the streets and in the supermarket. Practically all rapprochement children throw temper tantrums, which camouflage feelings of helplessness, vulnerability, and impotent rage. When all proceeds relatively well in the crisis, however, the healthy toddler gradually realizes that he is only a child, that mother can be both "bad" and "good," and a myriad of contradictory emotions become integrated.

According to Mahler,[30] in normal separation-individuation phases, the child becomes increasingly able to respond to the "whole mother," and to understand that the same person can both please and anger him. A friend of mine saw this development in action with her toddler, Marjorie, whom she had just scolded for not eating her spinach. The little girl ran to her "good mother" screaming "Pick me up! Pick me up!" as she looked for comfort from the abuse administered by her "bad mother." The rapprochement phase is a period of integration and consolidation. A different type of synthesis occurred when my son Zane was surmounting the *rapprochement crisis*. I made the mistake of saying to him, "What a big boy you are!" He answered, "No, I'm not, Mommy. I'm a tiny little boy, but I'm getting bigger."

Bergman states[31] that a separate sense of self clearly emerges during the rapprochement period. At that time, the toddlers' explorations at the center took on new meaning, as they wanted to share all their new achievements with mother. But the mothers could not always be available, which led to rage and frustration on the part of the children and frequent misunderstandings between the two. Instead of emotional refueling, the toddlers now needed mother to respond to their newly acquired skills and appreciate the objects from the outside world they brought to her lap. The toddler frequently responded with rage to mother's lack of satisfactory response. "Often mothers could not satisfy their toddlers, no matter how hard they tried," Bergman says. Both mother and child seemed to experience the loss of their earlier way of being together. Mahler hypothesized the beginning of depressive moods during this period.

Senn questioned how one could help children get over the rapprochement crisis. Mahler answered that the most important factor in predicting a positive outcome of the crisis is the earlier mother/child relationship. She advises informing parents, teachers, and pediatricians that the crisis is a normal stage of development and not to get too excited about it. It will not last forever, she said in typical Mahlerian fashion, and they should be told that it is nobody's fault. "At that period of infancy," Mahler went on, "*the child is normally nice, an angel of a child at one moment, and then, the next minute, he may appear to be a kind of monster of a child.* The mother may feel that either she is unnecessarily tormented by the child, and does not deserve to have such a monster of a child, or else that she is not an adequate mother." If they can be taught that it is a particularly vulnerable age, much distress can be prevented in both mother and child. After mothers are given an explanation of their child's behavior, Mahler says she often hears remarks of relief, such as, "I'm so happy to be told that one can expect a child who has been happy at fifteen to seventeen months to suddenly become clinging and touchy at eighteen months!"

Anni Bergman describes the rapprochement subphase elegantly in her paper, "Revisiting Rapprochement," when she says,[32] "Rapprochement captures that human condition of never being satisfied." She continues, "Rapprochement is a period that entails disruption and misunderstanding, and the importance during this phase is how mother and toddler can repair the disruption and thereby enrich rather than disturb their way of being together." Despairing parents may find consolation in learning that no matter how frustrating the child's behavior during "the terrible twos," the misbehavior itself in the long run is unimportant; what matters is how well the participants are able to rectify the damage.

The separation-individuation process completes itself in the fourth subphase, the open ended stage that Mahler called "*on the way to object constancy*." In this period, from twenty-five to thirty-six months, the normal child gradually experiences an increasing ability to separate from mother. As he or she learns to speak, new language skills replace more primitive means of communication. Mahler's wording of the phrase "*on the way to object constancy*" is illuminating, as she believed object constancy is an ideal that is never fully reached. Even the erudite Dr. Justin Call was once corrected by Mahler in his use of the term. He said,[33] "Margaret insisted that no one ever achieves full object constancy but they do reach relative object constancy, one of the many fine little vignettes that Margaret bestowed upon me." Similarly, Mahler told me[34] that the period of object constancy never ends, but continues to develop throughout one's lifetime. She also believed that as one's personality matures, its central core remains the remnants of the earliest infant-mother relationship.[35]

Verbal communications improve greatly during the rapprochement period, as does the ability to tolerate frustration and to endure separation. Because the beloved is internalized, the physically absent mother is not lost to the normal child. In contrast, the tragically abrupt loss of an infant's symbiotic partner through death, abandonment, or withdrawal does not permit the gradual working through of separateness experienced by the normal child. A toddler experiencing so great a deprivation will struggle throughout life to master the catastrophe.

Mahler believed that until the rapprochement crisis is successfully navigated, the child is psychologically unfinished. According to her, the separation-individuation process endures throughout life. Like any psychic process, it continues to resonate throughout the life cycle. "It is never finished," she says,[36] "but remains always active; new phases of the life cycle see new derivatives of the earliest processes still at work."

For example, a second mighty leap in separation-individuation takes place in healthy teenagers during adolescence. Successful achievement is most apparent when they are able to develop their own identity within the confines of a good relationship with their parents. According to Geuzaine, Debry, and Liesens (2000), independence is realized when the adolescents are able to feel separate while still being connected,[37] an observation that is true at every level of the separation-individuation process.

The results of the Masters Children's Center research on human symbiosis were published in numerous scientific journals, and culminated in 1968 in the monumental book *On Human Symbiosis and the Vicissitudes of Individuation: Infantile Psychoses.*[38] Psychoanalysis and the theory of child development have never been the same since.

11

Dr. Mahler's Advice to New Mothers (1979)

How can knowledge of separation-individuation help new mothers to cope with their changing infants? In a remarkable video interview in Mexico City,[1] Dr. Raquel Berman asked Dr. Mahler how the knowledge of human development can help any parent in any country in caring for the emotional well-being of the child. I think Mahler's words of advice are priceless, and should be available to all parents. Hence, with Dr. Berman's kind permission, I am including them in this book.

Mahler responded to Berman's question with the remark that infantile psychosis is a very rare disease, and the mother should listen to her inner voice. "The most important rule," Mahler said, "is that she really love the child and have enough confidence in her ability to read its signals. Mothers are much maligned these days. The frailty of the infant makes them anxious, and she doesn't realize that psychologically and emotionally she can handle the child better than anyone. They read books and listen to the neighbors, and don't grasp that if they would only listen to their instinctive knowledge of how to be a mother, it would go along with the world of the child.

"The first dialog," Mahler continued, "begins a few weeks after birth, with the child giving cues. The mother will know very soon when the infant cries out if he is hungry or uncomfortable in wet diapers. The very young baby soon realizes that there are certain cues the mother does not act upon. These cues will drop out.

"During the symbiotic phase," Mahler went on, "the baby has a vague sense that comfort comes from the outside. It is essential that the mother satisfy the child's needs as soon as possible. Some mothers are not available to the infant. Nor should mothers intrude when the child has no need but to be left alone. Such children never learn that help comes from the outside. Neither too much nor too little is good.

"In the differentiation period, the child has to find out the difference between mother's body and his own. In one case, a mother got very upset when her child touched her hair. The baby has to learn 'This is mother's hair and this is my hair,' one of the most elementary distinctions between the self and mother. Later on, the child plays at his mother's feet. It is critical that the mother be there, but does not interfere. When the child starts to creep and crawl away, the mother can be sure that he will come back.

"The differentiation phase," Mahler said, "slowly glides into the practicing phrase. It is very important that the mother not be too anxious if the child is a late walker or speaker, unless he is very deviant. She must be aware very early of what the norms are, in order to tell what are dangerous deviations."

Throughout the entire separation-individuation period, it is the love of the mother for the child that is primary. According to Mahler, "A baby thrives according to the sparkle in its mother's eyes. No sparkle, no growth spurt."

Dr. Berman then asked a question which is uppermost in the minds of most new parents: "What recommendations would Dr. Mahler make to parents about the spacing of siblings so as to interfere in the least damaging way with the child's development of object constancy?"

"That is very difficult to answer," Dr. Mahler responded with a knowing smile, thinking no doubt of her own reaction to the birth of her sister. "From the point of view of the older sibling, there should *never* be another child. It would be good if the mother is exclusively the mother of the one child in the first few years of life. Envy and jealousy would not disappear from the world. As Anna Freud said, the siblings are here to stay.

"Object constancy divides mental health and pathology, whether it was or was not achieved in growing up. According to Hartmann, the baby at three or four months has already reached the first step and has learned to wait. When he sees the mother unbuttoning her blouse and making preparations to feed him, he will stop crying. He will follow the mother's movements and will wait. The child is gaining confidence in the mother's ability to be there when he needs her, and will become a grownup who has object constancy. The image of the good mother remains in mind and is available, even if the mother is angry with him or goes away. He knows the mother is good and can be counted on to come back. The mother becomes a symbol for all other relationships."

Berman then asked, "Some mothers have to work and cannot be available all the time. How can such mothers help their children to develop object constancy?"

Mahler's answer must be reassuring to the millions of mothers who have to work. "By no means do mothers have to be with a child for twenty-four hours a day," she said. "The child is much less happy if the mother feels she is tied down to him. Mothers can be wholeheartedly with the child even for a very short time, like a couple of hours, to relax and come down to his level and play with and be with him. It is important to love the child, not kiss it all the time. It is not important, for instance, that the child go to sleep at eight o'clock. The mother can be with the child at eight o'clock. What is important is the quality of the relationship when the mother is available."

Berman asked, "What about the times when the mother is not available?"

Dr. Mahler said, "I have a pet idea that I have had for a long time. I learned of an ideal kind of daycare for babies in Scandinavian countries, especially Norway. The children who are dropped off in so-called day care or day mothers seem to have a wonderful time. They love it. The day mothers are elderly women. The ones I met have five, six, or seven children. If not dropped off there, the children miss it. If they have to leave day care for the summer, they can't wait to return. That would be ideal here, but it would have to be done on a large scale economically. These women feel useless. They love children and have grandchildren. They have lost their families. I think these elderly women if healthy and well screened could be used for an entirely new kind of day care. It would solve two very important problems for two completely different groups of people. The babies would have somebody who loves children and knows how to care for them and to help them grow up. The old women would feel useful and would enjoy themselves with the children." Then Mahler gave the first indication that she wanted to leave her money to the destitute aged. She said, "One of my deepest wishes is to leave whatever money I have for such projects."

Berman then asked, "Could you make some recommendations that would improve day care centers?"

"The child should be able to make a connection between home and the new site; for example he should be permitted to bring a transitional object with him, like a toy animal that he or she can take back and forth," Dr. Mahler answered. "Nothing is more important than that. Also, there should be one main person to whom the child 'belongs' and develops a special relationship with, to whom he can say hello, and will tuck him in at night. There are certain people who can hire such a person with more confidence than others, but there are not many people like that. They seem to know from birth on how to pick up the child, put him down, etc. People hiring them should watch how they pick up the child and put him down. How such a person handles children is the best diagnostic means. A certain minimum of intelligence is required. You do not need a sophisticated person to care for children; in fact sometimes the less sophisticated the better."

"What is the role of the father?"

"That is a good question which is coming more and more to the fore. He is much more specific than the mother. From very early on, much earlier than we used to believe, at the beginning of the second year if not the end of the first, the boy wants to emulate him. You can see the baby boy making exactly the same movements and gestures as the father."

"In some homes the father is absent," Berman said. "What would you recommend in order to compensate for the lack?"

"We know very little about it, except from analyses," Dr. Mahler said thoughtfully. "I would suggest squeezing out every drop from the male environment, an uncle, a neighbor, the hired man, the doorman, and especially other male members of the family. It seems not to be life threatening if the father is not around, but it can be just as dangerous and cause as great emotional disturbance and character distortion as a deficient mother. Some men think it unmanly to take part in the growing up of children, but I believe it is much more manly to do so. That is the difference between the American and the European father. Generally, in Europe, men wouldn't set foot in the kitchen."

"With your contributions to developmental psychology, is there any moment in the life cycle where the development is accentuated, when preventive intervention is of most benefit to the child and the adult?" Berman wanted to know.

"There is *no* point in the life cycle that constructive intervention would not be feasible and useful," Dr. Mahler answered. "We are never quite ready, development goes on from the cradle to the grave, just as we never can be without a mother. This is the dilemma of the human being; from the cradle to the grave we are longing to be one with the one from whom we are born and whose body we have lost. But at the same time, we are afraid we will lose our identity. All our lives, we oscillate between the two."

These last words of Mahler's are particularly moving because they were spoken from her heart, out of her primary conflict in life, the clash from infancy on between longing for and fearing the mother who bore her.

12

Alma Bond, Participant Observer (1966)

I Meet Mahler

When this writer was a young student of psychoanalysis, I admired the work of Margaret Mahler as no other psychoanalyst except Freud. In both a professional and personal sense, she was all I wanted to be, a great analyst, a brilliant researcher, and a prolific author who was original, creative, and famous. I knew from her articles that she had developed an unusual research plan in which she studied the relationship between young mothers and their babies, and the process by which they grew out of a oneness with their mothers and became their own persons. I learned that in her work at Masters Children's Center, she used what she called "participant observers" in her study of well babies and their mothers. These junior investigators were usually young female psychologists who either were volunteers or received a small salary. They watched the babies and their mothers one or two mornings a week and recorded their observations. Mahler studied their comments, reflected on them, and used them to further her theory of development. I saw from her published articles that young staff members, such as Anni Bergman and Kitty LaPerriere, often coauthored articles with the doctor. I had no publications at that point, except for a poem I had written and published at age eleven. I looked up to the participants almost as much as I did Mahler and dared to dream that someday I might join their ranks.

Overcoming my anxiety, I wrote Dr. Mahler a letter in which I said that I was fascinated by her work, and asked to be considered for a position at the Center. I walked around the block three times before mailing the letter. Then I forgot about it, never for one moment believing that the great Margaret Mahler might be interested in me. To my surprise, I soon received a response in which she asked me to contact her.

For some unknown reason, I didn't answer her letter. The woman frightened me, as if I had a premonition there would be complications if I were hired as a participant observer. Three weeks passed without my taking any action. To my amazement, I received another letter from Dr. Mahler demanding to know why I hadn't answered her letter. I hastily picked up the phone and dialed her secretary. She made an appointment for me to meet with Mahler at her apartment on Central Park West in a few days. The year was 1966.

I was greeted at the door of Mahler's elegant, European-type apartment, which was filled with comfortable beige chairs and sofas and large leafy plants, by the maid, who ushered me into the small office where Dr. Mahler was sitting — behind a large desk which took up most of the room — flanked by her attractive middle-aged associate, Dr. John McDevitt.

Dr. Mahler was a heavy, thick-waisted woman of 69, with straight brown hair, rather thick features, and canny dark eyes. I thought she looked like a European peasant. It appeared to me that she had little sense of style in her clothing and obviously wore a tight girdle which made her look uncomfortable. She was not a particularly attractive person, and no one would take her for a famous physician. She looked more like a maid or housekeeper. To me, her maid looked more like a famous researcher than Mahler did. I was always surprised when people I interviewed spoke of her as "beautiful" or "elegant." I never saw it. One well known analyst, on being interviewed by me, exclaimed, "Margaret Mahler is an empress." An empress, yes, beautiful, no. Strangely enough, I didn't realize until this moment how much she resembled my mother.

Mahler indicated for me to sit down on a small chair at the base of her desk. She sat in a large chair behind the desk, while McDevitt sat in its twin to her left. I wondered why she needed another person there to interview me, as if she didn't trust her own judgment. Not much happened during the meeting. Apparently, I had already been hired in her mind before she met me. She spent most of the interview describing what I would do at the Masters Children's Center. Participant observers, I was informed, were required to provide weekly descriptive reports on each mother-child pair, focusing on highlights of ongoing development. The individual qualities of each mother-child pair in both quality and quantity of interaction were requested, as the child went through different phases of separation-individuation. Reports were to include notes of illness or home events, comments of the mothers, and outstanding features of the child's behavior, such as whether they were particularly aggressive that day or had begun to walk. The mother as a person was also to be observed, including her moods, her feelings about herself and the child who was being followed, as well as about other family members. Great flexibility was given to the participant observers, Mahler added, to allow them to piece together their own versions of the mother-child couple. I liked that very much. McDevitt spoke little, and added nothing to the meeting that I could see. I was told to report to the center every Thursday morning, where I would become one of the envied "participant observers." There was to be no salary.

The center was located in two nice old houses with a new modern-looking front on Horatio Street in Greenwich Village. Both buildings were already equipped to be nursery schools and the ambiance retained much of the charm of an earlier era. In those days, Dr. Mahler used to drive to the center and park in front of the buildings. It was rarely necessary to display her sign, "Physician on Call," on the dashboard of her neat four-door Chevrolet. By the time I got there, the research had been going on for five years, and the design of both the research itself and the interior of the building had changed considerably. A dining room and kitchen were on the first floor, and the research center was largely on the second.

The floor was divided into four large quarters, which (going counterclockwise) consisted of the Interview Room, The Staff Room, the Infant Room, and the Toddler Room, to which I was assigned. The arrangement provided a warm, friendly gathering place for the mothers and children, where mothers could be together while keeping an eye on their babies. It reminded me of a comfortable living room, or mothers gathering around a sandpile in the park. I remember thinking that I would have enjoyed participating in the study when my children were infants. The mothers in the Toddler Room could see their children through the one-way mirror and take care of them as needed. They could talk with their neighbors, have coffee and cookies, read, or interact with their children, as they wished. All the rooms except the Staff Room were equipped with observation booths, through which the participant observers could follow the children's activity in the rooms, but be invisible to them. The children's bathroom, equipped with pint-sized toilets and sinks, was at the end of the suite, as was the bathroom for adults. The Toddler Room opened onto a hallway, through which the children were free to approach their mothers in the Sitting Area for mothers in the Infant Room next door, and to return when and if they pleased. It was a lovely set-up for mothers and children, and I envied those who had been chosen to take part in it.

I spent several pleasant Thursday mornings in the Toddler Room, where

I conscientiously recorded my observations about the babies and their mothers. I enjoyed the work and hoped the great lady would approve of it and me.

We Become Friends

Dr. Mahler seemed to value my contributions. A few weeks after I had begun to work there, she invited me to lunch at the Café des Artistes, a lovely restaurant on Central Park West frequented by the wealthy and the famous. I, of course, was thrilled, and assumed that she had invited me because she wanted to know me better. The food was delicious, especially the chocolate mousse, which she recommended. Nevertheless I didn't eat very much; I was too excited. As I tried to eat, she gave me a typical Mahler look, a quiet look, an unostentatious look, and I knew that she had taken in the situation. She didn't eat very much, either.

Dr. Mahler was by nature a rather silent person, Or rather, it seemed to me that she really wanted to say a great deal, but, characteristically, refrained. There is a lovely picture of her taken in 1967, which illustrates her customary restraint. In it a small child is reaching out and grasping her large black beads. Mahler is smiling rather lovingly at the boy, but remains motionless, with her hands at her sides. The ambiance of the photo, at least to me, is as if she wanted to take him into her arms but inhibited the gesture. It says a lot about her that the photo was one of her favorites, which reminds me of something she said to me in her car one day when she was driving me home. It seems that one of the mothers at the center had tried to kiss her good-bye. Mahler was indignant that anyone would dare. One simply did not kiss the great Margaret Mahler! I was glad she had told me the story. I had the impulse to kiss her on the cheek the last time we parted, but successfully resisted it. Could she have read my thought?

Although she asked few, if any questions, during out lunch there was a quality about the great analyst that encouraged me to talk. I found myself telling her that even though she was the originator of separation-individuation theory, I found it the single most important insight in psychoanalysis today and there was nothing I was more interested in. She nodded with her quiet look again, and I felt understood. I told her about my actor husband, who was about to play the leading role in *The Big Man*,[1] a play at the Cherry Lane Theatre in Greenwich Village. She said she would like to see the play when it opened, and I told her I would arrange for tickets. We spoke of the financial difficulties he, like most actors, was having at the time. Surprisingly, she told me she empathized with me, that she had made much more money than her chemist husband, who was now deceased. To spare him embarrassment when he couldn't pay the bill in a restaurant, she said, she used to pass him the money under the table. I sympathized with the great lady whose husband was so far beneath her professionally.

Although there was a huge age difference between us, I felt we were on the same wave length emotionally, probably both stuck at one of the symbiotic phases of development. I felt very close to her, and hoped that the lunch meeting would be the first of many to come. She seemed to return my feelings. At the end of the meal, Dr. Mahler implied that she liked my work and offered me a paying position as a participant observer at the center. I was ecstatic, and without missing a beat accepted her offer.

We left the restaurant, and she said she needed exercise and would like to take a walk. She invited me to accompany her. I was overjoyed to be walking up Central Park West with my idol. Every time we passed a pedestrian, I looked to see if they recognized that I was walking with the great Margaret Mahler. (Nobody noticed.) She walked slowly and laboriously and tired after a few blocks. Sixty-nine years old and much too heavy, she moved like an even older woman. But that didn't deter my feelings for her. I felt about her the way my little son felt about me when he was two years old, that I was the most wonderful person, the most beautiful, the most charming person in the whole world.

Nothing of much consequence went on for me at the center for another month. One incident sticks in my mind. Dr. Mahler was in the habit of driving me and several other staff members uptown after each session at the center. Once the seat beside her was empty and I was about to take it. But thinking she might prefer one of her closer colleagues to sit next to her, I suddenly jumped around into the back seat. Mahler gasped and looked shocked. I guess she expected me to sit next to her.

Hilary's Story

I continued to make my observations and hand them in for the doctor's perusal. Then one day, an exciting drama took place between eighteen-month-old Hilary S. and me. The episode is included here because I believe it exemplifies the work done by the participant observers at the center and also reveals as much about the psyche of Margaret Mahler as it does of Hilary's and mine.

For some unknown reason, the child selected me from a number of adults in the Toddlers' Room to approach. Many of the young children at the center made contact with the observers, but not Hilary. She had the reputation there of being notoriously unresponsive to female staff members. If spoken to by one of them, she seemed not to hear. If approached directly by a woman, she "looked right through her." If the attempt at contact continued, Hilary ran away. Most obvious of all, Hilary ignored her mother. This was apparent to all the staff, one of whom commented, "Mrs. S has made remarks about how Hilary never notices her, and I often have the feeling that she seems a little rejected by this."

To me, Hilary was a sad little girl who for all emotional purposes had no mother. She neither saw nor reacted to her. She showed little pleasure in being with her mother and did not turn to her in time of need. In contrast to the other children, who by and large seemed to enjoy their mothers, much of Hilary's time at the nursery was spent in masturbatory activity, in which she would sit or lie before a mirror and watch herself rock back and forth.

The healthiest aspect of her upbringing seemed to be Hilary's relationship with her father. She responded with love and attention to him, as she never did with her mother. In his opinion, she was a healthy, normal little girl who gave him nothing but pleasure. I could not help but think of the young Margit Mahler, who experienced a very similar relationship with her parents. Like Dr. Schoenberger, I believe Mr. S. had an importance in his daughter's life which probably saved her from a life of pain and sorrow.

Detailed records at the center tell us that Hilary was weaned abruptly and traumatically, for the convenience of her parents rather than in accordance with her own need. At the time of these observations, Hilary was not yet fully toilet trained, although Mrs. S. was working on it intensively if not consistently. It was important in Hilary's development that a little sister was born to her when she was fifteen months old, just three months before she confronted me in the Toddlers' Room.

Hilary and I had never met before. I was talking quietly with another staff member when Hilary came up close to me and then stopped. In a strange gesture, she draped a semicircular little hand over each of her eyes and then darted away. I didn't understand her action and wondered whether the sun was in her eyes. Hilary soon cleared up the mystery. Several moments later, she approached me again, with her hands in the same odd position. In one quick motion, the tiny girl grabbed a large white platter that was sitting nearby, thrust it at me, and bolted out of the room. I felt honored by the "gift." Then I questioned whether the attempt at intimacy had been too much for her to tolerate.

About twenty minutes later, she approached me again. This time she handed me a top. "Thank you," I said with obvious pleasure, the two of us in an eye-lock. Then she abruptly turned to the playpen and leaned over the rails in a vain attempt to pick up a large cuddly teddy bear. I reached for the stuffed animal and handed it to her. She lovingly clutched it to her chest, swaying gently from side to side, murmuring "Bear ... bear ... bear...." "Yes, bear," I said, deeply moved, as we remained locked into each other's eyes. I believe that relating to me was an important milestone for Hilary, for it was the first time she had shown any interest in a woman at the center.

At our next meeting, I held out a little plastic doll to Hilary that I had brought for her. With obvious joy she came closer, vocalizing in monosyllabic rapture. She then moved right next to me, but stood there silently. She did not reach out for the doll, but obviously was waiting for me to put it into her hand. I was afraid that if I gave it to her she would dart away. So I waited, still holding the doll. It took only a brief instant until she grabbed it and chortled joyful sounds. Then she turned to me with a dazzling smile and said a warm and poignant, "Hi!"

Thus began a fascinating interlude, which I characterize as the "whither thou goest" period. It began when Hilary went over to the sink in the toddlers' kitchen corner, seeming to know I would follow. For perhaps thirty or forty minutes, as she played with the little doll, she clearly communicated what she wanted and felt by grunts, pointing, monosyllables, and maybe even thought transference. I responded with a steady stream of whatever felt right. When she wanted the water turned on, she grunted and pointed, and I turned it on with, "Uh-huh, you want the water on." When she pointed to a cup, I reached it for her, similarly commenting on her wish. Once, she took the little doll, on whom practically all of her play centered, and put it in a cup of water, continuing to emit sounds of pleasure. I said, "Umm, it feels good to be in water, doesn't it?"

Once, I went out of the room after Dottie, another child at the center, had marched off with my pocketbook. "I'll be right back," I said to Hilary as I left. She smiled and resumed play in the same vein when I returned. But shortly after, another interruption brought quite a different reaction. Again Dottie wandered in. She managed to get stuck in the closing door and began to cry. I got up and opened the door for her. This was the unforgivable sin to Hilary, older sister of a three-month-old baby. I, like her mother, had betrayed her with another child, and she was not about to forgive me. She abruptly threw down the doll (where it lay soggy and forlorn the rest of the morning) and ran out of the room. I went to the observation booth to watch her through the glass and saw that she had reverted to her characteristic narcissistic behavior. She was lying on her stomach watching herself in the mirror as she rocked her body back and forth.

I must admit I felt pretty bad about the whole thing, and that prob-

Mahler flanked by her "daughters," Anita Kolek and Maria Nardone, in 1983 when they were traveling together in Cannes. (Courtesy Maria J. Nardone)

ably is just the way I was supposed to feel. As I see it, Hilary would accept only a mother person who was together with her one hundred percent. But at the first breech of unity, mother was "wiped out," and no longer existed psychologically for her. Such was Hilary's revenge, and such was my punishment for disrupting the union. But in a distorted way, her vengeance also served as the means of keeping the relationship going. I found myself upset that she had pulled away from me and was tempted to pursue the child, in a manner reminiscent of Hilary's mother. Fortunately, I resisted the impulse.

Hilary had her ways of making sure that the mothering person remained preoccupied with her. When she bluntly broke off contact after a period of delightful intimacy, she left her "victim" emotionally stranded, faced with the choice of being flooded with longing for a lost paradise or of relating intensively on a sadomasochistic basis. Yearning for someone, chasing after that person, and pathetically searching in vain for some sign of her "love" makes for a time-consuming, all-absorbing relationship. It is understandable that Mrs. S selected that choice. It is also possible that my willingness to tolerate the first state enabled Hilary to establish a new type of relationship with her mother, in which she became a normal child with a mother she trusted to love her, with no need for the pathological manipulations designed to force Mrs. S's attention.

I believe that the interaction between Hilary and me was a direct repetition of the original relationship she had with her mother. The compre-
hensive records kept at the center reveal that the nursing couple had
experienced a deep, warm, all-exclusive preoccupation with each other during Hilary's early infancy. Mrs. S was frequently observed stroking, holding, and murmuring to her baby. Then, when the child was four months
old, the mother abruptly withdrew her breasts. After the weaning, there
appeared a sharp change in her attitude toward her daughter. She no longer
seemed relaxed with Hilary, nor enjoyed her smile, talked to her, or kissed
her. Thus, shortly after Hilary was weaned, an observer noted that "Hilary's
face is turned away from her mother during bottle feeding." No longer was
the child's adoring gaze locked into that of her mother's, as it had been with
mine. It seems likely that Hilary's reaction to her mother on being weaned
was a direct prototype of her response to me fifteen months later. The door-
closing incident with Dottie must have felt to Hilary like a reenactment of
the "dumping syndrome." For such a child, there is only the symbiotic
mother or no mother at all.

Mrs. S herself showed mixed feelings about intimacy, which could have
led to the abrupt and untimely weaning. For instance, within a relatively
short period, she was heard to say to Hilary, "I'm going to put whipped cream
all over you and eat you up!" This was followed shortly by her statement,
"I didn't want the Goddamn baby dependent on me every minute of the
day!" Apparently she was able to allow intimacy with Hilary briefly, and then
felt compelled to terminate it abruptly. The initial union was replaced by a
distorted version, in which Hilary literally as well as figuratively led her
mother a merry chase.

Insofar as our relationship was concerned, I may have been "dead and
gone" for Hilary, but she was not ready to bury me permanently. After her
withdrawal from me, she remained preoccupied for a while with watching
her body in the mirror as she rocked away. I had given up on her for the
time being, and sat there writing my notes.

Hilary was playing with the doll crib when I looked up. She looked at
me (I would swear) knowingly, and went again to the sink. Somehow, silently,
I had been summoned. She had forgiven me for my abandonment. We stayed
at the sink again, and she began showing me cups, pitchers, and so forth,
which she pulled out of the water. She handed me each particular item and
watched as I responded with pleasure, until her mother came to take her
home.

Two weeks later, Hilary's mother was away for the day, and there was
no one to bring the child to the center. So I went to visit her. A maid reluc-
tantly let me in. Hilary was sitting in a high chair between the tiny foyer

and kitchen, smeared with the remains of a large bowl of applesauce and some crackers. When she saw me, she lit up in recognition, and then closely examined the crackers as she squashed them to pieces. I stood nearby watching. She smiled at me again, and then looked down at the crackers and kneaded them to mush. She then put a bit of cracker in her mouth, and said, "Poo," her word for feces. She curled her hands up over her eyes, as she had done at our first meeting. I waited. Then suddenly, fully, characteristically, she opened her fingers wide, peeked out at me, and burst into gales of laughter. I put my hands over my eyes, peeked out at her, and began to laugh, too. We laughed and laughed together.

Freud tells of an eighteen-month-old child (the same age as Hilary) who flung away his yo-yo and pulled it back again, saying "o-o-o-o," "da," "gone away," and "there." According to Freud,[2] the child was symbolically sending away and then bringing back his mother. In his play, *he* was in charge of when she left. The abandonment was *his* doing, not hers. Freud ascribed the game to the "instinct for mastery" of a situation that was overwhelming to the boy. He also said that the flinging away of the yo-yo was the gratification of an impulse to revenge himself on his mother for leaving him. In a similar way, Hilary seemed to be saying to me, "Now you are gone, now you are back" again and again and again.

When I took her down from the high chair, the excited child began to dash back and forth from one wall to another. She ran to the TV set, which had been turned on throughout my visit, and announced that the man shaving in a commercial was "da da." Then she dashed to the door and urgently pointed. "Mama. Gone. Car," she said, with better speech than I had ever heard her use. Next she ran to her parents' book-lined bedroom, where the dog was lying on the bed, and said, "bow wow." Her last stop was to visit her own room, where she reached through the crib bars to ask for one and then a second of her dolls. After that, she picked up her nearly empty bottle and began sucking on it.

She then picked up a lampshade. Still sucking on the bottle, she put the shade over her head and shoulders, so that she seemed enveloped in it, held by it, contained within it. From deep inside, she sucked on the bottle, swaying rhythmically, as she murmured in sensuous tones, "ma ma ... ma ma...." Absorbed in herself, walled off from the world, she looked so very tiny. Then, with the now familiar spontaneity, she dipped down the shade, peeked out at me, and laughed and laughed. As before, she played the game again and again and again. Then, her anxiety conquered, she came out from her womb nest to be with me.

She went over to the two dolls, kept one and handed me the other. Together we held the dolls in our arms. Together we hugged them with affection. Then she put her doll down on the bench, said, "wee wee," and went over to her potty chair and urinated. After that she came back to her amply endowed baby doll, laid the top part of her body over it, and placed her open mouth on the breast of the doll. So she lay for a long moment, her finger resting on the mouth of the doll. Then she turned the doll over and hugged it from the rear. She examined it closely, fingering a pimple-like nodule on its buttocks, saying "poo poo." But this time she did not carry through her stated intention. Instead she came to me and hastily climbed on my lap. Time seemed to stop as she sat there frozen for a moment. And then she hastily climbed down from my lap, and went to her parents' room.

What a morning it had been for Hilary! She had accepted her need for closeness to a mother person, had spoken many new words, urinated on the potty, and symbolically hugged and was hugged by me, defecated, and allowed herself to nurse at my breast. And now of her own volition, she had come and climbed onto my lap. Her achievements were truly monumental, and she had earned a rest.

I saw Hilary only once after that, and then only briefly. For reasons that were unavoidable, it had been a month since our last meeting. In the meantime, I had heard through the grapevine that a striking change had occurred in Hilary in her interaction with other staff members, and, even more, with her mother. Reports were that she now persistently longed for her mother, followed her about, yearned for her when away, cried for her, and seemed to delight in her company.

A brief contact with Hilary confirmed these rumors. On this occasion, Hilary passed me in the hall. She was crying for her mother. "Mama, mama, mama," wept this child whose vocabulary had not even included a word for mother until after our meeting. "Mama, mama," she entreated me plaintively. I took her by the hand and said, "Let's go find Mama."

I wondered how long she could maintain her newfound relationship with her mother, who, after all, had not changed. Mahler herself spoke of the difficulties of doing therapy with a child whose mother was not in treatment.[3] I speculated on the possibility that our time together had given Hilary enough gratification that she was willing to risk the pain of longing. Perhaps it helped her discover that the ego of an eighteen-month-old child is strong enough to tolerate pain that is overwhelming to an undeveloped infant. If so, I hoped she would be able to grow up in an emotional sense with two parents instead of one. But all in all, I remained skeptical that her progress would be permanent.

Shortly after this incident, Mahler abruptly changed her attitude toward me. From feeling like a dear friend, I now became invisible to her. I never did find out why. Although I asked everyone I interviewed who was at the center at the time I was, nobody could answer the question. To make matters worse, it seems that her change of heart was contagious, and the other associates closed ranks behind her and ignored me, too. The frostiness of Mahler and company became unbearably painful. As Benedict Carey described in his article, "Bullies in the Workplace," I experienced "a sudden chill of isolation that is all too real,"[4] and felt forced to leave the center. Although I thought of Hilary often after that, I heard no more of her and her progress.

It seems my misgivings about her subsequent development were unfounded. Six or seven years later, I happened to meet Mrs. S at a party given by a mutual acquaintance. She didn't recognize me, and had no memory of the incidents I've described. I told her who I was and how we had met. Then I asked her how Hilary was.

"She is wonderful!" Mrs. S exclaimed. "She is a happy child and an excellent student. She is doing better than either her brother or her sister. In fact, she is the best adjusted person in the whole family!"

What can we learn about separation-individuation from these observations of Hilary? According to Mahler, emergence from the twilight state of symbiosis customarily occurs at eleven months of age. Hilary did not have the opportunity to outgrow the symbiosis with her mother because its premature termination required Hilary to separate forcibly during the subphase of differentiation, which is advanced mainly by motility. As the infant becomes increasingly able to move away from mother it becomes increasingly conscious of being a separate person and, in Hilary's example, prolonged dashing to and from mother kept them both locked into a distorted symbiotic period.

Mahler believed that a disturbed body image robs a child of his or her identity, which she defines as "the earliest awareness of a sense of being ... not a sense of who I am, but that I am." A person who has not separated sufficiently from her mother necessarily suffers from an insecure sense of self. Hilary's obsession with the mirror, hoping to discover who she was, seems a perfect demonstration of the behavior of an insecure child.

Infants generally like to move away and stay just a small distance from mother. As soon as they are able, they slide down from the mother's lap. They play it safe by remaining as close to her as possible, preferably playing at her feet. Hilary had a greater need than the average child to break out of her passive lap-babyhood, because it was painful.

The optimal psychological space between mother and child during this stage of development allows the practicing infant to inspect his or her exciting new world at some physical distance from the mother, who continues to be needed as a home base for emotional refueling through physical contact.

Hilary did not have this vital experience, and kept her mother in the picture by leading a merry chase indeed.

The differentiating toddler soon begins to vocalize syllables, grunts, and gestures, the number and quality of which differ notably among infants. Little by little, they begin to exude nonsense syllables expressing such diverse emotions as love, fright, surprise, joy, anger, alarm, pain and suffering. This primitive prattle provides the basic elements out of which symbolic language eventually is formed. If the mother remains quietly accessible and shares the toddler's adventures on an emotional level, communication in syllables and gestures subsides and words gradually become primary. When we first met, Hilary did not "talk" at all, which deprived her of another opportunity to connect with her mother. She first started grunting and talking in my presence, which provided the impetus she needed to begin acquiring symbolic language in the usual manner.

The third and most important subphase, rapprochement, occurs at approximately fourteen to twenty-two months. In contrast to the child's behavior in the practicing period, when mother was used as a "home base" for physical and emotional stability, at around fifteen months mother turns into a person with whom the toddler wants to share the expansion of their world. They demonstrate this chiefly by lugging back numerous objects from explorations and dumping them in mother's lap. The toddler seems to need to share every new acquisition of skill, and experiences pleasure in functioning to the degree that they have succeeded in capturing mother's interest. A responsive mother at this point may well have overcome Hilary's withdrawal. But during this period of Hilary's toddlerhood, her mother was preoccupied with a new baby. Unlike the ordinary child, Hilary did not bring trophies back to her mother as children ordinarily do, but seemed to be pressed to go through the stage with the author. Living out with me this phase of sharing behavior that was missing in her relationship with her mother may have allowed Hilary to continue her development in the rapprochement subphase. The separation-individuation process ordinarily completes itself in the open ended stage that Mahler called "on the way to object constancy." In this period, from twenty-five to thirty-six months, the average child experiences an increasing ability to separate from mother. As they learn to speak, new language skills replace more primitive means of communication. Verbal communication proliferates greatly during this last subphase, as does the ability to tolerate frustration and to endure separation. When the beloved is internalized, the physically absent mother is not lost to the child. In contrast, the tragically abrupt loss of an infant's symbiotic partner through death, abandonment, or withdrawal, such as Hilary experienced, does not permit the gradual working through of separateness experienced by the emotionally healthy toddler. A child experiencing so great a deprivation will struggle throughout life to master the catastrophe. Hilary was more fortunate. With a bit of cooperation and genuine interest from me, her language skills greatly improved and she apparently learned to tolerate frustration and to endure separation. Thus she was able to return to her mother and experience a healthy rapprochement period, "on the way to object constancy."

Would Hilary have developed normally had the disturbed relationship with her mother continued? Mahler stated that a normal separation-individuation process is essential for the development of a sense of identity. The rapprochement subphase is at the crossroads of development. It is then that the well adjusted child learns to delay gratification, to tolerate separation, and to integrate conflicting feelings of love and hate. When the phase is executed successfully, the fortunate toddler goes on to develop object constancy. In contrast to cases of traumatic separation such as that experienced by Hilary, the process of individuation ideally takes place when the maturing child is ready for and takes pleasure in independent functioning. Such progress requires the libidinal presence of the mother. According to Mahler, one can best assess the normality of the individuation process by observing the quality of the baby's wooing behavior with mother. A toddler like Hilary who displays a complete lack of interest in her mother's attention is a deeply troubled child. Mahler believed that a referral to psychotherapy for such a mother and child should be considered. Given that Hilary's mother was unresponsive, that Hilary lacked the typical interaction with her of a rapprochement-age child, that she engaged in provocative, sadomasochistic behavior and did not speak, it is difficult to see how Hilary's development could have proceeded in an optimal fashion without intervention.

Mahler's Change of Heart

Hilary had done better with me in establishing a symbiosis than I had done with Mahler. The first unmistakable indication of Mahler's change of heart toward me came when my husband opened in his play, *The Big Man*. He received wonderful reviews. Delighted, I sent them to Dr. Mahler, who had said she wanted to see the play. I called to invite her to a performance. The woman was surrounded like a fortress. First, one had to get through the first line of defense, and, if found satisfactory, the caller was then connected to her secretary. Since it was too much to ask that I be permitted to speak with the great lady herself, I left a message with the secretary saying that I would like to invite Dr. Mahler to see my husband's play. The secretary said she would deliver the message. Mahler never responded to my invitation.

The truth was so painful that it dawned on me only gradually that my days as Margaret Mahler's colleague and coworker were over. When I finally understood, I was filled with a dark oppressive feeling. I didn't understand. She was so interested in what I had to say, had liked my work so much, took me to lunch, offered me a salary to work at the center, drove me home from the center, and then, bingo! She dropped me like the iron that had scarred her sister's cheek. I didn't understand why. Couldn't she have explained to me the reasons for her change of heart?

I, like Hilary and Mahler herself, had been weaned traumatically. In terms of healing the repetition compulsion, I had to relive my infantile symbiosis and have it end differently, so I could overcome the ill effects of the trauma and pick up and go on with my development. I needed such a relationship so I could outgrow my yearning for my early mother and be free of the need for a symbiosis. But, typical of the results when the repetition compulsion is reenacted, here was my substitute symbiotic partner repeating my own mother's behavior.

But to my surprise, the miserable experience led to a totally unexpected result. Up to that moment I had lived in unconscious terror of "falling apart," and kept myself in a constant state of physical tension in the attempt to hold my body together. After the alarming experience, I could say, "My worst fear has come true and I have fallen apart. But I did not really disintegrate; It just *felt* that way." Now I knew in the essence of me what the six-month-old Alma couldn't possibly have known: that even though the present experience appeared as vivid and lifelike as if I had fallen to pieces, it was only a feeling that seemed real. There was nothing in reality to be afraid of. Sticks and stones will break my bones, but feelings cannot hurt me. For the first time in my conscious life, I was able to really relax. There was a dramatic change in my musculature, so that my husband said I had become a well-adjusted, happier person. Such was the therapeutic genius of Margaret Mahler. It seems that our relationship, painful as it was for me, was a therapeutic symbiosis. Although her "technique" was a bit drastic, it turned out to be a "cure." I suppose I should be grateful. She saved me a lot of analysis.

There is a sequel to this story. About six months after I left the center, I wrote up another version of the incident with Hilary and sent it to Dr. Mahler. I asked if she minded if I sent the paper to an analytic journal and made sure to add that if she had any objections I would not send out the paper. I received the following response:

MASTERS CHILDREN'S CENTER
Sponsored by the Masters Nursery
75 Horatio Street
New York, NY 10014
November 3, 1966

Dr. Alma H. Bond
1040 Park Avenue
New York, N.Y. 10028

Dear Dr. Bond:

I want to acknowledge receipt of your — strangely enough — certified mail.

I will read it with great interest, because I am interested in your thoughts (and always have been), but I will have to frustrate you again because I am more pressured than ever, and it might very well be many weeks before I can carefully evaluate it and react to it.

Very sincerely,

Margaret S. Mahler, M.D.

MSM/es

Why she thought she had frustrated me before, I have no idea, unless that was her intent. I held up on the paper for about six more months, and then discussed the situation with a group of my colleagues. They unanimously agreed that Dr. Mahler was *never* going to respond to my letter, and insisted that I send out the paper on my own. I did. It was accepted immediately and published in *The International Journal of Psychoanalysis*, 48, no. 4, 1967: 597–602, "Sadomasochistic Patterns in an 18-month-old child." I never heard from Mahler again about the paper or anything else.

An amusing sidelight to the story came up as I was perusing the archives of the Mahler Collection at the Manuscripts and Archives Library at Yale University. Mahler was a packrat, who saved one hundred and eighty-seven boxes of paraphernalia, including what looked like every Christmas card, rent receipt, and communication she ever received. There was even an Alma Bond file which contained a lone announcement of an appearance as a discussant I had made somewhere. Missing from the file was a copy of my letter to her and her response.

13

Mahler's Need for Dual Unity (The Present)

The Many Faces of Margaret Mahler

Winnicott once said that without the mother there is no baby.[1] One can almost say that, in the case of Margaret Mahler, without another person to melt into there was no Margaret Mahler. According to Anni Bergman,[2] the chief participant observer at Masters Children's Center and Mahler's longtime associate:

Margaret had an enormous need to work with other people, she couldn't work alone. I think this was very fortunate for her colleagues, at least I consider that it was so for me, even though working together wasn't always so easy. She always needed someone to think with, that was my role. The best times we had working together were at her country house in Connecticut, which she loved, but eventually had to give up. Underneath her brilliance, there was an insecurity, and a great need for constant feedback and praise. She was full of contradictions. She was both possessive and very generous. A lot depended on her mood and you never knew how she would be.

She had an ambivalent relationship with the psychoanalytic establishment of her time. She wanted to be fully accepted, and recognized by the establishment, but she also wanted to follow her own ideas, and be recognized separately from it.

Dr. Arnold Richards, to his surprise, also found Mahler an insecure person. He said,[3] "At the Kernberg Bat Mitzvah, what struck me about it — I was very young — Margaret Mahler seemed to feel that I was important, that she should get to know me. She thought I should recognize her, that I was one of the up and coming analysts and she should be recognized by someone so much younger. She chided me for not talking to her. I felt, 'Who am *I* to be talking to *her?*' But she felt left out that I wasn't paying attention to her. There was an incredible distance between her idea of how I should be relating to her and mine of how I should react to her, as if she wanted all the important young people to recognize that she was Margaret Mahler."

It is most difficult to define her as an individual, because she was a different person in almost every important relationship. She seemed to have as many sides to her personality as there were people to whom she related. Peter Neubauer[4] said, "Margaret had a differentiated response to all of us, because she handled us each one differently. That is not what I assume but what I know." Bluma Swerdloff corroborated Dr. Neubauer's observation, when she said,[5] "Dr. Mahler was always nice to me, even though she wasn't to many others. She was different with everyone, nice to some people and not so nice with others."

When asked why she thought Mahler was always nice to her and not to others, Swerdloff responded, "I think she was always nice to me because I didn't work with her."

As if in illustration of her theories on symbiosis, Mahler and each individual she was close to blended into each other and established a union that was different from any other. Mahler reminded me of the little boy in Walt Whitman's poem, "There Was a Child Went Forth,"[6] in which "the first object he looked upon and received with wonder, pity, love, or dread, that object he became."

An analyst and co-worker who wished to remain anonymous said, "*It was almost impossible for her to work alone, as she was unable to think for herself. All her writing came out of a dyad.*" For people close to her, as with me, a relationship with Margaret Mahler often served as a litmus test for unexplored parts of their personality. In this chapter, I shall attempt to illustrate "the many faces of Margaret Mahler" in the convictions of the friends and colleagues who knew her best.

Mahler's Dearth of Ego Boundaries

Fred Pine, her collaborator and research associate, explained some of Mahler's behavior by the lack of boundaries between her and other people.

He said,[7] "The concept of a symbiotic phase and the separation-individuation process came from powerful sources somewhere deep inside of her, and she knew about it personally. Like other creative pioneers in psychoanalysis, Freud among them, Mahler was able to take her distinctive sensitivities and convert them into an important contribution, but *was not able to excise it from her character. The negotiation of boundaries between herself and people who were close to her was always hard for her.*" Mahler herself said that with her "separation-individuation complex, she tended to go back home."[8]

Ilo Milton also spoke of Mahler's lack of ego boundaries.[9] She said:

I worked for her as a research assistant in the apartment on 66th St., where the only boundaries were a door that was open most of the time. A lot of the work was done in her bedroom, or in the hospital. I wouldn't call it work, because the boundaries between personal and professional were so murky. The secretary, accountant, and her women friends were all there, so there was a lot of stuff going on. I don't know how well I knew her. I thought I knew her more than I wanted to know. I wished that the boundaries had been firmer. I think Dr. Mahler wanted something so deep in her life. There was something missing and she didn't know how to ask for it. I said please ask me what you need. Her needs were very mother-child oriented. She was annoyed that I couldn't read her mind. It was very upsetting. You expect more from someone in her position. She was the grand dame with all these young woman around her, and you expected her to set the boundaries.

One day something really humiliating happened. Usually she had all these people looking after her. Once when there was no one else there she said, "Listen out for me, I will be in the bathtub." In the back of my awareness a bell was ringing. It turns out that Dr. Mahler was ringing a bell, a call for me to come help her. I had never heard a bell before in the house. She wanted me to come help her out of the bathtub. I didn't know that was her sign. She started screaming at me. When people came back she started talking about me as if I wasn't there; "Do you know what this idiot did?" I was so upset I went into the bathroom and cried. She did leave me an apology note on my typewriter later.

Another time there was a board meeting and I was preparing all the paperwork stuff for the meeting. I worked for her thirty hours a week, in addition to fifteen hours at a clinic. I never had lunch at Dr. Mahler's. It was going to be a long day and I had to come back from seeing patients at the clinic for the meeting. The next day she was really not nice to me, and asked me to hand her a film canister. She said, "That's no way to hand a film canister to an old lady!" I said, "You are so angry with me that the canister can't be what's wrong." She said, "You didn't offer to make me lunch yesterday." I said, "I didn't know you wanted any. Why didn't you ask me?"

It was a very sad moment. She had all those women around to anticipate her needs and she would just blow up if anyone didn't. When I was hired I lived five blocks from her. I was on the phone one morning when there was a knock on the door. It was her previous assistant, Mary, who said, "Dr. Mahler sent me over because she couldn't reach you by phone." Mary sat down with me and begged me not to take the job. She said, "I know it seems like an opportunity, but don't take it, don't be seduced by her." I didn't know she was such a difficult person, I thought it was me. I felt better when I realized that other people thought so, too.

People call me Miss Boundary, if someone had loose boundaries they would say, "Go talk to Ilo." I probably learned that from being with Dr. Mahler. I was very aware that with her you needed them or she would consume you. I understood how frustrating it could be, like having an intruding mother. Intellectually it was crystal clear, but emotionally someone had to keep the boundaries. Once I set the boundaries she treated me well, and everyone else poorly.

Fred Pine perhaps understood Mahler as well as anybody. She battled constantly and stubbornly with him. He said,[10] "I was a consultant for Margaret Mahler. That generally meant that I met with her in a group one evening a week for a year during the time our book was being written. I wrote the first two chapters and Mahler modified them. When I wrote the next chapter on autism and symbiosis, she was very unhappy with it, to say the least, and she rewrote it. I was just as unhappy with the way she wrote it, and at that point we agreed to part company."

"What didn't you like about her version?" I asked.

"Her writing on those stages was obscure and noncommunicative," he answered. "It was part of an ancient psychoanalytic world where one could say whatever one wanted, under the authority of The Psychoanalyst. That chapter later became the primary negative example of what is wrong with psychoanalytic theories of infancy. I elaborated on the subject in a response to Peterfreund's critique in a paper published in 1978 in *The International Journal of Psychoanalysis.*

"She respected my decision not to continue with the book," Pine continued, "but also felt I was important to the book, and wanted me to remain connected. It was not easy for Mahler to be connected at a distance, but we managed it. So I remained a coauthor, but we specified in the preface which parts I was involved with."

"What was the relationship between you like, after you stopped working on the book?" I asked.

Pine responded:

I dropped by her house and saw her at parties. I would periodically visit with her and spend an evening with her and talk. She was very difficult, very angry, and at times very icy, but she was capable of great warmth. She was interested in the family and the kids of colleagues. She was interested in me and my growing position in the field. We didn't talk intimately, because she was not an intimate friend of mine. But we were very comfortable together, especially in the later years when we didn't have to struggle together over the book. In the working years, we were both very strong-minded, and battled very much. She appreciated those battles. That's why when I told her to take my name off the book, she absolutely insisted it remain.

She gave me a reprint of a lecture she had given, and inscribed it, "To Fred, my belovedly stubborn associate, with resentful appreciation." And that conveys the relationship in the period we were working together. Later, ambivalence fell away and it became a nice relationship.

She showed her anger at me by coldness. At all times I had a career completely independent from her, which is how I differed from some of her other coworkers. I was an associate professor with tenure at Einstein, I had been an associate professor at Downstate and had my own research. I was not dependent on her and that's what made the relationship possible. She always wanted to possess more of me and I am not easy to possess. She wanted to own me, to have me be part of her world. Yet she appreciated the separateness. The warmth was there but the two of us had to negotiate together. Twice we were very distant and she wouldn't talk to me for months, except at meetings, and both times she felt rightly that I had withdrawn. Once I withdrew because I objected to having my name on the chapter she produced because I disliked it so thoroughly, and prior to that because I had gotten an honorific research award. It didn't allow me to earn any income from outside sources, so I cut back my time with her and didn't accept any remuneration. She not incorrectly read that as a personal withdrawal. In both instances I withdrew because I wanted to possess my own life. But I valued what she was doing and was happy to have a hand in it. I still think it was important work.

Some Who Hated Her

Dr. Leo Madow said[11] that Margaret Mahler was one of those people you either loved or hated. Joan Jackson, Mahler's longtime assistant, was one of the latter. She found Mahler "cold and ungenerous." According to her,[12] "Mahler had very severe back pains, and was on Percodan a lot. When she wasn't she was not a happy person. I was young and just had to steer clear of her. When she had her rages people would just bypass her. She was bitter about a lot of things. She talked about her divorce, and that she had gotten all his relatives out of Germany during the war. After she got divorced they shared custody of the dog."

A colleague who did not wish to be identified cared even less for Mahler than Jackson did. He said frankly, "I didn't like her personally and I didn't like a lot of the nonsense that went on around her. She was bright, but very exploitative of people. I didn't like how she exploited my friend, Manny Furer. She tried to use me to push Manny aside. I refused to go along with it and ultimately just left Masters Children's Center. When I quit I told her that she was exploitative."

Lucia Wright,[13] an artist with a Ph.D. in performance studies at New York University who worked for Mahler briefly, also found her difficult to like. Wright was an administrative assistant to Mahler in 1978 while Mahler was recovering from surgery and bedridden. Wright described the scene and her experiences:

When you came into the main room there was a large dining table and a window at the far end. The table was always covered with papers and books in progress. A live-in caretaker did the heavy work, and I was supposed to help with the writing. Sometimes if her help was out I would make her a sandwich for lunch." "Mahler was very unpleasant," "She seemed overly self-important, and was in a bad mood most of the time. I didn't like being around her. I remember once she dictated a letter to a person new in the field who had sent her a paper. Mahler got all bent out of shape because this person had attached a note saying, "I'm sending you my paper, as you requested." She, Mahler, said she had not requested the paper, but that the person had asked her to read it. It seemed like such a petty thing to get upset about. Oh, the politics of Academia!

Wright explained that she did not work for Mahler very long:

I was on a night schedule at the time and found it hard to get up in the morning. I often got there late, and it really upset her. She would say things like, "I need you to be here on time. I was waiting for you," which is understandable but I was not motivated to make the extra effort required. I even told her I had a sleep disorder in order to get her sympathy! One day I just didn't show up and then I never really told her I couldn't make it anymore, it just petered out. She was never nasty or mean to me. I just remember her being very cranky and needy and it was too much for me, it was unpleasant. She was very critical of everything, including her colleagues, and her philosophy seemed to be "just focus on your work." I think that's what kept her going, sitting up in her bed and doing her work, as if that's the only thing that kept her alive.

Mahler and Anni Bergman

Further illustrating the diversity of her responses to different friends, many of the people I interviewed mentioned the relationship of Mahler and her longtime associate, Anni Bergman.[14] Kitty LaPerrière, Mahler's assistant and coauthor, was one of the interviewees who commented on Mahler's mistreatment of Anni Bergman. LaPerrière said,[15] "Mahler had a way of reducing everyone to their lowest functioning level. She humiliated people. Once, she invited me to dinner in front of Anni and said to her, 'You can come for dessert.'"

Swerdloff echoed LaPerrière's statements about Bergman. She said,[16] "Mahler treated Anni very badly. Mahler loved clothes and talking about them. Once, when I came to see her in the hospital, she had on a very interesting robe that we talked about, an oriental style. We were chatting away and she was so rotten to Anni that she went out in the hall and wept. This was in contrast to how nice she was to me. Anni tolerated all this because she and a number of others had their careers made by Mahler. She was nasty to Anni all along, and at the same time helped her to get a degree. She had no degrees when she met Mahler."

An anonymous child analyst and researcher also mentioned Mahler's treatment of Bergman. She said somewhat angrily, "Mahler criticized Anni Bergman, and made it very difficult and embarrassing for her."

Whatever the reason Bergman allowed herself to accept Mahler's abuse, it is apparent the two women were locked into some kind of ambivalent relationship. If Anna Freud is right that libido binds and aggression separates, the relationship between Mahler and Bergman may well have served Mahler's needs both for closeness and emotional distance.

Bergman herself made some interesting comments about Mahler's destructiveness:[17]

> Margaret had an enormous need to work with other people, she couldn't work alone. In a way, I have inherited that from her. I always like to work with other people. But what I don't wish to inherit from her was the way she could be very destructive to people and very demanding. *She needed other people to think; she was unable to think by herself. That was my role. Whether about the design, the results, or the individual children, she always needed someone to think with.* Underneath her brilliance there was a tremendous insecurity. She had a terribly unfortunate temper, had rages, you had to be a very special person to be able to tolerate and appreciate her good sides. She had a desperate need for people, and could never be alone. She was full of contradictions. She was both possessive and very generous. A lot depended on her mood. You never knew how she would be.

Adding to the stories of people who were suddenly dropped by Mahler, Bergman said, "She could suddenly turn on you and you would get the feeling the relationship was over forever, and a few days later she would call you as if nothing had happened."

Some Who Loved Her

Despite Mahler's difficulties in relating to people, she had many friends and associates who loved her. Yet, for a woman who had many friends, she confided in surprisingly few people. With a few colleagues such as Harold Blum and Selma Kramer, Mahler was intimate and let them into her deepest needs and fears.

Blum, with whom Mahler had a relatively unconflicted relationship, learned a great deal about her in their personal discussions that is not generally known. He said,[18] "We had a private conversation about her mother, who was murdered at Auschwitz. Mahler told me this as if she were revealing a dark secret. She said she would never forgive or forget her mother's murder, and had a memorial put up for her in the Hungarian cemetery which said, 'She died a martyr of the holocaust.'"

Blum[19] confirms that Mahler had a difficult relationship with her mother. He said, "*Mahler made peace with her mother after her death, which spurred on her creativity.* There was an evolution in Mahler's work. First she was a traditional analyst, when she again wasn't accepted by the inner group. Then after the war she began to evolve into Margaret Mahler. The development started right after World War II, when she learned about her mother's murder. The knowledge had a formative influence on her creativity, as she was honoring her mother in her research."

"I think another aspect of her work was compensation for being childless," Blum continued. *"It was Margaret's way of being a surrogate mother, and was also in identification with her mother.* It is a deduction on my part about a very complex individual."

Selma Kramer was one of Mahler's first Philadelphia students and dearest friends. Selma adored her teacher and their relationship took over her life. Kramer's daughter, Karen Berberian,[20] felt quite differently about Mahler than her mother did, and may well have paid the price for Selma's love of her mentor. Kramer and her colleague, Leo Madow, with support from Mahler, began the yearly Mahler symposium. In addition, Kramer was one of the founders of the Margaret S. Mahler Psychiatric Research Foundation. According to Berberian, the symposiums were her mother's gift to Mahler, whom she worshiped as a god.

"When I think about Margaret's impact on the child analysts in Philadelphia, and the degree to which she was revered as the source of all wisdom, I picture Moses and the Ten Commandments," Berberian said, and continued

> Margaret, of course, was God. I see my mother as Moses, and all of her students were to study what was written on the clay tablets. My mother felt empowered through her relationship with Margaret. I suspect that the self-confidence that she and the others gained from Margaret played a role in their success in treating patients, in addition to any role played by separation-individuation theory. I wonder if I have communicated how much these people felt "special" and "right" about everything, as if there was only one way to treat children (their way), and the rest of the world was wrong.
>
> Last week, I finally decided to go through my mother's Rolodex. One card had Margaret's name, date of birth, and date of death. There was nothing for my grandparents. This sums up my mother's relationship with Margaret.
>
> Margaret gave my mother something that she never got from her parents; she made her feel special and important. My mother gave Mahler her endless devotion and admiration. The symposiums were her great gift to Margaret. It was never clear to me if other people were involved as much with her as my mother was. Cal Settlage didn't need Margaret in the same way my mother did, and felt free to go off on his own. My mother was less ambivalent. She was a card carrying member of the Margaret Mahler club. She was always so pleased when Margaret visited. She might say, "Yes I know Margaret can be difficult," but that was the most critical remark I ever heard her make about her.
>
> This person stole my mother away from me, [Karen poignantly added]. "Once my mother started her analytic training, she was grabbed by it and gone from me. Mahler just made a bad situation worse. My younger brother, Jim, didn't feel the same way. When I was a baby, my mother practiced medicine a little but was with me nearly full time. By the time my brother was born, she was so immersed in her psychoanalytic training that she hired a succession of housekeepers and babysitters to take care of us. I don't think my brother experienced the loss I did, because he had a less intense relationship with our mother from day one. My mother even hired a woman to come to our house at night to take care of my brother's nighttime bottle feedings. This was so she could sleep through the night and be available to her

patients the next morning. I was eighteen months old when my mother started her psychoanalytic training. Speaking of rapprochement crises....

When I was little the psychoanalytic community was the total focus of our lives. Most of the people we socialized with were analysts. I still remember being compared with the other analyst's children, not my cousins. In the '50s, analysis was very current. Before managed care, my mother felt she was doing something so special, it was almost through her association with Mahler that she became royalty, too. All the Philadelphia analysts socialized with each other, summer vacations, and so forth. Margaret went down to the shore with my mother.

My father devoted his life to Selma, so she could devote her life to psychoanalysis. Some of the other analysts were resentful, indicating that if they had the level of support my mother did they could have been as successful as she was.

My grandmother was uneducated and unsophisticated and never provided my mother with important things that she needed. Margaret was my mother's Prince Charming, who rescued her from scrubbing pots. I sometimes thought about the erotic element in their relationship. They didn't have a lesbian relationship, but it was intense and passionate. My mother loved having Margaret as her mentor. Although my mother was a mentor to many students, she was never as excited about being a mentor as she was about being Margaret's mentee.

It was very hard for me. There was nothing I could do as a child that elicited the same level of passion from my mother as she invested in Mahler. My mother was there when I had my tonsils out or broke up with my boyfriend. She seemed to do all the right things. But there was nothing I could do to compete with her love of Margaret. I could whack my brother if I wanted to, but there was nothing I could do to compete with her love of Margaret. I could whack my brother if I wanted to, but there was nothing I could do about psychoanalysis.

The pain of Karen's feeling about her mother's friendship with Mahler continues to the present day. When I asked Karen if she wanted to see a lovely letter her mother had sent Margaret, Karen declined. She said,[21] " I don't want to see any of my mother's letters to Margaret right now. It is still painful to be reminded of their relationship, from which I was excluded."

And yet, Karen's envy of Margaret Mahler does not tell the whole story. As I was getting out of the car in which the hospitable Berberians had driven me to the railroad station, Karen said, "I have something to show you." She took out her key ring and handed me a silver medallion engraved with the initials M.S.M. Mahler had given the key ring to Selma. "Isn't it strange?" Karen said. "Margaret Mahler nearly ruined my life, and here I am carrying her key ring around with me. I guess this says something about the intensity of my wish to be a part of that very special relationship."

I thought Karen and her son Josh would be surprised by a remark her mother made which is recorded in the Neubauer, Kramer, Mahler video of February 13, 1982.[22] Kramer said, "Margaret has become a grandparent to my kids." When I showed Karen this comment, she disagreed with Kramer's idea of her children's affection for Mahler. She added, "Here is the more accurate version of how Margaret came to be 'Grandma Margaret'":

When my brother and I were young, we were told to address Margaret as "Auntie Margaret." This was a bit strange, since we called our other aunts Aunt Carolyn, Aunt Mimmy, and Aunt Bebe. I can speculate on the reasons for my mother's choice of "auntie." Perhaps the word sounded fancier than "aunt." It made Margaret seemed special and different from my other aunts. I also wondered if my mother was thinking of the flamboyant *Auntie Mame* character. When my children were little, they were introduced to Auntie Margaret but felt that she looked old enough to be a grandmother. My mother recalled Josh saying, "That's no auntie, that's a grandma." After that, Margaret became Grandma Margaret to Josh and Jeremy. My mother's remark that "Margaret has become a grandparent to my kids" reflected her wish, not the actual role played by Margaret in our lives.

Although Susan Schwartz (pseudonym)[23] also loved Mahler dearly, she had a much less ambivalent relationship with Mahler than Selma Kramer had. Mahler adored Susan, and treated her like a beloved grandchild. "Margaret loved me," Susan said,[24] "and was lovely to me. She was like a grandmother to me and gave me many beautiful presents that I treasure. She was often upset about things, but many people are. I was fortunate in that she never seemed upset about me."

The English analyst Anna-Marie Sandler[24] was not on intimate terms with Mahler, but got along well with her. She also had a charming Mahler story to tell. She said, "Margaret was attending a reception in our house in November 1971, when our eldest daughter and her husband joined us with a number of photographs of their young baby. Margaret became enchanted with one particular shot. She asked if she could use it for her book, *The Psychological Birth of the Human Infant.*[25] We were, of course, delighted to oblige and so our first grandson made his appearance on the front cover of Margaret's famous book."

Par for the course, Dr. Bernard Pacella functioned differently with Mahler than any of her other close friends. He served at times as her psychiatrist. He said,[26]

If Margaret had a problem she would call me in to talk about things. I listened. At one time she told me she felt sick and would like to come into the hospital. I said, "What do you think is wrong?" She said she didn't feel well, and didn't know what it was. I got to know her so well I knew when she was feeling off. I knew it was a depression, not a physical illness. But she just said she needed a rest. She wouldn't admit it, but she was in a depression.

She had episodic depressions that you could not detect. One time she had a prolonged depression, but said she just felt sick. I was young, and had an office in a really large medical building with sixteen floors of physicians at 115 E. Sixty-first. They had a four bed hospital. I admitted her and talked with her a few times a day. She never talked much about her father, except that she loved him more than her mother. I kind of became her father. Her husband had problems. She told me about her husband and a sexual problem. She never wanted to talk about it very much. It became a distant relationship with the husband.

She never was angry with me. She was angry with a lot of people, but not with me. It can't be that she was afraid of me, she just didn't want to antagonize me. I was kind of her substitute husband, if she got into trouble she would call me up and I would come over. Lot of this was unknown, I never told anybody about it. She got depressed years after her husband left. She wasn't manic depressive, but sometimes she would be solemn and moody and some times gayer, a miniature type of manic-depression, which I wrote a paper on.

Mahler's moments of deep depression were also referred to in a letter written to her late in her life by her dear friend Darline Levy,[27] who spoke of a "terrifying state of melancholia" so profound that she feared for Mahler's life. Levy wrote Mahler, "I become desperate about this temporary condition, which unquestionably will pass; instead, I should be celebrating your steady progress out of a state of despair that was life-threatening, and where you might have been lost for all of us forever."

Mahler called Levy, who arrived in Mahler's life when she was in her eighties, one of her best friends. In a letter to Margaret, Darline wrote,[28] "I will never forget a beautiful little passage in a letter you wrote to me, at the end of last summer. 'I must talk with you (about part-self-object images)— as about many other things. Darling Darline — if you can accept me with my great weaknesses and dependencies?? Would you want to...? The greatest human strengths are rooted in and develop out of great weaknesses and dependencies.'"

The friendship seems to have cooled off shortly thereafter. The loving letters and cards ceased. "We remained friends until after the archives project was completed, although I didn't see her as much," Levy said,[29] "I was living in Paris with my husband and children during the academic year 1983–1984, on a sabbatical research leave, and she died in '85. We did speak on the phone as she got weaker. She needed help and support that neither Peter or I could offer at a distance of three thousand miles."

A very feminine woman psychoanalyst who was a close friend of Mahler asked to be quoted anonymously. The two often spent time together doing "feminine" things, like shopping for clothing. The analyst considered Mahler a very feminine woman, as did Ilo Milton, who said,[30] "The thing was that she was very feminine, and I really liked that. Her nails were done, her interest in flowers, the vases. Once, when I went into her bedroom, her hand was draped over the side of the bed. A hand embroidered handkerchief was hanging down over the bed. I think the dramatic hand dripping over the bed with manicured nails was the counterpoint to some of the hardness in her personality."

Although both women found Mahler quite feminine, other people, like Dr. Bernard Pacella, felt that Mahler was bisexual.[31] In my opinion, both sexual identifications were aspects of her personality. Which one was uppermost was brought out by unconscious elements in the person she felt close to at the moment.

When asked if Mahler had ever treated her badly, the anonymous analyst vehemently replied: She wouldn't have dared! My experience with Margaret was very positive. It went on for a long time. I was married at the time and she wasn't.

> She was very lonely. "We spent many evenings together and talked. Everyone who knew her would tell you about her moods. She was really hungry for companionship. I got to know her in a different way. She told me about her mother and sister, with a kind of bitterness. I had had similar experiences with my mother and father. We talked about how this left an imprint on people forever. She was characterized by a great deal of loneliness. She was really fearful of being interviewed without support. Margaret never knew how much she would reveal, how much she could trust the interviewer. She refused to be interviewed without me, which gives you a feel for the hunger she had for support.

Another colleague and friend of Mahler's, Justin Call,[32] cared about her deeply and felt compassion for her. He remembered a poignant and revealing anecdote about Mahler which suggests that her "tantrums," at least at times, were caused by feelings of inadequacy. He said:

> I first met Margaret Mahler in the early 1960s. That was my first meeting of her in a scientific forum and she was there jointly with Kitty LaPerriere. When it came time for questions and comments from the audience, I challenged her theoretical position on using the term *normal autistic phase* in the early weeks of life. Later on she explained what she meant by that, rather than implying that there was something pathologically abnormal as shown in autistic children.
>
> I knew and associated with Margaret Mahler and read and taught her publications to my students. I saw her frequently at meetings on the East Coast and had one or two visits with her in her apartment in New York. Also, she stayed with me at my home in Newport Beach for a couple of nights and I arranged for her to lecture to my students and to talk with her about her work when she came to California for a rest. I would say that I knew her moderately well.

Call also wrote to me:

> I always found Margaret pleasant, interesting, and easily engaged. She was sincere and thoughtful, in my experience. I am not sure whether Margaret helped me in my career or not. I think she had a good opinion of me and I am sure that she spoke with our mutual friends in a positive tone about me. I certainly did about her. Yes, I do believe Margaret was generous of her time and her thoughtfulness and the enormous work that she had produced for all of us to read. I think her writing was good and always highly informative, helpful, and clinically relevant. She also gave me the feeling that we were friends and I do think she was attentive to my work as well as being interested in sharing her work with me.
>
> I never encountered any temper from Margaret, but I remember an incident in Boston when I had organized a conference and she was there to participate as one of the major presenters. When it came time for her to present, she just sat in her seat. It was really for me very amusing and interesting, but I had been primed by Eleanor Galenson that Margaret was sometimes difficult and I utilized what Eleanor told me

by going into the audience where Margaret sat on an aisle seat. I sat down next to her, putting my arm around her, and reassuring her about the importance of her work, even though there had been others who presented before she did. She responded very well to this approach, so I was not the object of any rageful expressions and of course she did present her work very well. Later on her presentation was included in the publication, which I had to fight for but was successful in getting her contribution published. This was in the book on *Infant Psychiatry*. I was always thoughtful of her work, as she was of mine. I have no idea what might have been the in-depth understanding of her so-called rage. I never experienced such rage or even terribly difficult transactions. Perhaps she had a problem with self-esteem. I only say this because others have said it.

Leo Madow, who found no difficulty interacting with Mahler, experienced her still differently from the others. He said,[33] "I found her a wonderful hostess, who was very pleasant. She gave nice parties and had good food. This was the same woman who was supposed to be a terror, who would pulverize people. But she never did that sort of thing with me."

"Why do you think she was so nice to you, in contrast to many of the others?" I asked.

"I think she saw me as the chairman of the department of psychiatry at the Women's Medical College and used to call me 'The Chief,'" he answered. "I think she had me in another category than the others."

"You were her boss."

"Yes." We smiled. "If anything, she needed me, and it didn't pay her not to be nice to me. But I think her friendship was genuine, I know it was. Mahler was one of those people you either loved or hated. Even though she was hard on some of our people, all of them loved her."

Mahler's "Daughters"

Margaret had a number of young women friends and colleagues, including Darline Levy and Maria Nardone, whom she considered "daughters." Although she loved all her "children," she characteristically treated each one differently. For example, her analysand, Bluma Swerdloff,[34] later to become a friend and the interviewer of Mahler's Oral History, generally found her kind and caring. With Judith Smith, Mahler's film editor who was also a social worker/psychotherapist in private practice, she was also helpful and accepting but cooly professional.

Smith said,[35] "Margaret Mahler was a very important person in my life. She was a strong, smart woman, who let me into her den in critical but limited ways. Her ideas were very important to me. They sort of formed the basis of my professional identity. It was nice being liked and taken into the world of psychoanalytic history. I worked for her probably from 1975 or '76 until she died. She couldn't tell me precisely what to do because she didn't know about filmmaking."

Echoing the refrain of other friends who put distance between themselves and Mahler, Smith said, "I was not one of the people she pushed around, probably because I had some autonomy and independence, and had a specific skill. I knew she was a difficult lady, but I didn't feel she impeded me. I think I didn't see her as my friend, I saw her as my employer. I got a lot from being with her and never wanted any more."

Like Margaret's sister, the beloved Suzannah who was secure in the love of her mother, certain "daughters" like Maria Nardone and Pat Nachman mysteriously remained untouched by Mahler's rages.

"I never got in the cross fire," Nachman, who is a developmental research psychologist and researcher and assistant clinical professor in psychiatry at the Mount Sinai School of Medicine, said. "She knew that I felt she had made a tremendous contribution, She left me out of the crossfire, and I was delighted. She liked fighting, and got full of energy when she was angry, including at the end of her life when she fought with everyone in the intensive care unit.

Nachman continued:

> I remember another story. We were invited to lunch and some poor woman brought her three-year-old along. The first thing, the little girl decided she didn't want to eat her peas. The mother started with, "One little pea, 2 little peas, etc." The silverware was marching around the table. I looked at Margaret and steam was coming out of her ears. She said something really harsh to the woman. To her she represented this whole new generations of mothers who were over-protective of their children. She lashed into this mother.

> "What happened?"
> "The child ate her peas."

Kitty LaPerrière, Research Associate at Masters Children's Center and collaborator of a journal article with Mahler, did not consider herself a daughter, but a collaborator and student. LaPerrière was somewhat more ambivalent and openly critical than the "daughters" and voiced her views, both positive and critical, more directly than the others. She said:[36]

> James Anthony introduced me to her. He said, "If you can forgive some eccentricities you will have an interesting time with her." She seemed to be a very intense person whose eyes could cloud over and hint at unhappiness. I thought I could be forgiving, and we agreed that I would come to work for her as a research psychologist. I had my Ph.D. already and didn't have to work for her if I didn't want to. Many people who worked for her did not have adequate degrees in their profession and had no choice of interesting employment. She had respect for me. She said, "She thinks like a man." That was the highest compliment she could pay any woman.
> Anni Bergman was the chief participant observer.
> We had a bad relationship. We probably competed. Mahler had me in a different

place. She used me as a cat's paw with the others. She would say, "LaPerrière would never do that." We would sit and have meetings every morning, where we would read the observations. She could reduce even a strong person like Imogene Kamakaio (another participant observer) to tears. When I was there nobody else had a Ph.D. The men all had MDs, and Mahler thought Ph.Ds were higher. I am a linguist, and speak French, Czech, and German, and studied Latin in school. Maybe that impressed her.

We weren't close, as Anni and Imogene were to her. I was very fond of Mahler, though, and maybe a little protective. She was a vulnerable, lonely woman. That was clear when she wanted you to work on holidays. Instead of saying "I'm lonely" and inviting a few people over, she would order you to come. If you refused, she would say, "Do you want to work here or not?" Shock and awe, in Baghdad was what people experienced with Margaret Mahler when they worked for her.

Mahler taught the fellows in child psychoanalysis in Philadelphia, some of whom were already well known. About four or five of them came and she taught them in her apartment. Once or twice she asked me to sit in. I remember once when she went out to make a phone call. The analysts behaved like a second grade class who made nasty comments and threw spitballs when the teacher turned her back. To me, the analysts were like demigods. In those days they would go to psychoanalytic meetings, where if you were well analyzed you sat motionless; nobody budged. You were supposed to be removed from all human emotions, to have eliminated all unacceptable drives and be all intellect and sublimation. Nobody scratched their nose. It was eye opening to see those four or five grown men letting loose!

Mahler seemed to have the same effect on her coworkers as she did on her students. Ilo Milton[37] told a story about a party she attended where twenty of Mahler's associates let off steam for an entire evening by "telling their worst Mahler stories." There was not much Mahler's colleagues could do to heal the psychic wounds she inflicted, except to gripe about it in groups where they found they were not alone in being victims of her abuse. Of course, they could always quit. Many, like Kitty LaPerrière, did. Mahler was notorious for the number of caretakers who came and went in her employ.

LaPerrière finished the interview by summarizing her feelings about Mahler. "In retrospect," she said, "I enjoyed her, but I remember that I felt very oppressed by the situation. I got myocarditis after being with her two years and needed to get out of it. So I quit and began to work with Nathan Ackerman. When people said Ackerman was difficult, I said, 'Not after Margaret Mahler!'"

Summary

According to the many friends and colleagues interviewed by me, it is evident that Margaret Mahler treated some people kindly and others quite badly. She adored her "daughters" and gave them lovely gifts, went shopping with a friend, confided in Harold Blum as she did to very few friends, and deferred to her "boss," Leo Madow. She used Bernard Pacella as her personal psychiatrist. In contrast, she battled constantly with Fred Pine and tried to possess him, was "cold and ungenerous" to a number of employees, was said to exploit Manny Furer, was "unpleasant" to Lucia Wright, established an ambivalent relationship with Anni Bergman, stole away Karen Berberian's mother, and behaved in a paranoid fashion with Leo Rangell, a relationship which will be further discussed in the next chapter. Perhaps there were other sides to her personality that we have no way of knowing about at this point. One conclusion, however, seems likely. It is doubtful that any one person ever was exposed to all the fragments of Margaret Mahler's personality.

Margaret Mahler achieved her life's ambition, and became the great researcher and teacher she had always wanted to be, despite her emotionally deprived childhood and adult experiences with the Holocaust. It is likely she took pleasure in that knowledge. But despite the fact that she had fulfilled her conscious goals, what remained forever unobtainable was her secret desire to be the infant partner in a relationship of dual unity. Although the dream as such was impossible to fulfil, she sublimated it in her famous research of the symbiotic union of mother and infant. In her life as a researcher, Mahler accomplished what she was unable to do in her personal existence: She brought together the two conflicting themes of her life, the need to live out her ambitions and to be smack in the middle of the mother-infant union. Margaret Mahler's genius for sublimation brought her closest to being an integrated human being.

14

Her Colleagues Remember (The Present)

Mahler's Rages

That Mahler was well known for her temper and seemingly uncontrolled outbursts of rage was confirmed by many people, including her friend Helen Meyers,[1] well known analyst, author, and officer of numerous psychoanalytic organizations. Meyers, who considered her friend's tendency to rages a harmless idiosyncracy, said:

> Once, in Portugal when we had a reception for her, she was the center of the whole thing. She saw Peter Blos Jr. and Eric Erickson in another part of the room and, a little hurt, asked, "Why is it that they don't come over and congratulate me?"
>
> Another cute funny negative thing that people laughed about, she wouldn't talk to somebody for months because they didn't come to a dinner. When she got insulted by a person she got mad at them and wouldn't talk to them for months. Once, she didn't talk to us for two years because we didn't visit her at her table. It didn't bother me because I am not a child analyst, and Margaret to me was a cute little old lady and not the power figure. How Mahler treated them was very important to other people, but I thought it was funny that she was insulted by me. When she was happy with me she called me "Helenitchka," the same thing my mother called me, which was very sweet. But when she was mad it was "Helen." There was a sort of a little girl quality about her.
>
> I found her quite loveable. I was very fond of her, and admired her greatly. We took her out to a lot of places, to the opera and the ballet, and at meetings when she couldn't walk we drove her about in a wheelchair. She was always very responsive to that and very sweet, and I'm sure she looked forward to it, as we did.
>
> My husband was particularly fond of her, as he is a child analyst, and felt her work was a breakthrough. Up to then, people talked mostly about the Oedipal complex. She made a big impact on earlier development. She brought the work with

psychotic children into the foreground of analytic thinking, and nobody had done that before she did. Before she developed separation-individuation theory, people talked about neurotic problems as starting with the Oedipus complex.

Lotte Koehler, Mahler's German friend, bore out Meyer's thinking. Koehler said[2] "Mahler had friends, and yet she was lonely. She sought people out, and then proceeded to offend them. *She hurt almost everyone who had personal dealings with her,* but always managed to reconcile with them. She could be very self-absorbed, but then when she became aware of it could switch around and listen with remarkable empathy to the other person's problems. Her sensitivity allowed her to empathize with this side of her patients."

When I asked her if she had ever been the object of Mahler's rage, Koehler replied, "Yes, I was. In 1978, I got a letter, as follows:

"Dear Lottchen: I hesitated for along time to write you again, because I can't be silent about the fact that all my trustees and most of all I am deeply disappointed and mortified, as you simply are not aware of the fact that we expected since years and especially now a significant donation of money or shares, according to your financial situation. We have increasingly difficulties concerning the archives, which cost us immensely much and is so rich, and there are many data which are not yet digested."

Koehler went on:

Then she continues writing about her severe disease and operation. It was written in German and I have translated it myself. This letter was an enormous mortification for me. I don't translate my answer, which was very frank. I described to her what a disastrous consequence for my life was the fact that I was the only daughter of a rich father, and that I had to continue his work in industry and could only in my leisure time be a psychoanalyst, and that I had thought that I was respected by Mahler and her foundation, because I was I and I was a good psychoanalyst, doing something for the work of Margaret Mahler, but not because of my money. Both my marriages failed due to that fact. I cannot find what she answered, but I guess it was some words of regret. But this affair did not disturb our relationship.

An anonymous colleague inadvertently may have given an explanation for Mahler's offensive behavior. In speaking of *why toddlers in the rapprochement crisis behave so badly,* he said, "The mother who understands this stage of development can see why the temper tantrums take place, why the screaming when you leave the door, as *a way children adapt to keeping the symbiotic web going.* It may well be that Mahler's tantrums were her way of 'refueling' a dying symbiosis."

A previously mentioned anonymous psychoanalyst agreed with the many people who spoke of Mahler's moods. "As far as personal friendship, you couldn't depend on Margaret to keep the same frame of mind for very long," she said. "Perhaps the people who did not have to depend on her and could take her for what she was could get past the criticism. They would ask, 'How do you know this?' Of course, she knew it. My sons talk about how fiery a character she was, and how she couldn't abide fools. They also knew John McDevitt well, and would laugh at how she had him in tow."

Mahler's students were terrified of her rages, according to Irving Sternschein.[3] He observed that, indeed, Mahler frightened her pupils, but in his opinion that was only part of the story. He said, "When she first came to this country, she began to do some teaching at Columbia in the child therapy division. She was not only revered but feared because of her skills as a clinician and her perceptiveness. Her opinions were made quite forcefully, she had a reputation for that. I consulted her at one point and was struck by how sensitive she was, how with a few pithy remarks she could size up an internal problem very well."

Jacob Arlow, the late "Grand Old Man of Psychoanalysis," said,[4] "I never saw her in a temperamental outburst, but she was not a woman who was easily crossed, especially if she was in control. She was a difficult person, but I didn't reach the degree of working together in intimate projects, where such flair-ups are likely to occur. *The lasting impression I have of her is kind of an embattled woman, and the word 'dour' comes up in connection with her.* There was always that aspect about her. I don't recall her kidding around, joking, or making word plays, but that might have been my own

The great Jacob Arlow, a dear friend of Margaret's, and his grandson (date unknown).

stiffness. I always felt there was a toughness about her that foreordained that a distance would be kept."

A quite different slant concerning Dr. Arlow's feelings about Mahler was given to me by Leo Madow. According to him,[5] "The story going around was that Arlow was in love with her." When I asked him about it, he said, "If so, I don't remember."

Although Judith Smith, the editor of the Masters Children's Center videotapes, said that Dr. Mahler was an extremely important person in her life, she did report that at times she could be painfully critical. She said:

> What I most remember is how she would point out my faults. Once, when I knew her for just six months, she called me and demanded that I come to her house right away. She said it was an emergency. She'd once had a fire in her house, and since then had a safe where she kept her most important papers. She had opened the safe and couldn't close it and was afraid to leave it open. She called me because I was the so-called "technical" person. I got there and couldn't fix it. She got furious, and said, "You are such a dilettante, you think you can do all these things and you can't!" Although at the time, I didn't feel devastated by her attack, I do hold on to her criticism of me as a possible dilettante.

Swerdloff spoke further about Mahler's screaming outbursts.[6] "She was known for having temper tantrums. The first time she started yelling at me, I walked away. She had a housekeeper who never said a word, a shadow of a person. Mahler of course found fault with everything the housekeeper did, but she stayed anyway." Swerdloff then told the story of the housekeeper who dared to bring in a cup with an unmatching saucer. Mahler raged at the woman and said, "*In my house we do it right.*"

Henri Parens, the author of important work on aggression and one of Mahler's early Philadelphia colleagues, experienced Mahler as "complex, fascinating, and impossible.... She was very fascinating, she really was.[7] I found her someone who understood a great deal, and really knew human dynamic processes. I didn't particularly find her easy to be with as a person, but I sure admired what she knew and was able to convey to us, her insights and knowledge; she was a great teacher and, I sense, a great clinician."

On the dance floor as well as in her life, Mahler had to be in control. Parens said:

> I once danced with Mahler. It was like I was dancing with a small, life size statue. To try to get her to move with the flow, I had to yield to her; I had to figure out where she wanted to go and guide her there gently. She was very demanding, but there was a real lovingness about her. *I really loved Mahler. It was the person I loved, difficult as she was. She could be a pain in the ass!* Mahler was very demanding of people's personal environment. She was very object hungry, but was very choosey about whom she would turn to. Certain people adored her and she adored them, and of those people she wanted more. Like Selma Kramer, Mahler's student and past-president of the Margaret Mahler Foundation in Philadelphia. Selma loved that Mahler wanted so much of her and was exceedingly demanding. Like with everyone else,

some people rubbed Mahler the wrong way. For those people she would find a crisp way of putting them in their place. She would make some comment which could frizzle a person.

Henri Parens also believes that Mahler's place in psychoanalytic thinking is secure. He said, "I admired her brains, her thinking, no question about that. Mahler was certainly one of the strong thinkers of the era, along with Hartmann, Anna Freud, and Rene Spitz. Later I would also add Winnicott."

Mahler's paranoid trend reared its head with Leo Rangell, the coauthor of one of her earliest papers, on Gilles de la Tourette's. He said,[8]

> We were socially and personally friendly, but it was a social relationship, not an intimate one. Basically, she was a mentor to my being a resident at the time. She never talked to me about her personal life, although she knew my wife and one child I had at the time. Mahler made a first birthday party for my daughter, Judy, who is now in her sixties, in her apartment on Central Park West. I have told Judy, with some pride, "Do you know that Margaret Mahler made you your first birthday party?"
>
> After Pearl Harbor, I joined the army. That is how Margaret and I separated. She was very disappointed. She had wanted me to write a book on tics with her. I would have done that gladly, if I hadn't had to leave. I never moved back to New York. In later years, I found out that she was angry with me for that, and said strange things, like I left her or rejected her. As if I had wanted to be in the army!
>
> She was also angry with me another time, after I was president of the American Psychoanalytic Association. Mahler was nominated for president. She was eager to do it, but at the end got cold feet. David Beres would be running against her. She began to say that I was the West Coast man for Beres, who was a close friend of Arlow, Brenner, and me. She believed I was their man on the West Coast, and would work against her. This was far from any truth. She was afraid that Beres would defeat her, so she withdrew. Beres was elected.

Early in her American career, Mahler wanted to write a book about child psychoses and asked Manuel Furer, the director of the Masters Children's Center project for psychotic children, to coauthor it with her. It was a collection of all her old papers, and Furer thought there was nothing new in it.[9] "She wanted to work all the time," he commented: "so I refused. She soured on me and snapped, 'All right, I'll write the book but you won't be coauthor.' But in the book, she says, 'In collaboration with Manuel Furer....' It was her way of making up for her guilt and bad feelings."

As my research continued, I discovered that more and more of Mahler's associates had experienced traumatic incidents with her. The apotheosis came at the previously mentioned party attended by Ilo Milton, where all of twenty women spent the evening discussing Mahler's tirades. Milton[10] said,

> I went to a party given by Mahler's personal secretary, who was retiring after twenty-five years in Dr. Mahler's employ. Unfortunately she didn't invite Mahler, but twenty other women, all her research assistants. Everybody was sitting around

telling their worst Mahler stories. At one point we looked at each other and said, "What did we all have in common that led us to work with her and stay with her?" We decided we probably all had a depressive piece and were looking to fulfill it. At the time I worked for her, my sister was working for an elderly female writer. I thought, *Why are we working for these older women?* I never had a grandmother and my mother was not knowable, you couldn't know her interior life. With Dr. Mahler, I knew too much, it became more complicated personally.

One day, when there were a bunch of people in the office, a young psychiatrist from Scandinavia came to see her. The door to her office was open and we could see inside. She was in her chair, and he was on one knee holding her hand like a proposal. He was telling her what a phenomenal influence she had made on his life. We all looked at each other with surprise at this archaic manner in which he expressed his admiration.

I worked in the apt on 66th Street, where the only boundaries were a door that was open most of the time. A lot of the work was done in her bedroom, or in the hospital. I wouldn't call it work, because the boundaries between personal and professional were so murky. The secretary, accountant, and her women friends were all there, so there was a lot of stuff going on. I don't know how well I knew her. I thought I knew her more than I wanted to know. I wished that the boundaries had been firmer. I think Dr. Mahler wanted something so deep in her life. There was something missing and she didn't know how to ask for it. I said please ask me what you need. Her needs were very mother-child oriented. She was annoyed that I couldn't read her mind. It was very upsetting. You expect more from someone in her position, she was the grand dame with all these young woman around her, you expected her to set the boundaries.

Actually she fired me two weeks after she hired me. Ruth came to me and said, "Dr. Mahler is firing you." I asked why. She said, "She thinks she is going to crush you." I looked at Ruth and said, "What are you talking about?" She answered, "You are so nice and she feels she is going to hurt you." I got enraged and said, "I'm going into her bedroom!" I went in and said, "Dr. Mahler, nobody has ever fired me in my life. If this is true that you are afraid you are going to crush me, I may not look it on the outside but I am tough as nails on the inside and won't let anyone hurt me." She said, "OK." That is not to say she didn't hurt me. She had a streak she was very well aware of.

One day something really humiliating happened. Usually she had all these people around looking after her. Once when there was no one else there she said, Listen out for me, I will be in the bathtub. In the back of my awareness a bell was ringing. It turns out that Dr. Mahler was ringing a bell, a call for me to come help her. I never heard a bell before in the house. She wanted me to come help her out of the bathtub. I didn't know that was her sign. She started screaming at me. When people came back she started talking about me as if I wasn't there. "Do you know what this idiot did?" I was so upset I went into the bathroom and cried. She did leave me an apology note on my typewriter later.

At one point she was talking about her dog. I am not a dog lover. She thought it was a personality deficiency. She didn't pry into my personal life.

Milton added that, although these comments sound quite negative, that was not the whole story:

as there were positive reasons why I stayed with Mahler for one and a half years! Working for her was not a bad experience, on the contrary, it was a rich experience. The first summer I was there she went to Shelter Island. I stayed in the New York office. I did inventory on the Masters Children's Center. I did work on the Yale collection, I just had to inventory it. I thought it was an incredible privilege to have the opportunity to have access to it. I had just finished my master's degree and thought what could be better. It solidified my knowledge about attachment theory and separation-individuation.

She was working on the paper, "The Constructive Use of Aggression," when I was there, and I was so impressed that her mind was so clear. I had never been prone to revisions of my own work, and here I had a model of someone who revised and revised and revised. I had to retype the whole damn paper. There were no computers yet, and she didn't like cut and paste and copy. It really had an impact on me that you can take the time, it is different in graduate school, and the process of getting ready and revising was enormously helpful to me.

She had an enormous influence on me. I could read her whole library. I was in analysis, of course, she had to give her approval for it. She didn't really pry, but I was not going to expose my personal life with her.

"I learned so much from Dr. Mahler about development, especially her work on separation-individuation stages, her thinking and understanding of Dan Stern's work; the opportunity I had to inventory all of the Master's Nursery files when the voluminous papers were being acquired by Yale was formative in my own appreciation of the exquisite details of the separation-individuation process. My interest in psychoanalysis was fostered by Dr. Mahler and I began analytic training while I worked for her. Her way of writing academic papers influenced me greatly, as her revisions demonstrated the necessity of fine tuning of ideas over time to create greater clarity of thought. I have come away with appreciating Dr. Mahler for her brilliance and not appreciating her style in our working relationship. Keeping Dr. Mahler in mind as a model of professionally accomplished woman, I have tried, and believe succeeded in, working hard to establish and maintain a kinder working model with professional boundaries enhanced by a kindly and empathic manner. At least I have less turnover in staff!

There were times when I thought there was a contusion in her mind between paid employees and people who cared. She thought she could pay for being given to, and didn't have to return anything. I think she was just a very lonely woman and wanted affection and cuddling and girly stuff and acted as if she expected it to just come to her, not because of who she was. She must have been lost in an earlier time in her life, and was repeating early problems, that's where the boundaries got lost. She was happy at those moments when all the women were surrounding her, talking about Magrit. She could consume you, and was very envious of your other life demands and interests.

When you hire a researcher you get those graduate students who throw themselves into the work and then in a couple of years are gone. That must be very hard when your personal life isn't fulfilling. I was one of those researchers. I felt cowardly when I quit, because I had waited for the incident that broke the camel's back. The matter of my quitting had been brewing, it was just a matter of when. But I became a *persona non grata*, and never heard from her again after I quit.

Joyce Edward[11] noted she was aware that Mahler could be very difficult, though she herself had not experienced this side of her. In commenting further about this, Edward remarked how difficult it was to understand how some people in our field can be so competent with their patients and live up to their ethics but be so difficult in their relationships with their colleagues.

A colleague who wishes to remain anonymous said:

She often was very demanding and treated a lot of people around her like servants. She would dress them down and mistreat them. She had a certain respect for me because I wouldn't be subservient, the way people like Robert Bak were. She never said, "I'm sorry."

One summer we invited her to dinner in our house in Wellfleet on Cape Cod. My son, who was adolescent at the time, was the driver who picked her up. Mahler was in the back seat. She must have been jealous, because from Central Park West all the way to our home in Wellfleet she berated me that I didn't care for her, was cold, didn't invite her enough, etc., etc. My son said, "What is the matter with that lady? Why was she so nasty to me?" She was speaking to me through my son. She knew that would hurt me more than if she had said such things to me directly. She would say things like that to me sometimes. I would look at her and know she was in one of her cruel, bitter moods.

She was not generally a warm person. We really were not intimate friends. You need to have more affection to consider a person a close friend. She kept herself apart. My suspicion is that she was very lonely, because she collected people, mostly women, all around her.

We saw a lot more of each other in Wellfleet during the summers. One evening we had six friends come up from New York for dinner. Margaret loved lobsters. We had several three pound lobsters for dinner, and cut them in half so that everybody could have a pound apiece. Margaret grabbed four pieces. She didn't notice that anything was wrong. We divided up the rest. Either she didn't understand the situation or she didn't care. I think she wanted a whole lobster and she didn't care. The men were furious, but the women said, "She is just a greedy little child."

Mahler punished a number of people interviewed for this book by suddenly severing relationships with them. Besides Pine and Furer, the list of victims at least temporarily on Mahler's "drop dead list" included Ruth Lax, Louise Kaplan, Helen Meyers, and me.

Dr. Lax, who is the senior author of several books honoring Mahler, said[12] she and Mahler were friendly for many years, until they sat next to each other at a dinner party. Margaret told Ruth that her husband had just died and she was very sad. Ruth said, "But you were divorced many years ago." After that, Mahler refused to talk to Ruth for two years. I asked her if Mahler had ever insulted her. She said, "Not unless you call not talking to me for two years insulting."

According to Louise Kaplan,[13] author of *Oneness and Separation*,[14] "Mahler was abusive to a lot of people, like Anni Bergman. Because they needed her they put up with it. She was not abusive to me because I didn't need her, just as Fred Pine didn't. She adored my husband. He was very charming and could make her laugh when no one could. When it came to a choice between me and Donald, she would always favor Donald. So she was reenacting the Oedipal situation, and taking her father away from her mother. That made us very close, from her point of view."

Although Kaplan said that Mahler had not been abusive to her, a letter she sent to Mahler confirms that she, too, had received "the iceberg treatment." Kaplan said she had completely forgotten[15] that, in a letter dated May 22, 1980, she had written:[16]

> Dear Margaret:
>
> I'm sorry that you are so irritable with me these days, but I suppose my time has come. The timing is particularly bad because of the personal difficulties I am now having. And I do remember that in the midst of it all, I worked for two solid months for the Foundation to get things set before you went to Portugal.
>
> I heard from Ruth Lax that you had been complaining to a number of people in Philadelphia about my lack of social graces. And then I was quite shocked at the idea that you would reprimand me in public and also call me a liar in front of the Altmans.
>
> However, I am scrupulous about replying to invitations and I also keep a record of these replies to make sure I have not overlooked anyone. According to my records I called Selma's secretary and expressed my deepest regrets and thanked her for the invitation on April 28th. On that same day I responded to the other invitation, which had no name on it, only an address and a phone number. The secretary there made note of my call. And when I get this month's telephone bill I will send you a copy.
>
> You seemed happy after all your festivities and celebrations and I was coming to congratulate you — when you so abruptly and rudely spoke that way to me I was truly shocked.
>
> I hope you have a nice summer and that whatever is bothering you about me simmers down.
>
>   Best,
>
>   Louise.

Joan Jackson had an experience with Mahler's physical attacks. She said,[17] "You know how heavy Kris's collected works are. When I told her I couldn't and wouldn't go away with her for the summer, she picked up Kris's book and threw it at me. It hit the credenza and left a mark. I thought, *Good! Now you will always have a reminder of what you did to me.*"

"When she had her rages, she was very scary," Jackson added. "She screamed and yelled. She had an enormous credenza, which she wanted moved to the other side of the room. She asked my husband to move it for her. He said it was too heavy, asked her to please take out the drawers. She refused and said, 'If you won't move it, I'll get Donald Kaplan to do it.' He moved the credenza and got a hernia."

"I have one more question," I asked. "Was there ever anything nice or generous she did for you that stands out in your mind?" Without missing a beat, she said, "No." I said, "That was quick." We both laughed.

Mahler and Optimal Distance

Mahler was less angry with people who maintained their distance from her. She got along very well for decades with her closest research associate,

John McDevitt, who, according to at least one observer, subjugated himself to her every whim. Regardless of whether this is the case, Mahler and McDevitt never were on intimate terms. "She didn't tell me about her personal life, and I didn't tell her about mine," he said.[18]

Like McDevitt, Ernst Abelin probably got along well with Mahler because he was "low key," and never was on intimate terms with her. Abelin, a research associate at the Masters Children's Center known chiefly for his article on fathers and separation-individuation, got to know Mahler privately and stayed in touch with her until she died. He said,[19] "I tended to be very low key and cautious with her. We had a friendship, perhaps because of my European background. My wife and I would invite her to a summer place we rented in New Rochelle perhaps twice every summer. Our children grew up with her. She gave them nice presents. I would often cook for her. I made goose, which she loved. It reminded her of Europe. She was very upset when my first wife and I separated. She knew us as a family and thought we had an ideal marriage. My first impression of her was that she was intimidating and severe, but I grew to admire her. *She got along better with men than with women.* She and Dr. Doris Nagel were good friends, but then they had a falling out, and Mahler dropped her."

Ruth Lax was another person who ordinarily had very little difficulty with Mahler. When asked why she thought Mahler treated her better than many of her colleagues, Lax replied,[20] "Perhaps because I never wanted anything from her. Perhaps she appreciated the two books we published about her theories and her work. I enjoyed being with her, and found her a very stimulating person. I was impressed with her ideas, and found that she had an amazing amount of energy, and was highly creative." Although Dr. Lax didn't mention it, she like, Abelin, immigrated from Europe, which established a common link.

Edgar Lipton,[21] a colleague who knew Mahler for twenty years, also experienced a relationship with her that he felt was unambivalent. He found her empathic to mothers and children, gentle, kindly, and understanding. In addition, he thought her "very smart and warm, a gifted and intelligent woman." She was generous to him with advice and helpful in his career, while he cannot recall being helpful to hers. Unlike many other colleagues, Lipton never found himself the object of her rage. His explanation of the causes of her temper was interesting. "She did not tolerate intelligent fools well," he said, "and was intolerant of pomposity. Many people envied her."

Darline Levy, one of Mahler's closest friends, said Mahler frequently used the term "optimal distance" to describe what she wanted in her friends.[22] "'Optimal distance'" was one of the services she rendered to a lot of us, not to get inappropriately close," Levy said. "She basically related to everyone as someone who had deep understanding of that dynamic."

Apparently, distance could accomplish what her ego was unable to do on its own and allowed Mahler's underlying *largesse* to surface. Except for the previously mentioned disagreement about financial contributions to the Philadelphia Foundation, Mahler did very well in her friendship with Lotte Koehler, who lived in Germany. Koehler told of how they became friends.[23]

> My case for graduating in the Swiss Psychoanalytical Society in 1974 was a borderline patient with a very chaotic transference, which I almost could not understand. That changed when I read the "Festschrift" for Mahler, edited in 1971 by McDevitt and Settlage. I could clearly understand now the course of the analysis as stages of a failed separation-individuation process. Because I was entering new territory, I decided to send my manuscript to Mahler. Mahler answered in a friendly manner and announced that she would lecture at the Freud-Institut in Frankfurt, where Alexander Mitscherlich praised in his introduction her excellent case histories. It was obvious that he did not know her research. But as in Frankfurt there was no time for a discussion. Not long after, Mahler asked me to meet her at a highway rest stop on the autobahn near Chiemgau. It was clear that she had read my paper carefully because she subjected me to a thorough grilling. Once she had satisfied herself that I was not a complete lightweight, she included me in her circle of friends. This, I understood, was not simply a matter of course for a Jew whom the Germans had treated so badly. but Mahler never made collective judgments, and she was willing to lecture in Germany. My friendship with her was tremendously enriching at the human and professional level.

Lotte Koehler agrees with the appraisal of Mahler's contributions made by Drs. Parens, Sternschein, Neubauer, and Smith as well as by. Bergman and Weil. She said, "I feel sure that Mahler made a lasting contribution to psychoanalysis, and especially to psychoanalytic developmental theory. It is difficult to place a person in a hierarchy of great psychoanalytic theorists, because one has to take the historical point of view into consideration."

Fred Pine[24] said, "Robert Frost wrote a poem called Fire and Ice.[25] It conveys what her coldness was like. [He recites it]:

> 'Some say the world will end in fire,
> Some say in ice.
> From what I've tasted of desire
> I hold with those who favor fire.
> But if it had to perish twice,
> I think I know enough of hate
> To say that for destruction ice
> Is also great
> And would suffice.'"

Margaret Mahler, like Frost, was capable of both fire and ice in her rages. Those she felt closest to were among those thrust into the fire. To others, like Helen Meyers, Ruth Lax, Louise Kaplan, and me, Mahler's habitual anger was expressed as ice.

Mahler, the Hungarian

Kurt Vonnegut said,[26] "If you have a Hungarian friend, you don't need any enemies." Was Margaret Mahler's contentiousness due at least partially to cultural sanctions? It seems that way when one realizes that she was not the only aggressive woman who was born in Hungary. Olympia Dukakis admires a group of such women in her memoirs.[27] "It was at the Boston fencing club that I first saw a team of Hungarian women train. These women were incredible! They were athletic, loud, fast, and very focused. I yearned to be as free and uninhibited as they were. It was inspiring to see women so unapologetically playful and competitive." That Mahler and her country-women were successful as well as competitive possibly may be attributed in part to their biological surplus of aggression.

Bluma Swerdloff also believed that Mahler's nationality contributed to her eruptive behavior. Swerdloff was not as hard on Mahler as some of her other colleagues. Swerdloff excused Mahler on the grounds that she was Hungarian. She said,[28] "I forgave her for all the things she did that she shouldn't have, like arguing — I felt it made her human. Having seen Rado having a temper tantrum, I just thought, 'She's Hungarian!'"

Helen Fogarassy, another Hungarian immigrant who worked for Mahler towards the end of Mahler's life, agreed with Swerdloff. Fogarassy said:[29]

> Mahler was very Hungarian, both the good and the bad. What basically drove her was that she was absolutely convinced that her mother hated her and preferred her sister. My grandmother was the same way, my mother was the oldest child and my grandmother just wasn't ready to have a child. I sat by Mahler's bedside for hours, and Hungarians make eye contact. We just sat there for hours looking at each other. It really was so satisfying to sit there and look into each other's eyes. The United States is not a gazing culture.
> She had a big craving to talk Hungarian. Once she called and I went to where she was in Martha's Vineyard because she wanted to talk Hungarian. She said it was old age that made her crave her native language so much. Sometimes she asked me to talk in Hungarian, just so she could hear a bit of it. It didn't bother her that I didn't understand everything she said because my vocabulary in my native tongue is limited. I nodded and shook my head and said "oh," depending on the tone of her voice because I got the message in that complex, evocative language. The image she held of herself was that of being a small child sitting up in bed with eyes wide open, not wanting to go to sleep.. She told me kids who are over vigilant are afraid their mothers want to kill them. The fear drove her to uncover whatever she could about children and their mothers.

Speaking of Hungarians, Paul Erdos told a delightful story about them[30] which the proud Dr. Mahler would have enjoyed. Two philosophers were discussing the possibility of life on other planets. One said that if such beings existed, they would in all likelihood be more intelligent than human beings and would have visited earth. The other philosopher said, "Where is the

evidence of their presence?" The first one said, "Shhhh! Here we call our-
selves Hungarians!"

Geza Roheim, who was an important friend of Mahler's, told her a
similar joke which she loved. Roheim was a great Hungarian Jew who liked
to make fun of himself. His favorite joke was, *Beyond Hungary, there is no
life worth living, and if there is, it isn't the same life.*[31] Hungary to Roheim
was the center of the world.

If Roheim's philosophy was characteristic of his countrymen, Mahler
was a true Hungarian, as demonstrated by this anecdote told by Helen Meyers.[32] "One day we were going up in the elevator in the building where the
science fiction author Isaac Asimov lived. He was in the elevator and I wanted
to introduce them to each other. I said, 'Margaret, this is Isaac Asimov, a
famous science fiction writer.' He said, 'Oh yes, Mahler, the famous com-
poser.' She pulled herself up to her full five feet four inches and said, 'I am
more famous than he!'"

The Sources of Her Rage

We know that Margaret Mahler was inclined to outbursts of rage, sometimes, it seems, with little or no provocation. But we do not know why. Was
the cause (or causes) genetic? Were the temper tantrums precipitated by her
abysmal early relationship with her mother? Her early weaning and the loss
at five months of her nurse? Was her temperament simply inherent in being
a Hungarian? Was it her poor health in her later years? Her loneliness? The
stress and agony of being a Holocaust victim? Arline Zatz, multi-published
writer and journalist, went so far as to suggest[33] it was Mahler's cruel treatment at the hands of her first therapist, Helene Deutsch, that was responsible for Mahler's temper tantrums. Zatz, who had undergone a similar
experience, felt Deutsch's rejection of Mahler was so outrageous that she
never recovered from it.

In my interviews with Mahler's colleagues and friends, I asked what
each thought was the underlying cause (or causes) of Mahler's outbursts.

Bluma Swerdloff[34] and her colleagues felt, as did I, that whatever the
precipitating factors of Mahler's rages, their origin lay in her earliest relationship with her mother. At least two of Margaret's childhood memories
seem to bear out this theory: her early fury when she saw her mother breast
feeding Suzannah and was told by Eugenia that she had not nursed Margaret, and her delight that her mother developed a breast abscess on nursing Suzannah.

Many of Mahler's colleagues and friends said that the desire for perfectionism lay beneath her outbursts, which occurred when she or others could not meet her own lofty standards. When asked his opinion on the sources of Mahler's tantrums, Leo Madow answered,[35] *"As a psychiatrist, my guess is that she was a perfectionist and was intolerant of imperfection and stupidity. She couldn't stand it if people around her were unintelligent.* We had a few candidates who were not the brightest. She was either impatient or would be nice to them. *If she was nice, you knew that she didn't think much of them."* Those she was "nice" to were people from whom she expected nothing.

Darline Levy agreed with Madow's explanation of Mahler's perfectionism. She said,[36] "Margaret didn't suffer fools easily, or foolish actions. She was a perfectionist and enjoyed having the language right. I found it fascinating to see Margaret struggling to get it the way she wanted. It was a joy, because I also have that sensitivity to the nuances of language. Although English wasn't her native tongue, she was a master at using the language in her profession. She was wise about preverbal behavior, and was capable of seeing infantile behavior in adult behavior adult gestures and body language."

The perfectionist explanation of Mahler's rages was also hypothesized by Anita Kolek, who worked for Mahler as a research assistant for several years before Margaret's death. According to Kolek.[37]

> Mahler was a perfectionist who achieved what she did by her determination and her perfectionism. She would always say to me, "It has to be perfect." She was quite critical. When we were editing, she would go over and over it word by word, not once or twice but again and again. I think her nastiness had to do with losing her family. She was very lonely but didn't really let people know that. The bitterness came out in other ways. I think losing her family and her loneliness made her bitter.
>
> Once after I left Dr. Mahler, Peggy Hammond went away and I spent the weekend there. It was not a bad experience. We talked about her family, how close she was to her father. I didn't confide in her because I knew she had a mean streak and I didn't want her to attack me. Sometimes at parties she would turn on me and say something nasty. I stood up to her, and said, "Don't treat me like that!

"Did it help?" I asked.

"No," she laughed. "And yet she also could be very kind. She gave me one of her books, *The Psychological Birth of the Human Infant*,[38] and inscribed it, 'To Anita, My right hand and cherished friend. Feb. 9, 1983.' She said to me, 'You are a very creative person. You should do something with it.' She would invite me for dinner or to the ballet. She was interesting to work for, if you could bear it! You had to have a thick skin. She taught me how I didn't want to be. I don't want to be a bitter person."

A person who insists on perfection at all costs is one with low self-esteem. Such an individual feels that only an infallible person is loveable. A number of Mahler's friends and colleagues, including Calvin Settlage, believe that Mahler's low self-esteem was behind her rages. He said,[39] "I personally did not observe or experience Mahler's reputed terrible temper or rage. This may be attributable in part to my reputation as being 'a nice guy' and my preference for avoiding hostile interpersonal conflict by not being given to provocation. *I think that Mahler's anger was evoked by what she perceived to be a lack of respectful regard for her thinking and therefore for herself. Speculatively, from what I know from Mahler about her upbringing, I suspect that lack of regard stirred up her sensitivities and self-doubts from early childhood about her loveableness and worthiness.*"

Mahler was very aware of her difficulties in controlling her temper. In a letter to Castilo de Padro on March 11, 1971,[40] she said, "Knowing myself, I ought to be careful not to upset the delicate balance. I tend to blow my top, you know." In an interview with Darline Levy and Selma Kramer,[41] Mahler's students and closest friends, Selma Kramer said that Margaret didn't get angry if you just said something dumb, "but only if you made a mistake that in any way could hurt a child patient." Kramer agreed with Madow that Mahler only got angry with people she cared about, and added that she and Cal Settlage soon realized that Margaret only hollered at people in whom she had trust and confidence: "Jim Delano, remember, nice, nice guy, whom Margaret never shouted at?" When asked if Margaret ever shouted expletives, Selma Kramer indignantly commented that she never would because she was too much of a lady.

Mahler then gave her own explanation of why she believed she hollered so loudly.[42] It fits in very well with Dr. Settlage's ideas on the subject. *She said that she wanted to impart the knowledge very, very badly, but wasn't confident that the way she said it would get through to the student, so she tried to do it with the volume of her voice.* If this is correct, and there is no reason to assume it is not, then as Dr. Settlage surmised, Mahler's rages stemmed from a sense of inadequacy and a feeling of helplessness when she was unable to reach her own standards.

I suspect that in some way Mahler enjoyed the image of herself as a person with a temper, that she thought having such a trait was an indication of a strong character, in contrast to the lack of confidence she said she felt. In one of our talks,[43] she told me how much she disliked therapists who were sticky sweet. She called them "psychosirupy," a word no one would ever use to describe Margaret Mahler, although her underlying fear may well have been that underneath her rages she was nothing but a marshmallow.

Another theory advanced by several people concerns Mahler's fear of closeness. Helen Fogarassy spoke of Mahler's tendency to say whatever she wanted, with no consideration for the feelings of the person she was insulting. Fogarassy said:

> She was *threatened by closeness*, and was more comfortable with people she wasn't close to. Those she could control. I had a typing business and one of my clients was an industrial designer. Her accountant, Bernice Apter, said, "I have a client who needs some help, she's had a hard time keeping people." Mahler was eighty-two or three at the time. I went and interviewed her. I wore overalls. At the end of the interview, she looked at me and said, "Do you always dress like a boy?"
>
> At the time, I was a struggling writer. At a birthday dinner, she said, "I don't understand how you can continue with a career in which you are such a loser." A few weeks later I sold my first story.
>
> She berated some of the people she loved most. Berating is kind of a Hungarian thing. Hungarians are protective of their emotions, so they kind of make fun or tease. My father used to call me "little ugly," you understood it was humor. Now that I am over it I understand it. Although I must say it took me years of analysis to get to that point. She was very much like that with the people she was close to.
>
> *Her rages could be to avoid closeness.* She had a high-strung nervous system and was very impatient. One of my favorite images of her was when she would say, "Give me that thing." I would reach for something, I would grab for it and she would say, "No, not that," as if I was supposed to read her mind. She was just impatient because she couldn't think of the word. It always reminded me of her work, a kind of magic thing, like your mother knows what you are thinking.

Fogarassy was one of the few people who knew how to handle Mahler's temper tantrums. I asked her, "Did she yell at you?"

"Yes, sure," she answered:

> I would yell back in the same way. It was OK, she understood it. It sort of defused her frustration if I responded in the same way: It made us equals. She didn't mean to hurt. Peggy Hammond, her companion, would say, "Dr. Mahler, calm down!" She would say things like, "That's stupid!" Most people would withdraw. Because of the way I was raised, I knew she wasn't trying to hurt me. And she apologized about what she said about my career.
>
> It made her human instead of inhuman. Hungarians are very passionate and intellectual, people of extremes. Dr. Mahler didn't know she was afraid of people she felt close to. She felt safe with yes people. Hungarians are very high-strung and fine-tuned, we try to figure out our passions and think we know ourselves. We are kind of isolated as a culture, related to the Finns. Both originated from Northern Asia. We kind of settled down in the middle of a bunch of Slavs and Czechs.
>
> Sometimes she got very frustrated and started venting and I would say, "OK, OK," and just touch her head. She would give me this look, "O God, I'm so impossible!" Then she would sit down and laugh. It was worthwhile to put up with her anger. She could also be so profound sitting there with me, just sitting there staring at each other.

With a break in her voice, Helen added, "She was a terror, a beautiful little terror."

In my opinion, Mahler's outbursts served another purpose which relates to the separation-individuation process. Since Mahler ostensibly suffered from a lack of ego boundaries,[44] I agree with Fogarassy about Mahler's fear of closeness, and believe she used her rage to put distance between herself and people to whom she felt threateningly close. I will illustrate from a memory of my own. I am the mother of twins. When they were perhaps three years old, they fought all the time. Once, Jonny threw a can at Janet's head, which broke her head open and necessitated many stitches. As if in retaliation, Janet stomped on her brother's forehead, and gave him a black eye. I asked my analyst what I should do about it. She answered, "Keep them as far apart as possible." I asked Janet why they fought so much. She answered, "*When we fight, we are not twins.*" Anna Freud said something not too different, albeit more technically, in her statement that *libido binds, aggression separates.*

Leo Madow had a different explanation. He said,[45] "The joke that went around was that if Mahler really liked you, she was particularly hard on you. If she didn't think you were talented, she was nice to you. She was very nice to me, but we were good friends. When I retired, she said to Selma Kramer, 'We'll never have a better chief.'"

I believe Leo Madow was correct in his understanding of Mahler's rages. In my opinion, Mahler's wrath also served to "refuel" a dying symbiosis. Robert Frost wrote, "Good fences make good neighbors." Mahler built an emotional fence of rage so people would keep their distance. If she was afraid of being submerged in a dual union, her anger supplied the boundaries which defended her against losing herself. On the other hand, if she was disinterested in a person, she was in no danger of being swallowed up, and didn't need anger as a protection. The tantrums, in a perverted sense, also kept people close to her in their anger. A good example is the way little Hilary kept her mother tied up with her. By keeping a distorted symbiosis going, Mahler was able to eat her cake and keep it.

It seems evident that Margaret Mahler never adequately resolved the rapprochement subphase of separation-individuation, when an open-ended stage is reached which she called "on the way to emotional object constancy." These observations were confirmed by Mahler herself. Lotte Koehler said, "A year and a half before Mahler's death, she told me that she herself had not resolved the rapprochement crisis. She always felt alone, even though she possessed a great talent for making friends and attracting collaborators."

Mahler believed that until the child could successfully navigate the rapprochement crisis, they were psychologically unfinished. She described the turmoil going on in a child's mind at the rapprochement stage of development. "*At that period of infancy the child is normally nice, an angel of a child at one moment, and then, the next moment, he may appear to be a kind of monster of a child.*"[46] It seems evident from the words of those who knew her best that Mahler knew this from personal experience. What better description could there be of the personality of Margaret Mahler?

Why Didn't She Control Her Temper?

Because of her deprivation as a child and the loss of her family and homeland in the Holocaust, it is understandable that Margaret Mahler had a deep storehouse of inner rage. What is not clear, however, is why a woman of so many strengths allowed herself to act on her anger whenever she felt like it. Many of us experience moments of fury, but the controlling functions of our egos do not permit us to express such feeling when it seems inappropriate. Why did Mahler's ego function so poorly in that respect?

There are certain rules of behavior and speech from which Mahler felt exempt. As her father taught her, she saw herself as an "exception." Mahler was a famous woman for a long time, a legend as well as a pioneer from many points of view. Her celebrity bore out her father's teachings that she was not of the common herd and therefore absolved from following the rules devised for "lesser" people. Like many celebrities (but not all) she had grown used to people abiding by her wishes: students and junior colleagues who were in awe of the great lady's talents and reputation, those who wanted to ride her coattails to fame, patients in the throes of positive transference, servants scurrying about fearing her wrath. They were just as confounded by her explosions as she was when they didn't do what she demanded. When she "requested" that a friend come see her immediately, even if it were in the middle of the night, it seemed perfectly logical to Mahler that nothing was more important than her loneliness. In previous times, one wouldn't have been surprised to hear her exclaim, "Off with their heads!" After all, she was Margaret Mahler.

Her thinking on that score was demonstrated to me during an incident that took place at the Masters Children's Center. The entire staff met after each morning of observations to have lunch together in the center's dining room. On one occasion, Mahler and I were the first ones in the dining room. She sat down and immediately grabbed a piece of fried chicken and began to devour it. I couldn't believe my eyes, for my mother had taught me that one doesn't begin to eat until everyone is seated at the table. I'm afraid my reaction was written on my face, for she looked at me and said, "I am Margaret Mahler. I don't have to wait for the others to join me to eat my lunch." Her rages had a similar implication. "I am Margaret Mahler. I can yell and scream and hit people whenever I feel like it." For underneath "the exception" lurked a rejected rapprochement-age toddler who felt justified in giving vent to her tantrums.

Robert B. Millman,[47] professor of psychiatry at New York Hospital–Cornell Medical School, has postulated a diagnostic category which seems to accurately depict the personality of Margaret Mahler. The diagnosis is so new it has not been included in DSM at this writing. Nor is it covered by the usual textbook definition of the syndrome, because its onset occurs well after childhood. It is called Acquired Situational Narcissism. According to Millman (p. 1), "The 'victims'—billionaire tycoons, movie stars, renowned authors, politicians, and other authority figures—develop grandiose fantasies, lose their erstwhile ability to empathize, react with rage to slights, both real and imagined and, in general, act like textbook narcissists."

Millman says that the life of a celebrity is not a normal one. Admiration is often deserved and extravagant, criticism is muted or nonexistent, and social control either absent or vicious. Such an unrealistic environment is not conducive to mental health even in the best-adjusted people. In this respect, Margaret Mahler was no exception.

In keeping with psychoanalytic theory, Millman does not believe that ASN begins in adulthood, but states that its appearance is merely an amplification of earlier narcissistic behavior, character traits, tendencies, and temperament. Celebrities with ASN already had a narcissistic personality long before it became obvious. Fame, power, and wealth only abolished the necessity to disguise the preexisting disorder. Millman's theory fits in with my conclusions that unrealistic support by her father in combination with her mother's rejection encouraged the early development of Margaret's narcissism.

Kathleen S. Krajco[48] (2004) adds to the definition of Situational Narcissism. According to her, such behavior can run to extremes, as it sometimes does in politicians and movie stars: It can be "insufferably haughty, arrogant, supercilious, exhibitionistic, vain, insolent, brutally inconsiderate of who gets trampled, and even contemptuous," all qualities we have seen in Mahler. But the situational narcissist is just full of himself, Krajco continues, and is not an evil person. He or she lacks narcissistic envy, and does not go around slandering people. Unlike the true narcissist, good things happening to others do not make such a person unhappy. Again, these characteristics were true of Margaret Mahler, who often brought about "good things" in the lives of her friends and associates, along with her abuse. Krajco believes that we are the ones who make celebrities celestial. The star isn't imagining his or her glory: reality is in accord with his delusion. Reality is the source of it. This was certainly true of Margaret Mahler, who was treated with so much deference, adulation, and awe that it is not surprising she herself came to believe it.

Yet there is another dimension to her wrath that needs to be looked at. Margaret Mahler overcame her early lack of a symbiotic mother, a failed marriage, and two great obstacles of the times—her sex and her religion—which

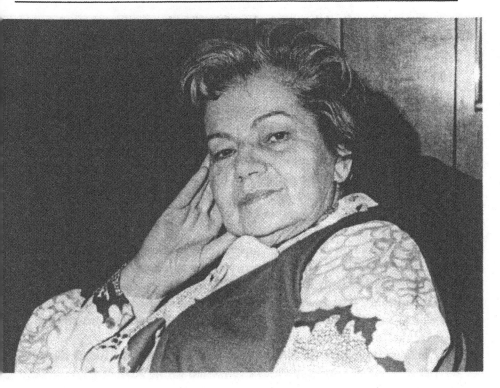

Mahler at age 80 in 1977, eight years before her death.

few women did in the early and middle 1900s. Mahler was a victim of the Holocaust. Her mother died in a concentration camp, she lost her whole family and homeland, her life and career were interrupted, and she was fortunate to have survived at all. Like Freud's "exceptions," Mahler may well have felt she had suffered so much in life that she deserved to get whatever she wanted and the rules didn't apply to her. Her rage at the world is certainly understandable, and may well be the force that saved her life. "I was, of course, a fighter all my life," she said, in discussing how she managed to be the first eastern Jewish woman allowed to study medicine in Jena.[49] "What I wanted to get I got,"[50] she said about her wish not to study or practice anymore in Germany. As she said to Nancy Chodorow,[51] "I survived through my 'chutzpah.'"[52]

Her Life Embodied Her Theories

Many people had asked me, on finding I have undertaken this project, why Mahler was so interested in symbiosis. Seeking to expand on my own ideas on the subject, I turned again to Mahler's colleagues.

Bernard Pacella, Margaret's close friend and sometime therapist, said, "I recall talking about why she was interested in separation-individuation. My own feeling is that it was her own personal problem, she never could be intimate with any person."

Harold Blum was more specific, in a way that would have pleased Mahler. According to him, her originality of thinking could be compared to the differentiation phase of separation-individuation:[53] "She emphasized more than anyone the infant's capacity for locomotion, which was not included in the libido theory, although it occurred in the anal phase," he said. "It does not even take place in a libidinal zone. Margaret was brilliant in this sense, and in my opinion a very original thinker. She explored the world of infancy in new ways, so that she was able to walk away from the mother theory, the libido theory."

Another example of Mahler's superb individuation was given by Manuel Furer.[54] He was struck by her integrity when she returned grant money to the NIMH, rather than spend time doing routine psychiatric work in the Albert Einstein Department of Psychiatry. She wanted to do the research she had in mind, and no amount of "free" money would persuade her to stick by the "mother" theory.

Because Margaret Mahler had an unsatisfactory symbiosis with her mother, the pull to remain symbiotic remained strong all her life. As a result, the road to individuation was long and hard for her and constantly threatened by regression. From her earliest relationship with her mother, who discouraged the formation of a symbiosis with her baby, Margaret Mahler fought to individuate and to develop into her own person. This was evident all through her life, from rejecting the idea that her mother had given birth to her, to breaking away from her family at the early age of fifteen to live on her own in Vienna, to her unusual ways of gaining knowledge — she was actually an autodidact — to her move to Philadelphia when she was not accepted as one of the powerful hierarchy of the New York Psychoanalytic Society, to her plea to psychoanalysts everywhere to encourage individuation in the younger generation of analysts and allow them to become themselves. Given the dreadful circumstances of her symbiosis with her mother and an Oedipus complex that wreaked havoc, the life of Margaret Mahler stands as a triumph of the separation-individuation process over the regressive pull.

Anni Bergman, in her eulogy to Dr. Mahler on October 6, 1985,[55] confirmed that Margaret's life embodied her theories of symbiosis and separation-individuation. Bergman said, "She did not like to work alone. She needed a sounding board. Margaret liked to write with others. The way in which she involved others in her work, the way in which she let others participate with her in her ideas, was her unique gift. In this way, it seems to me that her life embodied her theories: symbiosis and separation-individuation. She wanted and needed others to be close to her and yet to maintain optimal distance. Out of this close working together — the Dual Unity — often so delightful, pleasurable and exciting, came for many *the sometimes painful, but often productive process of separation-individuation.*"

The healthy infant's "personality" is at one with mother. As the child develops, he or she gradually becomes a separate person. Because Eugenia Schoenberg rejected her child, Margaret was unable to proceed through the normal stages of separation-individuation. As a result, she was like Walt Whitman,[56] who wrote:

> Do I contradict myself?
> Very well then I contradict myself,
> (I am large, I contain multitudes.)

She had to make do with putting together whatever pieces she could in whatever manner she could. It is a miracle that she was able to become the person she was.

Margaret Mahler's persona was like a stained glass window which is made up of shards and chinks. The fragments are precariously soldered together, but have no real connection with each other. Odd that such disparate pieces could result in a creation of beauty. Odd, too, that the essences of Margaret Mahler, like a stained glass window, evolved into a work of art. It reminds one of Thomas Wolf's remark: "A beautiful disease of nature, like a pearl in an oyster."

15

Aging and Death
(circa 1970–1985)

The Lonely Old Lady

What was Margaret Mahler like as she aged? What kind of old age and death did she have? In the opinion of many people, including Dr. Lucia Wright,[1] who worked for Mahler during one of Mahler's later illnesses, Mahler had a hard time of it. She was practically helpless and all but abandoned.

Wright said:

> I got a pretty lonely feeling when I went into the apartment. Maybe there were a few professional friends that came by occasionally, but it was not a lively household. She couldn't walk, that's why she needed an attendant. I don't remember ever seeing her walk. Her assistant would help her to the bathroom. She sat there propped up in bed and had everything she needed around her (like an analyst). I don't remember whether there was a wheelchair. I remember distinctly that she was bed bound and couldn't get up. I would sit by her bed and take notes. She was just concerned with letters she had to write, like to young people, I don't get the idea she was doing anything of importance.
>
> She was quite pathetic, she made me sad. I don't think I was the right person; I couldn't be there for her. It didn't seem like the right match. But I felt bad about it. I felt sort of sad, to see such an important life come to an unimportant, lonely end. I remember feeling surprised.

Anita Kolek had similar feelings about Mahler's last years. She saw Mahler as a very lonely old woman who didn't want to let people know it. Although she had a few friends like the Blums and the Sternscheins who continued to visit her, she felt alone and abandoned most of the time.

Arlene Richards agreed with Wright and Kolek on Mahler's loneliness in her late years. According to Richards,[2] "Mahler really didn't experience anyone being there for her in her old age. That was sad and lonely for her. A tragedy of all narcissists."

Research assistant Ilo Milton also spoke of Mahler's loneliness. She said,[3]

> I think she wanted a constant companion. She was very lonely, and the only way to get the companionship she wanted was to hire it. There were times when I thought there was a confusion in her mind between paid employees and people who cared. She thought she could pay for being given to, and didn't have to return anything. I think she was just a very lonely woman and wanted affection and coddling and girly stuff and acted as if she expected it to just come to her. She must have been lost in an earlier time in her life and was repeating early problems, that's where the boundaries got lost.
>
> She was happy in those moments when all the women were surrounding her, talking about the artist Magrit. She could consume you, and was very envious of your other life demands and interests. She was always disappointed. When I left she always said, "What time are you coming back?" I felt you could never satisfy her.
>
> When you hire a researcher you get those graduate students who throw themselves into the work and then in a couple of years were gone. That must be very hard when your personal life isn't fulfilling. I was one of those researchers, but I became a *persona non grata*. After I quit I never heard from her again.
>
> [Interviewer]: Did you miss her?
>
> [Milton]: (Sighs) No. I worked with a supervisor who was a Mahler replacement. Mahler made me feel good a lot of the time, and I got to read everything. But not with the replacement."

The concept of Margaret Mahler as a lonely woman comes up again and again, even when Mahler was relatively young. A participant observer at the Masters Children's Center who asked not to be identified told me that one Passover Mahler called her up and said she had nowhere to go for the holiday. She said, "I have nobody else to ask and I don't want to be alone tonight. Please invite me to your family seder." The image of a forlorn victim of the Holocaust pleading for an invitation to a seder haunted me. I found it distressing as well as poignant that so famous and highly esteemed a woman felt friendless.

Dr. Ruth Lax confirmed the impression of Mahler as a lonely old woman. She said:[4]

> In the last years of Margaret Mahler's life when she was really quite sick I was visiting her. Selma Kramer was sitting next to her and holding her hand. Selma said, "I have to go home." Margaret was very upset and wanted her to stay. But Selma said, "Ruth is here," and left. Margaret told me how lonely she felt. People were visiting her less and less and had started to forget her. Her worst fear was that she would lose her English and revert to Hungarian, which would make it very difficult for her to communicate. She eventually found someone who knew both English and Hungarian, who would be there for her if she forgot her English. I greatly sympathized with her and told her that as far as I remember, I always spoke English, which was

The Seder in 1977 to which Margaret invited herself.

my mother's language, and German, which was the language of my governesses. I didn't know which language was my first one so I didn't know which I might forget. She was quite interested in that and diverted for a little while speculating about it.

Dr. Arnold Richards[5] spoke of a different kind of relationship in which Mahler occasionally was able to assuage the loneliness she experienced in her declining years. According to him, "Margaret was close to Chuck Fisher. Both suffered from insomnia — Betty Fischer was still alive then — and the two of them would lie in bed together and talk about their illnesses. They would stay up talking and keep each other company. They had in common an incredible fascination with their physical complaints. A kind of regression. That became the important subject with them and their preoccupation. He was a very tortured person — it was very sad."

In her interview with the famous feminist, Nancy Chodorow,[6] Mahler spoke of the problems of aging without a man around. Chodorow asked if Mahler found advantages or disadvantages in being a woman analyst. Mahler answered, "I only see that it is terribly difficult to become old, and even middle-aged ... in the big city of New York ... and not have a man around. I mean it's unbelievable, from the taxi chauffeur to the usher to the I don't know what. There are exceptions. Just yesterday I had a class here of ten people, men and women, from the Pilgrim Psychiatric Center, and the adjunct was worried about whether or not I was tired. But this is an exception. Otherwise, I have to take a taxi, for example, when I go to the Lincoln Center. It is very near. I pay more for a limousine than my economic circumstances really warrant, because I cannot stand the abuse that I may meet more often than not. I tell them they'll get a dollar extra because it is such a short trip, but it doesn't help. And that does not change in New York. I'm getting old and I'm more invalided, and after all, I had, I have a broken hip."

Chodorow asked if Mahler experienced similar problems socially. Mahler said, "Socially not at all, socially they make too much fuss about me. There I am the living legend by now."

Did Mahler have people she was close to who didn't think of her as a living legend, but purely as a friend? Chodorow asked. "Oh, sure. Sure, sure. If I had a better mercantile sense," Mahler added laughingly, "I could make a lot of money about the legend."

Despite her fame and great success, Mahler indicated once more that she never got over feeling like a rejected child. "I'm curious about something in your history," Chodorow said. "When did it happen that you went from being basically an outsider and feeling like you weren't being recognized, from the extremes of the Deutsch thing to being a living legend?"

Mahler answered, "I always remained an outsider for the original Viennese."

"Still?" Chodorow asked, as if she found such a feeling uncomprehensible in the great Margaret Mahler.

"Yes. Yes. Yes," Mahler answered vehemently. "It is only since about ten or fifteen years that I don't give a damn. Because I am Margaret Mahler."

"Right. So you are not part of this kind of Anna Freud International Child analytic.... Are you connected to her or in touch with her?"

Mahler's answer was at odds with her earlier thinking and the reports of many of her colleagues such as Jacob Arlow on the subject. She said, "For a very long time I sent Anna everything that I wrote, and she was very appreciative. When I gave my first paper in Amsterdam, she came to me and said, 'This is a very good paper.'"

Frank Hernadi, one of my readers, who is not an analyst, had the most practical explanation for Margaret Mahler's loneliness as an old woman. He said, "Of course, it is no surprise that if someone lives a life of a prima donna, humiliating the heck out of others and alienating even the most loving people, that person will die a lonely, miserable death."

The Death of Margaret Mahler

On September 27, 1985, around 10:00 am, Hurricane Gloria made landfall on Long Island with winds sustained at eighty-five miles per hour and gusts of ninety to one hundred mph.[7] The eye of the storm passed ten miles east of Kennedy Airport. Hurricane Gloria ranks as the 13th costliest and the 16th most intense hurricane in the U.S. up to that point in the twentieth century. September 27 was the day that Margaret Mahler, who never made life easy for her intimates, "chose" to be admitted to Lenox Hill Hospital for the last time. The winds howled and screamed, as though the very heavens were protesting her imminent death. I remember the day well. The wind was blowing so hard it was difficult to stand upright. I was walking home from my son's school, which was two blocks away, and had to brace myself along the building walls in order to remain on my feet. As high winds can cause loosened objects to become missiles that shatter glass, batter walls and cause numerous deaths, the residents of New York City were ordered to stay indoors. When Maria Nardone heard that Mahler had been admitted to the hospital and was deathly ill, she attempted to go to the hospital but had to turn around and go back. Although she was filled with anxiety because she knew her dear friend was dying, she had no choice but to remain at home.

Anni Bergman managed to get through to the hospital in spite of the hurricane and was one of the few people who were present at Mahler's death. Bergman said:

> Margaret Mahler died in the hospital, where her Hungarian friend was with her. Outside there was a hurricane, and I struggled to get there, which I did. When I saw her at the hospital I realized that this would be the last time. She was in terrible pain and there was no hope she would recover. During the time I knew her she had many health crises and several surgeries.
>
> Underneath everything she was always very insecure. Once, she said to me, "You don't really love me. You just love my mind." After she died I missed her. In some ways, though, I felt that I had my life back.
>
> There were many things you could be angry with her about. She didn't leave her estate to anyone close to her, although what she gave us and left us with is more valuable than money. And the Mahler Foundation is continuing to honor and develop her work. She left her archives to Yale, where she felt they would be best protected, I guess. She liked having them in this prestigious place, although it makes them difficult to use.

In delivering Mahler's eulogy, Bergman spoke kindly about her longtime employer. She said, "Margaret Mahler always had the courage to act on her intuitions, her own judgement and her convictions. She was never bound by conventional attitudes or prescriptions.... She had an inexhaustible zest and capacity to enjoy life as well as an insatiable desire for human contact.... Her deep human involvement and her lucid mind never faded with age."

According to all reports, Mahler's chief assistant, John McDevitt, was not present during Mahler's final days in the hospital. In his characteristically laconic manner, he said,[8] "I never saw Margaret in a wheel chair. I never even saw the wheel chair. She died from an obstruction of the intestines. She was in a New York hospital. She had a heart problem, and may have died of that."

According to Helen Fogarassy,[9] Mahler remained a typical Hungarian woman à la Zsa Zsa Gabor almost to the end. She said, "Mahler was constantly talking about getting old and how she hated being old. But whenever she had a visitor she primped and flirted. She could be very charming, with very bright, expressive brown eyes."

Helen anxiously waited out Mahler's last hours. She said,[10] "Peggy Hammond and I stayed in the waiting room because Mahler kept asking for one of us. She didn't want to be on any life support system. I said, 'But she's not on life support!' Peggy thought she was suffering, but I said, 'She's not.' You can feel the death coming on. It is sort of a superstition in Hungarian, a premonition. I think Dr. Mahler felt that way very much. Peggy said, 'She is ready to let go of struggling and anger.' She was terrified of her mind being trapped in her body, where she'd be conscious and her body wouldn't be able to move. I remember Peggy and I arguing about that in the hospital. She said, 'It must be terrible for her.' I said, 'No, she's changed her mind, she wants to get better.'"

Perhaps Mahler's constant pain in her last years or her increasing identification with her disgruntled mother made her more disagreeable as she aged. Her friend Jack Arlow[11] used the words "embattled woman" and "dour" in describing her.

Patricia Nachman, who was at the hospital when Mahler died, felt that she wasn't much different than earlier in her illness. She said:[12]

> She was very alert to the end. I was there up to the end of her life. She was probably the same Mahler, only she worried more toward the end of her life about her work being misunderstood. She felt the same way about other people's work. She questioned every word in a paper; which almost drove us crazy but gave me an enormous respect for the precision she attached to the meaning of words. We would have research meetings once a week, she would go over a paper which was usually chosen by John, and she would pick on every word, with questions like, "Why is this in?" and "Why is this out?" She became increasingly vulnerable as she aged, and grew even more irritable and questioning than she was before. But her thinking was sharp and she remained focused up until the very end of her life.
>
> I was there when she died. I went in and saw her. By that time she was out of it. I kept on saying, "It's Pat, it's Pat!" and she did respond. I squeezed her hand and she squeezed mine back. There was this little girl side to her. You felt the child part of

her. Here we were all studying children, and the biggest one of them all was right before our eyes. This woman who was such a child herself at core was studying children, and no one got it. She was a tyrant, but probably no one got the fact that she was probably the biggest child of them all. Maybe when she was dying you could tap into that, but it was pretty hard when she was the dictator of the crib."

Despite her compassion for her, Nachman must have been very disappointed with Mahler's will. Mahler had promised Nachman that she would leave money to enable her nursery research to continue. She said,

> Mahler said at board meeting after meeting that she wanted the nursery to go on after she died, and that she wanted me to head it. But as Margaret became older she became interested in the aging process and the elderly. She had a housekeeper nurse companion, who was also interested in aging. They would have many discussions about it. While her whole interest at the scientific meetings formerly had been in early development, she changed her focus. She became interested in what functions are lost in aging and what functions stayed. She saw that as an interesting intellectual question. What is retained and what isn't. She was profoundly committed not only to the physiological remains but also psychologically, that the mother once again becomes very prominent.
>
> As she got older and physically more frail, she got angrier and angrier and didn't want to acknowledge her frailty. She was terribly frightened of losing her mental faculties.
>
> [Nachman told an amusing anecdote which was typically Mahler:] Once she had some severe cramps and her companion Peggy said, "We must go to the emergency room if you are in such bad condition." Mahler went but within a short time she became furious because she had to wait much longer than she had expected. Finally, an attendant came in and said, "Margaret, we'll be with you in a minute." "Margaret," she said indignantly. "Why are you addressing me by my first name?" This apparently was more than she could take and apparently worse than her stomach cramps. She got up and within minutes dressed and stomped out of the emergency room.

Nachman, who knew Mahler very well, told another anecdote, one of my favorite Mahler stories: "Once for an outing I took her for a walk along Central Park West. She was in a wheel chair. When we got to a curb that didn't have a ramp Margaret got angry with me for not being able to get the chair over the curb. I tugged and pulled and tried several times to lift her in the chair over the curb and couldn't. She got exasperated, got out of the chair and hoisted it up and over the curb and then calmly sat down and signaled me to continue pushing her. After she died we all sat and told stories for two weeks. Like sitting Shiva."

In contrast to Mahler's statement that Anna Freud told her she had to be more competitive, a colleague who wishes to remain anonymous believed that Mahler remained competitive until the end. "Margaret was a very competitive person," the colleague said. "When she gave a party, she made sure that only certain people were invited. Some people were invited sometimes, but not everybody every time. She always got dressed up, put on her best blouse."

Arlene Richards agreed about Mahler's competitiveness. Richards said,[13] "I didn't know her very well. I met her at a dinner party given by Marilyn and Bernard Brodsky. She was a very competitive lady. She said to me, 'I used to be thin, thinner than you.' I didn't say a thing, just sat there dumbfounded. I couldn't imagine why she was competing with me. She was the superstar and I was the new kid on the block."

Mahler's old friend Leo Rangell felt she had changed a great deal as she aged, and not particularly for the better. He said,[14] "By the time we met for the last time, which I believe was in Cannes shortly before she died, she had become bitter and feisty, with the same paranoid streak, and wore a self-satisfied look She felt she did not get the acclaim she deserved. She was a forceful, difficult, and important person who didn't get enough recognition. She was not as sweet forty years later as she had been in 1941. I remember her positively from those early days, which became blemished in later years."

Several analysts spoke of positive aspects in the manner in which Mahler aged. Irving Sternschein described her as a person who remained very careful of her health. We can picture her as a feisty old lady bawling out her physicians she saw as inept. "As one would expect," Sternschein said,[15] "she was not someone to tolerate slipshod medical treatment. She got rid of several outstanding internists. She believed that it didn't matter whether you were old or not, but demanded the same attention. She knew her body very well. She was knowledgeable medically right along, not in arrears, with modern medicine, and alert to what was going on."

Sternschein noted other healthy aspects in the way Mahler aged. He said,[16] "She really did very well as she aged. She could still do some occasional consultation work over a patient, but wasn't too active with that. She was more involved with research and papers. She became more and more feeble and confined to a wheel chair, but she could be very pleasant. My wife and I dropped over one New Year's Eve and enjoyed a glass of champagne."

Patsy Turrini was more understanding of Mahler as a cantankerous old woman than most of her colleagues. She said:[17]

Dr. Mahler was under severe criticism for her defense of the concept of symbiosis. She still is. Both Brazelton and Stern had refuted the concept, and met with her to get her to change her position. She held steady. She was surviving aging and ill health, and had a tooth digging into her jaw over a long stretch. Her fortitude in the face of major disagreement from several sources and her frailty offered a good role model. She stood her ground. The concept of symbiosis offers a rich way to understanding attachment theory, the more popular theory today.

Dr. Mahler told us that Gertrude and Reubin Blanck made her famous. They extrapolated from her work to develop techniques for treating severely ill borderline people. That she gave them credit is a credit to her.

She hired a good secretary to work with her in her final years, and kept working and teaching. She was energetic and vigorous in her last years.

Ernst Abelin, a friend of Mahler until she died, admired how she kept working until the end of her life. He said,[18] "I saw her for the last time in her apartment, when she already was bedridden. Margaret tried to do as much work as she could. She kept looking things up and became very interested in the problems of aging and the Gray Panthers. I think she died of intestinal problems. She had an interesting caretaker, an American Indian woman, who was quite mysterious, beautiful, and discreet."

Cal Settlage also believed that Mahler did well with the aging process. He said,[19] "I visited Margaret during her later years, but was not with her during the time that her life drew to its end. She did not like but accepted the increasing limitations of aging and gradually failing health. I felt that for one so committed to life, she aged and died remarkably well."

Fred Pine was another of Mahler's colleagues who remained friends with her. Toward the end of her life, Pine went to visit her. He stressed that she hadn't lost her sense of humor. He said,[20] "We spoke about people in the field, her illness. She said two things to me about aging that I remember, both quips. She said, 'At parties people always say to me that you are looking very well. I know they mean you are looking well for your age.' About cognitive functions, in regard to the slippage in old age, she said, 'People say, in Stage 1, *you* notice. In Stage 2, you notice and other people notice. In Stage 3, others notice but you don't.' At that point I told her, 'Margaret, you are at Stage 1.'

"I didn't see her during her last bedridden period at home," Pine continued. "I went to visit her in the hospital the day before she died. I walked in and said, 'I'm Dr. Pine.' I didn't mention that I was a Ph.D., so they let me in. Her physician, however, soon asked me to leave. Margaret couldn't speak by then. She was either in a coma or was heavily medicated." He said sadly, "She didn't know I was there."

Selma Kramer, who loved Mahler dearly, was distraught when she died, according to Karen Berberian, Selma's daughter.[21] Karen said, "My mother jumped on a train to go to New York when she heard that Mahler was dying. I don't think she made it in time to say goodbye. She was very upset about Margaret's death. My maternal grandmother was sick and dying at the same time, and I think my mother was more affected by Margaret's death than by her own mother's death. This bothered me a great deal. However, my family and I accompanied my parents to Margaret's memorial service. My father drove and miraculously found a parking spot right next to the funeral parlor. They played *Schubert's Unfinished Symphony*, which had been chosen by Margaret. The place was packed." A few people had only amicable words to say about Margaret Mahler. Judith Smith felt kindly about Mahler right to the end. She said,[22] "She was very happy that I was getting married. She wanted me to get married, to have a child, etc. She was supposed to come to my wedding, but was too sick. She died a few days later."

According to Justin Call,[23] "In her later years in the casual conversations I had with her, she knew that she wouldn't live forever and she was concerned about the status of her work after her death and was frightened that people would forget about it." (Mahler said something very similar to me, as early as 1966, when she said, "I'm not dead yet, and people already are forgetting about my work.") Call continued, "I don't know if this was true or not. Perhaps she was charming me a bit and making sure that I wouldn't be one of the people who would forget her work, so I am a somewhat skeptical person about that. Writing, of course, provides the illusion of immortality. I guess it is true to some extent that people don't quote Margaret as often as I think they should, especially in the field of infant psychiatry. I have been very critical about editors who have excluded her work from the work they are doing. I have not found anyone who has a clearer understanding of the stages of separation-individuation and the achievement of relative object constancy and the role of language in achieving that level of psychosocial development. I thought her concern about being forgotten was over-determined."

Lotte Koehler told a charming story about Mahler in her last years, indicating that Margaret Mahler remained Margaret Mahler almost to the end of her days. Koehler said,[24] "I remember her at breakfast time in her bed in one of the best hotels in Cannes. Berry Brazelton and other famous analysts, one after the other, came into her bedroom to say 'hello.' It was a levée like those of the Kings of France in former times." Margaret Mahler was indeed receiving the homage she commanded as the Royal Empress of Psychoanalysis.

The prescient Lotte Koehler found Mahler preoccupied with the significance of the death drive at their last meeting in 1984, the year before she died. "The thought alarmed me," Koehler said.[25] "I asked whether she was talking about the yearning for merger. She answered in the affirmative." Mahler never got over the yearning to be reunited with her mother. She herself wrote that it is part of human nature to long for symbiosis.[26] "The symbiotic origin of the human condition ... creates an everlasting longing for the ... state of primal identification, for which deep down in the original primal unconscious, every human being strives."

When Koehler got home she sent Mahler a poem by Maturana that describes death for some as a time of anguish for the "self-asserting ego" and for others as peace, calm, and nonbeing. Mahler thanked her, ending her letter, "love as ever." When Koehler called in October 1985 to schedule a visit, she was told that Mahler had died suddenly a few days before. Koehler ended her comments to me with, "The cream of American psychoanalysis attended her memorial." At long last Margaret Mahler had achieved complete acceptance by the psychoanalysts of the United States.

Patricia Nachman has vivid memories of Mahler's final days. She said,[27] "Ultimately she had no one who was truly close to her when she died, relative or friend. She also died in a feisty way. A few of us came to the hospital and Peggy stood by her, but when Mahler knew that she was deteriorating she was a handful in the intensive care, pulling out tubes, she knew she was dying and didn't want it to be a long process. She put up a fight."

Susan Schwartz, whom Mahler cared for as a beloved grandchild, was extremely close to Mahler during her last years. She said:[28]

> I was with her the last ten years of her life, until she died in 1985. She was very kind and generous to me, and taught me a great deal about psychology and life. I loved that she was so interested in me and my personal life.
>
> Margaret was working on another will before she died, but I don't know how it would have changed her bequests. I think it was something Peggy wanted. Harold Blum was there a lot, too, with his wife, Rachel. [Here Schwartz added Blum's explanation of Mahler's mysterious will that was quite different from what he said to me about it.] Blum believed Mahler felt the problems of children were recognized elsewhere, while the elderly were neglected, so she left a lot of her money to the Gray Panthers.
>
> A nurse used to come and give Margaret a bath, sometimes she came every day. Bernice Apter came and did the payroll. Another young woman, Anita Kolek, also worked with Margaret. Helen Fogarassy came and wrote letters for her. I don't know exactly how they met. When I heard Margaret was dying, I ran to the hospital.
>
> Margaret was eating Chinese food before her final illness. She was always very careful about what she ate, broiled filet of sole, boiled potatoes. She and Peggy were eating a Chinese dinner. They were having a great time when Margaret was stricken with a bowel obstruction. Dr. Henry Solomon was her cardiologist. He sent her into emergency surgery for the bowel obstruction. She'd had a pacemaker installed and died of a heart attack precipitated by her surgery. I don't know if her bowel perforated, but she was in terrible pain. She was in the hospital the day Hurricane Gloria struck in September 1985, so I couldn't get to the hospital and had to wait until the weather cleared up the next day. She died a week later.
>
> The hospital wanted fewer people there. When we went into intensive care we saw that Margaret was on a respirator and was trying to pull it out.

It seems Margaret Mahler was ready to die. "We waited in the waiting room," Schwartz continued. "Three or four young people, Anita, Helen and myself. Peggy asked us to leave so that she could stay, so we did. Anita, Peggy, and I were in the hospital when Margaret died. I saw her before her death, but I was not with her at the moment she died. I felt very sad when she died."

Thus Margaret Mahler died as she had lived, leaving bitterness and anger in her wake, along with deep, abiding love.

16

The Mysterious Will of
Margaret Mahler (1985)

A strange phenomenon occurred at the end of Margaret Mahler's life. Instead of leaving money to research and her longtime associates, as her friends and coworkers expected, Mahler did a turnabout and left most of her money to the Gray Panthers. It is the "why" of her choice, not its humanitarian aspect, that still keeps colleagues and friends guessing many years later.

The executors of Mahler's will[1] were her financial assistant, Bernice Apter, her beloved "grandchild," Maria Nardone, and her lawyer, Bernard Fischman (now deceased). The major bequests were: To the Gray Panthers, $761,821.12, to be used for indigent scholars and academicians over the age of seventy, other legacies of $232,845.00, including Yale University for processing and maintaining the Margaret S. Mahler Personal Archives and making them available to scholars, $40,000, to Mahler's companion, Peggy O'Neil Hammond, $35,000, to Mr. Ferencz Kornfield of the Sopron Jewish Community for perpetual care of family graves, $25,000; and to Mahler's cousin, Anna Bogicevic, $25,000; and a special bequest to Walter (last name unknown), her husband's nephew who lived in London. Included in her legacy were jewelry valued at $7,072, furs appraised at $4,035, and fine arts assessed at $25,750. Mahler directed that her remains be cremated by the Garden State Cremotorium [sic] in North Bergen, New Jersey, and that the urn of her late husband be buried with her own ashes next to her father's grave in the Sopron Cemetery. She further specified that her wearing apparel, jewelry, motor vehicles, household furniture and furnishings, books, silverware, glassware, works of art, and all other personal and household effects be given to her executors, with the request that they carry out the written or oral expression of her wishes. All further income from her estate, including royalties from her books, were to be added to the Gray Panther Fund.

The money, of course, was very welcomed by the Panthers, who no doubt considered the bequest to be a completely altruistic act. According to Denise Galatas,[2] of the Southern Mutual Help Association, Sister Anne Catherine Bizalion, one of the cofounders of the organization, was a recipient of the Gray Panther Margaret Mahler Award.[3] She passed away in 1997. Sister Anne was a rural Dominican nun who came to Louisiana in the mid-fifties to begin work to end poverty in Louisiana. She was the first Catholic nun with a master's degree in social work from Tulane University and was the first professional social worker at the TB Annex of the Lafayette Charity Hospital. She created and was director of the first Headstart Program in one of the poorest parishes (counties) in Louisiana. She also cofounded the Southern Mutual Help Association in 1969.

Sister Bizalion assuredly did a great deal of good with the contents of her award. But one cannot help but wonder whether humanity would have been served at least as well by further research in child development.

Mahler's surprising will promoted speculations which ranged from her wish for revenge, to her unwillingness to allow her research to continue without her, to her desire to support old people, to her disappointment in certain friends and associates, to the fact that she didn't like what was happening in the foundation, and to the conjecture that she was committing scientific suicide. The consensus was that the will was an act of recrimination and revenge.

Anni Bergman was one of Mahler's closest associates for twenty-five years. Everybody believed she would be Mahler's natural heir. When asked about the will, Bergman said,[4] "She left me the nameplate for the Masters Children's Center, which I really value, and a still life of a scene in the woods, which she gave me the chance to choose from among her paintings. I don't think I expected more."

Judith Smith feels that Mahler didn't leave the foundation any money because she didn't want it to continue without her. According to Smith,[5] "Mahler's final interest was in aging. The foundation was not going forward. It was too parochial; she saw it closing in on itself, so she didn't leave any money to the foundation. The rumor that circulated that she had bypassed a second will with the foundation as beneficiaries didn't shock me. I think in some ways she didn't want the foundation to go on without her, partially because she wouldn't let it, and partially because she felt that nothing was being done there." Darline Levy believes that Mahler didn't leave any money to the foundation because she was disappointed in it. Levy said,[6] "I think her will expressed Margaret from the beginning to the end. I like to think of it as exercising her aging prerogatives, when the individual remains alert. She was frustrated by her inability to make her body hold together as the vehicle for her thinking. Leaving her money to the Gray Panthers makes a certain sense beyond her own work. She undermined the furthering of her life's work, but she had radical ambivalence about the foundation, which I wasn't in any position to affirm or dispute. It was complicated, and the people were all working very hard on their own personal lives, *pro bono* for the most part. Although disappointed with the foundation, her pride was evident when something went well, like the symposiums or a film." Margaret left Darline her portrait in oils, in which she made a reflective gesture under a lamplight. It was painted by a Hungarian artist whose work Mahler collected.

Karen Berberian, the daughter of Mahler's disciple Selma Kramer, remarked, "People joked that Mahler changed her will so that people would feel angry, rather than feeling sad and missing her. I doubt that this was her motivation, either conscious or unconscious. My mother was upset because she felt that Margaret's will took away funding that should have been left to the people doing research on separation-individuation theory. I don't think my mother ever felt absolutely secure about her role in Mahler's life and whether she was as important to Mahler as Mahler was to her. When Mahler died she left behind a mink coat. My mother thought she was going to inherit it, but it went to someone else. I know that my mother was disappointed about this."

Ernst Abelin felt empathy for Selma Kramer. He said,[7] "That was a crazy thing Mahler did, disinheriting the Mahler foundation. Selma Kramer must have been very upset." Abelin had little else to say about the will, but was pleased that Mahler left him some vases from Vienna, which he proudly keeps in his office.

Harold Blum said, "In her will, Mahler left lots of little gifts specifically chosen for the recipients. For example, I received an autographed copy of *Separation Individuation*."[8] Mahler left many such little gifts, such as her *Selected Papers,* to Selma Kramer, inscribed "To my personal and professional confidante and heiress of my work (in her internalized manner) and from her most beloved friend, Her devoted Margit Mahler. 1979/80." She also left Kramer a second casting of the statue her friend Beni Ferenczy had sculpted.

"Surprisingly, she bequeathed no money to her foundation in Philadelphia, or to Masters Children's Center," Blum continued, "or to her closest coworkers for many years. Instead she left the bulk of her estate to the Gray Panthers, an organization who take care of the aged. My deduction is that she felt abandoned and lonely at the end. She was angry with colleagues for neglecting her, and presumably didn't want them to benefit from a bequest. Her will suggested an aggressive act of revenge in response to her feeling abandoned.

Peter Neubauer added his thoughts about the will. He said,[9] "She was very disappointed in Philadelphia in that they didn't do what she wanted them to. She was critical of her major associates, John and Anni, and disappointed in how they spent their money. Bernard Fischman advised her about her will. She also called me over and wanted to discuss it with me. At the end she turned away from her children. McDevitt stayed away from her, so that is why she was disenchanted with everybody but Selma Kramer."

Bernice Apter, one of the three executors of Mahler's estate, also spoke of Mahler's disappointment and act of revenge. She said:[10]

> I think she appointed me executor because she trusted my ability in finance to handle things. She must have had at least seven wills. She kept changing them. Even the day before she went into the hospital for the last time she asked me to take out her will. She read it and handed it back to me and said that is fine. But she never signed the will.
>
> She spoke to me about the will and said that she didn't want to leave her money to the foundation because she was angry with them and lost her trust in them. She had her moods, one day she liked you and one day she didn't. That was her nature if she got angry with someone. She was a wonderful person in so many ways, but she had her shortcomings. Her lawyer, Mr. Fischman, tried to get her to sign the new will, but she couldn't, as she was in a coma. She gave me a signed copy of *The Selected Papers*, both volumes. She inscribed it: 'To my beloved irreplaceable good friend and confidante, Bernice Apter. With gratitude.'

Manuel Furer agreed with Blum and Apter that Mahler used her will to get even with her associates because she felt they had deserted her. He said,[11] "Margaret was a bitter, angry woman, and showed that side of her in her will. She felt abandoned in her last years, and her will implied, 'The hell with you! I'm not leaving my money to you, but to the Gray Panthers, people who fight for the elderly!' She left a host of memorabilia, but without paying much attention to whom she parceled out the stuff. She didn't leave me anything in her will. She gave me a picture of herself when she was young and had black hair and was good looking, but I imagine she gave it to lots of people."

Ruth Lax, who, with Sheldon Bach, and J. Alexis Burland, edited two books in Mahler's honor—*Rapprochement: The Critical Subphase of Separation-Individuation*,[12] and *Self and Object Constancy: Clinical and Theoretical*

Perspectives,[13] was one of the recipients of Mahler's memorabilia. Unlike most of the beneficiaries, she was very pleased with the bequest. Lax said, "I was very surprised and pleased to receive a book of Kathe Kollwitz's drawings in her will."

Like Ruth Lax, and unlike some of Mahler's beneficiaries, such as John McDevitt, who were puzzled as to why she had selected a particular gift to leave them, Louise Kaplan was quite happy about the gifts Mahler had willed her.[14] "She left me this statue in her will, which was a gift to her from the N.Y. Society of Freudian Psychologists," she said, enthusiastically holding up the lovely statue for me to see. "It is a Copenhagen porcelain called 'Mother and Child,' made in 4-24-77 and inscribed, 'With Great Appreciation.' She also left me a silver cup engraved 'To Margaret Mahler with love from the Masters' Board.'"

Her will was a big surprise to everyone at the foundation, according to Irving Sternschein. He said,[15] "She was, I think, perceptive in a way. She was not confident that her efforts would be valued in the long run and accredited to her. Harold Blum got involved, and she knew he is a very wise and bright person, but he was not a factor in all this, except for her knowledge that he valued her work. The will resulted in a split in the foundation. Anne Lipton, the treasurer, and I in essence left our roles as officers. The Philadelphia people had a coup and took over, Selma Kramer, Henri Parens, Leroy Byerly, and a few other people like that took over. I turned over all the things to them. I think the will largely had to do with her experience as an elderly widow, teacher, and professional. I think she identified at the end with others not as fortunate as she was. It may be that Fishman counseled it. or that her judgement was affected. She was terminal at the time."

Dr. Sternschein then tied up the matter of Mahler's will with her major life interest. He said, *"True to her theoretical emphasis on separation, she dreaded the thought of dying, of approaching death without anyone there.* She was really comatose when I got there. She may have known that a number of us were in the vicinity, but not as individuals. She suffered before, a lot of stress and back pain."

Dr. Sternschein completed the interview and we hung up the phone. A few moments later, he called back with another (and kinder) point of view. He said, "I've had second thoughts about her will. She was very sensitive and smart and she may have thought that if she left money to any of her coworkers, there always would be people who would be deeply wounded. Everybody had a professional transference to her, and would have been very hurt. The only thing not understandable was why she didn't leave to the foundation. but to leave money to some people would be very offensive to anyone left out. I'm putting a good spin on it now, but didn't feel that way originally. Again there would have been a lot of wrangling on how the money would be used. There were a lot of people who wanted to grab hold of that kind of support. She did something that everybody would be hurt by but would get over. Equal treatment for everybody."

Mahler left nothing in her will to Sternchein, but he managed to obtain a keepsake of hers. He said, "I happen to have a rug that was hers. The people who were disposing of her effects let me have it. I didn't expect or need anything, but the rug was a bit personal. It wasn't a great oriental rug."

Leo Madow also had an altruistic justification for Mahler's bequests. He said[16] that although Mahler's will did not include the foundation, he thought she had wanted to change it. He said, "The word I heard was that Mahler was all ready to change the will back to include the foundation, and the change was never accomplished."

Helen Fogarassy was at Mahler's bedside when she died, and confirmed Madow's observation that Mahler intended to change her will. "Peggy Hammond was supposed to be her executor," Fogarassy said,[17] "but it remained the old way." Fogarassy added, "$35,000 is a nice chunk of change but it's not much compared to all Peggy lost with Dr. Mahler's death. She'd been virtually family, understanding Dr. Mahler and making decisions for her. Then suddenly she had no say in the process of how the Mahler legacy would be disposed. She was quite suddenly, completely and soundly displaced. As was I, which is probably why I empathize so much. Margaret's lawyer was coming over and I was called into the room to be the witness to sign the new will. While we were waiting for him she got worse." (She pauses.) "I can't remember any more details. I got a big rush of emotions. I was called into the room to be the witness to the new will, but it was too late." (She stops talking to regain control of her emotions.) Then she said, "Dr. Mahler left me nothing in her will, although she left a meticulous list of her belongings for distribution. We had kind of a love-hate thing, she didn't know what to do with me. She hadn't made any decisions about the will, and didn't know whether she could trust me or not.

I was supposed to have done her autobiography, but I prefer to have her in my heart."

Dr. Bernard Pacella had some information about Mahler's bequests, of which no one else I interviewed seemed aware. He said:[18]

> She became attached to me, for some reason I don't understand. She left a trust for me, the Mahler Trust, a hundred thousand dollar trust, with me as the trustee. I'm supposed to use the income for psychoanalytic research. It was separate from her will, a trust for me. Although it enabled me to use the income, I never took anything from it. I am thinking about what kind of research program can I develop. I am waiting until there is a hundred thousand dollars, so that it develops a certain income, and accumulates a certain amount of interest, like five or ten thousand a

year. I have to decide whether I want to give it to Columbia or some other research. When it accumulates, I thought I would name a prize in her honor. With a team, I would gather together the papers or research and ask the psychoanalytic division of Columbia who is the best writer or did the best work in psychoanalysis that year. I would contact the APA and request the name of a person who deserves a prize, to whom I would give the five or ten thousand dollars.

She left it to me for research. The problem is how to start it, I haven't taken any money from it. As a trustee, I can take a certain amount of it. I think she knew that I wouldn't do that and would have to abide by my own principles and restrictions. Harold Blum is upset that Mahler didn't leave him any money.

Again Pacella said something that no one else had, which makes Mahler's bequest to the Panthers seem less strange. He said, "Margaret was always interested in the Gray Panthers, even before she got old." Mahler also left Pacella a copy of the bust sculpted by her friend Beni Ferenczy.

Dr. Sylvia Brody sympathized with people she felt had been mistreated by Mahler in her will. She said angrily,[19] "Margaret promised Pat Nachman to leave her something in her will and she didn't. I'm shocked that she didn't leave any money to Anni Bergman and John McDevitt. They were really her lapdogs, her poodles."

The brilliant and forthright Dr. Helen Meyers[20] made some fascinating comments about Mahler's last years, in particular about her shocking will. She said:

> I was very fond of her, and despite the fact that she was a brilliant, smart, creative woman who contributed a lot to psychoanalysis, there were also funnily enough some negative things about her. But her negative traits did not outweigh the positive. Despite the fact that she was basically a good, warm woman who was very kind, there were these little negative things about her. What I meant was that she sometimes became angry for no apparent reason about things that didn't warrant getting angry about. She was an admirable, creative, even kind and warm person, and these funny little incidents were not her main character. She was at times angry, absolutely, but mostly she was very sweet and kind and very enjoyable.
>
> *When she died, I think Margaret was symbolically committing a sort of scientific suicide.* When I say I think that she was committing scientific suicide, of course I am only referring to her will. I do not mean an intentional suicide, but that it worked self-destructively, as she was unconsciously being destructive to her own heritage. She left a big intellectual legacy about her theory of "Separation-Individuation," but I felt that one of the problematic things at the time of her death was that she was angry about something and it interfered with the way the heritage should have been. She should have left her money to the Mahler Foundation and to people like Anni Bergman and John McDevitt. Instead, she left all her money and heritage to the Gray Panthers, who had very little to do with her, and gave no money to the Margaret Mahler Foundation, which consisted of a group of people who were intensely devoted to her and committed to maintaining and furthering her scientific contributions in the psychoanalytic and the childhood education worlds. Without money, the foundation was rather stymied and extremely limited in what they could do, They could have done a great deal more if they had some money, so that her will contributed to destroying her scientific heritage.

She was no longer in the forefront at the American Psychoanalytic Association. She was instrumental in destroying some of her impact because she was angry in her will. She was destroying her heritage, because, at the time, the American Psychoanalytic Association was paying little attention to Separation-Individuation issues and we repeatedly had trouble getting the topic on panels at the programs. I do not mean by that that nobody remembers her work. We certainly all do, or practice along her lines. But it could have grown so much more.

We all on the board felt very bad about it, because we didn't want to destroy her very important contribution, but it was already done in her will and we couldn't get to change it and we had little money. However, now the fact is her work has been revitalized, as there have been analytic panels comparing Separation-Individuation with attachment theories. Just last fall I participated on such a panel cosponsored by the American and the Mahler Foundation.

I also think that she did mean to change her will and would have done so if given the time, but she was probably angry when she originally made the will. I think her annoyance was one of the conscious motivations for the unexpected distribution of her money and the destructive aspects for her scientific heritage were the results. Probably in expressing her anger at her followers, who she did not feel were doing a good job, she was simultaneously and unconsciously damaging herself.

Margaret was angry that Anni might not do the right thing, perpetuate her memory in the right way. When Margaret was in the ICU with a coronary occlusion we sent somebody in to see if she wanted to change the will. She almost changed it. I don't think she thought she was going to die. I think she made that will to annoy us and expected to change it, but she died too soon. She had this coterie of people following her around, who she felt wanted to live off her fame. She was very complicated and contradictory but a very interesting lady.

Although many analysts were puzzled and angry that Mahler's bequests overlooked her colleagues, she was not alone among analysts in ignoring psychoanalysis in their final bequests. According to Kirsner,[21] many wealthy European analysts who professed loyalty to the profession left no legacies to the Institute. Kirsner states that Otto Isakower, who made a great deal of money in his profession and successfully invested in land near the shore, left all his wealth to the Hebrew University in Jerusalem. Similarly, Lillian Malcove, his closest colleague, left her million dollar collection of Russian Orthodox icons to the Toronto Museum. Of all the senior analysts at the New York Psychoanalytic Institute at the time, only one, Grace Abbatte, left a considerable sum of money — $80,000 — to the Institute for a fund to advance child analysis. As with Mahler's colleagues, many analysts were furious that numerous members who professed loyalty to psychoanalysis left nothing to the New York Psychoanalytic Institute. This was a particular hardship to the organization, which was facing bankruptcy at the time because of the high cost of its library, lawsuits against it, and water leaks in the building which revealed an underground stream. Kirsner said, "Leaving nothing at all to the NYPsaI probably reflected the Europeans' lack of loyalty to the NYPsaI and their contemptuous view of most of its mainly American members who, in their eyes, were not really doing analysis."

Mahler's reasons for her bequests differed from those of the New York Psychoanalytic Institute's members, in that many of the coworkers she overlooked, such as Selma Kramer and Anni Bergman, were of European origin.

The most realistic comment about Mahler's will, however, was written not by an analyst, but by Frank Hernadi,[22] one of my readers, who said, "The Mysterious Will is very factual but really does not come as anything mysterious after getting to know Mahler's difficult personality. I can visualize her thinking, *Do you want to keep the darn Children's Center going? Earn it yourselves. I came here with nothing and I made it from nothing. I'm not going to spoil you by letting you have it any easier.* Of course it is no surprise that if someone lives a life of a prima donna, humiliating the heck out of others and alienating even the most loving people, that person will die a lonely, miserable death."

In my writing of this book, another likely source of Mahler's mysterious will has occurred to me, the origin of which possibly remained in Mahler's unconscious. In taking care of the elderly, Margaret Mahler was identifying and merging with her beloved father at his best, the philanthropist who looked out for the indigent aged. Her father, Dr. Schoenberger, almost singlehandedly was responsible for building an old age home in Sopron. A plaque there still says, *This is the home which was erected under the leadership of Dr. Gustav M. Schoenberger.* Mahler had mentioned to Lotte Koehler that as she aged she was drawn toward the death instinct, and agreed that the wish for a merger was uppermost in her mind. What better way to merge with her beloved father than the one Mahler chose?

Dr. Meyers is correct in her statement that Margaret Mahler was a complicated and contradictory lady. She died as she lived, leaving *sturm und drang* interspersed with love as her legacy. Whatever else resulted from her bequests or lack of them, one thing is certain: decades later, people are still angry with her or grateful, rarely in proportion to what their relationship with Margaret Mahler had led them to expect.

17

Margaret Mahler Today (The Present)

Her Colleagues Speak

Where does the work of Margaret Mahler stand today in the hierarchy of psychoanalytic theorists? While there is no question that her works are not taught as much as they were in her prime, can we still consider them vital to psychoanalytic thinking? In this chapter, I will give the answers supplied to me by many well-known analysts, along with the thinking of important researchers in the field of infant development today. I would like to stress, however, that a complete report of their research exceeds the purposes set out for this book. Interested readers are advised to consult the original sources listed in the bibliography.

Dr. Justin Call, well-known child analyst and Mahler's collaborator, believes that her major contributions are still viable and will survive. "I feel very privileged to have known her and eagerly read her works," he said.[1]

I continue to insist that they have a prominent place in basic textbooks which I had participated in editing. I thought her writings were unique and helpful. She confided in me about the critique she had experienced with others concerning her theories of early development. I listened carefully to what she had to say and did not think that she was too far off base, but I do think her major contributions will survive, even the detailed phases of separation and individuation from six months of age to the point of relative constancy. I was also intrigued by her synthesis of language development as it influences the capacity for object constancy.

In my memories I am most impressed with Margaret Mahler the person, the writer, the creative individual, her charm and intriguing personality. She obviously had an excellent mind, was a very good listener, could speak clearly about what was

202

being brought to fore, and had an acute clinical understanding of infants and grown-ups. I do think Margaret's contributions will be maintained. *I think that she belongs in the forefront of great psychoanalytic theorists.*

Dr. Peter Neubauer expressed somewhat similar feelings.[2] "Margaret Mahler made a very profound contribution to psychoanalysis. For me her work not only stands up, but becomes more and more significant. Today a lot of analysis concerns the first years of life, as in attachment theory. It deals with the consequences of the failure of attachment on the future development of the child. For me it is extraordinarily significant that she named her work separation-individuation, which concerns not just the way the child is attached to the love object but how he goes about finding his own identity. Attachment theory deals only with separation, not individuation. *In my opinion her work is continuously significant.*"

Henri Parens also believes that Mahler's place in psychoanalytic thinking is secure. He said,[3] "I admired her brains, no question about that. Mahler was certainly one of the strong brains of the era, along with Hartman. Anna Freud, and Rene Spitz. Later, I also would add Winnicott."

Irving Sternschein agreed with Parens' estimate of Mahler's contributions. He said,[4] "I used her theories, observations, and explanations in my analytic work. Her constructs were very useful in analyzing adults as well as children. Some of the more classical analysts weren't as conscious of that." Sternschein thought so highly of Mahler's work that he placed her in the top echelons of psychoanalytic history. "*I think Mahler was one of the top psychoanalytic theorists, on a level with Anna Freud,*" he said. "She was not quite the initiator that Anna Freud was, but contributed greatly and was very influential in child analysis."

Judith Smith still teaches Mahler, within the framework of theories of development of early life. She says[5] that within the social work literature Mahler is acknowledged but overall not given major prominence in any of the social work journals or texts.

Lotte Koehler agreed with the appraisal of Mahler's contributions made by Drs. Parens, Sternschein, Edward, Call, Neubauer, and Smith, and added the names of Bergman and Weill as well. She said:[6] "*I feel sure that Mahler made a lasting contribution to psychoanalysis, and especially to psychoanalytic developmental theory.* It is difficult to place a person in a hierarchy of great psychoanalytic theorists, because one has to take the historical point of view into consideration."

Koehler continued with a remark that would have warmed Mahler's heart. She said, "Mahler made, I feel, an even greater contribution to psychoanalytically oriented developmental theory than Anna Freud, even though some of the viewpoints of Mahler's are now outdated by newer knowledge."

Psychoanalyst Helen Gediman believes that Mahler's theories have great historical significance. When asked where she thinks Mahler stands in today's hierarchy of psychoanalytic theorists, Dr. Gediman responded,[7] "I think she is absolutely indispensable, for historical reasons. If I had to choose the most important theorist today, I would choose Daniel Stern over Mahler, but I do not think I could appreciate Stern as much as I do without being thoroughly grounded in Mahler. He could not have been where he is now if it were not for Mahler's work. Like Freud, she had the ideas first, which others developed, and then say, 'This is better than that, and so forth.' They would not be where they are today if not for their predecessors."

But a number of prominent analysts and theoreticians feel very differently about the matter of Mahler's standing in the field today. A different appraisal is offered by Harold Blum, one of Mahler's close friends, who feels that *separation-individuation remains an important addition to developmental theory*. But, surprisingly, he expresses reservations about separation-individuation theory, and gives detailed reasons for his opinion. He believes that there is no evidence for the existence of a symbiotic phase. He says,[8]

> Like Hartman, Margaret Mahler was once so popular that hardly a paper was written without a reference to her. Both have been relatively obscured, for different reasons. Hartman's writings were very abstract, difficult to read. People are now inclined to talk about others as human beings, but not about energies. The language he spoke is regarded today as obsolete. I wonder if he hasn't in a major way been greatly diminished in the psychoanalytic institutes. He is hardly being taught.
>
> A rugged individualist, Mahler was very influenced by Hartman, Kris and Lowenstein, and the ego psychologists. She didn't hesitate to depart from theory she regarded as needing modification or change. She remained very much a Freudian, and considered herself an ego psychologist who wanted to study the foundations of ego psychology through observation.
>
> During Freud's lifetime, the Freudian group emphasized the oral phase in the development of object relations. The baby bonded to the breast and then to mother, sucking, feeding, and seeking oral gratification. Then Spitz introduced us to the importance of the smile, which was not related to nutrition, the concept of the social smile, stranger anxiety, and so forth. Spitz was beginning to think in terms of what we now call object relations.
>
> The baby's smiles have an effect on the mother. Margaret began to add to libido theory, formulating a parallel theory. I told her that the concept of a stimulus barrier was antiquated as a theory of earliest life, because it didn't take into account the feedback in the smile and the mother-infant dialog.
>
> She gave up the autistic phase, because the evidence was very much against it. Others were beginning to write about mutual stimulation, that the baby is born to respond to mother's presence. A better choice of words might have been to call it the barrier to overstimulation, or stimulus filter.
>
> Mahler assumed in conforming with accepted theory all the way back that the first five months were undifferentiated, and postulated that after the autistic phase came a symbiotic phase. While we cannot enter the baby's mind, psychoanalytic developmental theory must be compatible with the findings of infant developmental research.

Mahler was both extraordinarily open-minded and at times closed and opinionated. She was intrigued by new concepts, but when it came to her own ideas, she maintained an intense narcissistic investment in her own formulations.

Blum then discussed Mahler's diminishing investment in the libido theory:

She saw herself as building and adding to Freud's theories. I don't think she realized how much she was moving away from the libido theory, which could not account for ego development and object relations.

Separation-individuation is a description of evolving object relations unlike the libido theory, which does not take into consideration the infant in the process of becoming a toddler. Mahler contributed to the theory of object relations, as well as ego functions and their effect on the relationship to the mother.

By emphasizing separation-individuation, Margaret took for granted the ongoing continuing relationship of the infant with the mother. Unfortunately, the concept of separation-individuation did not elucidate the crucial complementary issue of continuing attachment. Current interest shifted from separation to attachment.

Researchers like Dan Stern strongly disagreed with the concept of symbiosis. I agree that there is no evidence for a symbiotic phase, so I no longer concur with the theory of such a phase in the normal infant. It is very likely that there are confused states in which mother and infant are amalgamated in the infant's mind, extreme states of dependency along with earliest differentiation. Emotional separateness and internal representations of self and object are not possible the first half of the first year. The infant can hardly deal with out of sight out of mind, and is unable to locate an object which is hidden behind a screen until much later in development. Mahler worked with symbiotic psychotic children and incorrectly assumed that their symbiotic state was relatively equivalent to a phase in normal children. Her assumption of normal symbiosis was based on evidence reaped from pathological development.

Fred Pine had further comments to make on the bypassing of Mahler's contributions. He says,[9] "I think in the U.S. her work was never really picked up by adult analysts. It was used primarily by child analysts, who really saw the value in it. When the critique of the whole theory of symbiosis came out, I think a lot of people felt, 'Oh good!' In a nonsophisticated way, they adopted the critique, even though they really had never studied the theory. There are places in the world, for example in Japan, where all they wanted to hear about was separation-individuation. They are more interested in the early mother-child relationship than Americans, and the mother-infant relationship is very important to them. *There was a time when Mahler's work formed a great new wave, but that wave has passed.* I think she has been bypassed, and many adult analysts have never picked up on her."

In an important 1992 article, "Mahler's concepts of 'symbiosis' and 'separation-individuation':[10] Revisited, reevaluated, refined," Pine reevaluates the doctrine of separation-individuation. He states that the concept of the *timing* of a normal symbiotic phase does not need alteration, but that of a symbiotic *phase* requires revision. According to him, the infant experiences significant moments of symbiotic closeness, but does not experience them as an ongoing state. He further states that there are individual differences in the degree to which merger issues are central in the life of the infant, and that they can serve various functions for different individuals. These refinements, Pine believes, are not inconsistent with the findings of infant cognitive research.

According to Anni Bergman, the present grande dame of separation-individuation theory, "There has been serious thinking about and reappraisal of the (separation-individuation) theory, which could lead to corrections and refinements." Much of the need for reappraisal is based on the emphasis of present day researchers on the relationship between mother and child, in place of Mahler's focus on development. "The study of the separation-individuation process began at the Masters Children's Center in 1959 at a time when analysts believed that one could learn about the psyche only within the psychoanalytic framework," Bergman says. "The research was modeled on the analytic situation in the hope that the eyes of the observers would reveal the inner processes at work in the children, as the ears of the psychoanalyst listened to the psyche of the patient in analysis."

Bergman continues with the statement that practicing becomes possible only after the child becomes aware that he and mother can share the experience, which allows him to move away from her. Bergman comes to the conclusion that perhaps Mahler would have done better to emphasize the inner forces driving the toddler toward the realization of a separate self rather than the normal circumstances for the development of the self.

It is interesting that Bergman, Blum, and Pine were among Mahler's closest associates. Are they differentiating themselves from Mahler after her death, as they were unable to do during her lifetime?

The Attachment Theorists

Attachment theory, which was developed by the great theoretician, John Bowlby,[12] differs from separation-individuation theory in that it stresses a universal human need to form close affectional bonds, in contrast to Mahler's emphasis on the individual development of the infant. At its core is the reciprocity of early relationships.[13] Bowlby postulates that the infant's attachment to the mother is based on instinctive behavioral systems that promote survival, that a child becomes attached to its mother independently of her feeding, cleaning, or otherwise comforting the baby. Bowlby's ethological approach is vastly different from Mahler's psychological approach, for whom attachment and separation are external counterparts to a development within the child. For Bowlby, the factors that promote attachment in mankind are not so different from what they are in other mammals. For Mahler, the distinctly human condition of "symbiosis" is a response to dependency needs that characterize human infancy.

Bowlby's main criticism of Mahler's theory[14] is that "Mahler's theories of normal development rest not on observation but on preconceptions based on traditional psychoanalytic theory and ignore almost entirely the exciting new information about early infancy." Bowlby is incorrect, however, in assuming that Mahler's theories on normal autism and symbiosis are based on preconceptions of traditional analysis. Those theories had nothing to do with preconceptions garnered from psychoanalysis, as people who have read chapter three, "Her Analyst" in this book know. Mahler came to these conclusions in the midst of her infantile psychosis studies at the Masters Children's Center, when she realized that these infants were very similar to two psychotic latency children she had treated privately.[15]

Emanuel Peterfreund, another advocate of attachment theory, objects to viewing psychotic conditions as regressions to normal infant states.[16] According to him, the infant's seemingly narcissistic behavior is normal for babies of that age, and bears little essential similarity to the narcissistic functioning of adults. To link the two denotes "superficial analogizing and a confusing adultomorphization of infancy" (p. 436). He gives other examples of both adultomorphization and what Milton Klein called "pathormorphization" of infancy, including Mahler's (1968) characterization of early infancy as "normal autism." He goes on to say that discussions of regression are often characterized by similar superficial analogous and confused thinking. As an illustration, Peterfreund says that when complex biological systems break down they do not necessarily retrace the steps by which they develop, and one must beware of viewing the products of a breakdown as regression to normal steps in development (p. 439).

Peterfreund illustrates his theory with the thought that while a man who has suffered a cerebrovascular accident and is unable to speak may be diagnosed as suffering from aphasia he does not have the same condition as an infant of two months. A normal two-month-old baby is not described as being in a "'normal aphasic' state of development. Nor would one say that the man suffering the cerebrovascular accident has 'regressed' to an earlier state of 'normal aphasia'" (p. 439).

Karlen Lyons-Ruth,[17] another authority on attachment theory and the work of John Bowlby, also disagrees with Mahler on the importance of internal conflict in the infant. According to Lyons-Ruth, recent research on attachment relationships suggests that ambivalent behavior and other forms of conflict in early toddlers are more related to difficulties in parent-infant interaction than to the normal "fear of engulfment." She adds that severe forms of infant conflict are found in the presence of maternal psychopathology. Lyons-Ruth believes that Mahler and Bowlby made very different assumptions regarding the developmental period from nine to eighteen months.

Mahler postulated a close relationship between baby and caretaker during the period she called *symbiosis*. She saw the developmental task from nine to eighteen months as that of increasing physical separation in the process of differentiation. In contrast, Bowlby postulated that developing a secure attachment relationship to the caretaker is the major achievement of the infant at the time when it is practicing crawling and walking, with the goal of maintaining close access to the caretaker. (Author's note: If this is truly the infant's goal, then why do so many toddlers walk away from mother, or take their first steps out of her presence?) The two theories have conflicting ideas about what is healthy or pathological in the young child. Agreeing with Bowlby, Lyons-Ruth insists that Mahler failed to distinguish clearly between normal and deviant developmental pathways, and adds that scientific evidence is obliging psychoanalysts to develop a theory of normal attachment behavior that is unconnected to pathological systems. Mahler also believed we must also develop theories of psychopatholology that are not based on ideas of fixation at normal developmental stages. Bowlby sought to formulate a theory of development that is not based on libidinal drives, but in contrast to Mahler's theory, which is based on ego functioning, his hypothesis rests on emotional maturation. He elaborated on a concept that stresses behavior and can be validated scientifically. His emphasis, according to Lyons-Ruth,[18] has led to a great deal of infant data that permits us to reevaluate the strengths and weaknesses of Mahler's theory of the separation-individuation process.

Like Winnicott, Peter Fonagy believes[19] the baby's development cannot be understood except in tandem with the mother. According to him, the seeking, smiling, and clinging behavior of the infant instigates such reactions in the adult as touching, holding, and soothing. These responses strengthen the attachment behavior of the infant toward the caretaker. Fonagy also stressed the importance of reflective functioning on rapprochement conflicts.[20] He theorizes that the mother thinks about her baby and reflects her thinking back to the infant. This encourages the child to become aware of the fact that their minds are independent of each other. The capacity for reflective self-functioning, Fonagy states, is closely correlated with early attachment security.

Harvard child psychiatrist and attachment theorist Edward Tronick suggests that mother and infant need to seek another way of being together.[21] The rapprochement period is characterized by disruption and misunderstanding. Like Mahler, Tronick believes that the manner in which mother and infant repair this rupture determines the future well-being of their relationship. Tronick finds scientific evidence of the importance of the mother/infant relationship, in contrast to the baby's individual development. "Clearly, the emotional state of others is of fundamental importance to the infant's emotional state," Tronick says.[22] Babies send their parents non-verbal messages, such as smiling when they are pleased, clinging for comfort, and following with their eyes when they are anxious they will be left. Tronick decided that the "I-smile-you-smile-back" kind of relationship could be an excellent basis for an important experiment. He and a colleague, Jeffry Cohn, asked mothers of three-month-old infants to remove all expression from their faces while looking at their babies. "The effect on the infant is dramatic," Tronick wrote. "Infants immediately detect the change and attempt to solicit the mother's attention." When the mother still did not react, the infants sucked their thumbs or looked away in an effort at self-comfort. "They reached for their best tools to engage their mothers," Tronick continued. "They smiled. They gurgled." When the mothers still refused to respond, the babies tried again and again. Then sadly enough, after a while, each child stopped trying.[23]

A Cognitive Theorist

Although Gyorgy Gergely has attempted to reformulate separation-individuation concepts using cognitive theory,[24] he nonetheless believes that *Mahler's work has had and still has a profound effect on the development of psychological theory.* In his reappraisal of Mahler's work, he agrees with the emphasis on the critical importance of the caretaker's ability to tolerate the infant's ambivalent behavior during the rapprochement crisis, and that the interpersonal experiences of the period may well be critical for the development of the ability to maintain identity of others in the face of ambivalence. While his conceptual reconstructions often involve radical departures from Mahler's theoretical views, Gergely states (p. 1222) that his recasting of her ideas "illustrate the continuing influence of her theories on current approaches to early psychological development."

Other Critics

1. Karlen Lyons-Ruth

Lyons-Ruth critiques the concept of the rapprochement phase,[25] and, indeed, questions whether it exists at all. She believes that rapprochement behaviors have a more complex understructure which is determined by earlier attachment strategies and the mother's sensitivity to the child. According to Lyons-Ruth, we must move on to a more complex, organizational view of adaptive behavior in toddlerhood. In her opinion, assertive relatedness rather than autonomy better describes adaptive behavior at that stage of development. Although Lyons-Ruth questions many of Mahler's concepts, she sums up her contributions with the statement,[26] "Although Mahler's theoretical concepts may need revision to accommodate new data, her vision in arguing for the relevance of direct infant observation has contributed to the dynamic rather than static nature of the analytic-developmental theoretical field. She was a pioneer in stressing the importance of the mother-infant relationship in contrast to the play of drives in infancy, and her clinical insight and careful observation of signs of maladaptation in early development have made her a uniquely influential contributor to psychoanalytic theory. Many of the influences she set in motion have contributed to the current array of new evidence that is reshaping our vision of the nature of early psychological development."

2. Jessica Benjamin

Jessica Benjamin's intellectual hypotheses frighten many readers to the point where Allan Souter wrote a paper entitled "Who's Afraid of Jessica Benjamin?"[27] According to him, Benjamin's background is different from that of other theorists, in that she comes from "an avowedly political framework — and is a feminist" who writes from a European philosophical framework and has a reputation outside clinical circles in contemporary social and cultural theory. Despite her differing background, Benjamin agrees with Fonagy "that the human mind is interactive rather than monadic, that the psychoanalytic process should be understood as occurring between subjects rather than from within the individual." She believes that the phase in which the infant discovers that other people have minds coincides roughly with Mahler's practicing period. In contrast to Mahler, Benjamin stresses that the infant's separation during this period proceeds along with the felt connection to the other person. "The joy of intersubjective attunement," she says, is that the Other can share the child's feeling. Mahler's "love affair with the world" is intensified for the toddler by the knowledge that mother is sharing it. Benjamin[28] also challenges Fonagy's theory of reflective self-functioning, as well as the concept of the resolution of the rapprochement conflict through internalization. She agrees with Winnicott, however, that the destruction of the object and its subsequent survival is of great importance in the resolution of the rapprochement crisis.

3. Janna Malamud Smith

Although Janna Malamud Smith believes that Mahler is one of the most studied psychoanalytic theorists of her times, in *A Potent Spell*,[29] she gives a most critical, even vicious critique of Mahler's work. Smith's evaluation of Mahler's work differs from that of the other critics in that it is completely negative. Smith says that Mahler and her ilk blame mothers for all of the misfortunes of humanity, without thinking about the needs of the mothers at all, for example "about how the absence of cultural respect, economic recompense, or companionship in her work might actually be depleting or depressing her (p. 154)." In addition to the one-sidedness of her observations, Smith thinks that Mahler's research in itself is flawed and "reflects a projective fantasy by the authors." According to Smith, Mahler overlaid preexisting psychoanalytic thinking about infant development upon the mother-baby couples she observed, and then elaborated upon them. Smith argues that the "research" is based upon Mahler's "idealized fantasy of a mother." But the theories were ungrounded to begin with, she says (p.149), and thus the "research" findings invalid. The researchers maintain that optimal maternal availability is essential, Smith continues, but never define it, including what maternal attachment means to mothers. "*For all the acuity of some of its observations,*" Smith says about Mahler's research, "*this famous psychological study is not science: it's religion.*"

4. Daniel Stern

The major criticism of Mahler's work, however, comes from Mahler's friend, Daniel Stern,[30] famous researcher, clinician, and author of *The Interpersonal World of the Infant* as well as numerous books and scientific articles, who believes that the normal infant does not go through an autistic phase, but rather that from birth on the infant is interested in the outside world, and is able to differentiate itself from the mother.

Maria Nardone met Dr. Stern at a conference where he was speaking, and told him I was writing a book about Margaret Mahler. He said she should inform me that he had something he wanted to tell me, and that I should contact him in Switzerland, where he teaches at the University of Geneva.

The following interview with Dr. Stern[31] took place by telephone on May 17, 2004. I am including the entire interview because of its importance to the relationship between Mahler and Stern, as well as its historical interest. The interview includes Dr. Stern's feelings about his criticism of Mahler and also shows what a big person Mahler could be.

"It goes like this," Stern began

One of the reasons this story is important to me is that a lot of Mahlerians were miffed at me that I was unfair to her and all that. When I was a candidate in psychoanalysis at Columbia, she was a very special person. We studied her works. Our professors would invite us candidates to parties. I always wanted to talk with her but was shy about it. She was always surrounded by a wall of men — she was short and they were tall — so I never talked to her in my life although I read a lot of her publications. Then I started to do my own work, which differed from hers. It was in 1974, or around then, at a conference at the World Association of Infant Mental Health. It went by another name then. It was in Istoril, Portugal, on the coast there.

Several weeks before the conference somebody knocks at my door, one of her assistants, and hands me a letter from her which said that she would be most interested in receiving a copy of the talk I was going to give. I didn't know what to do because I have never written down my talks, just a brief outline. So I sent her back a note saying I had nothing written but would be happy to send her my notes, if she could make them out. She didn't respond to that, so I go to Portugal. I was to be the first speaker. It was a special conference to honor Mahler and Eric Erickson, so I get there early in the morning to make sure the mike was working and so forth. She walked on to the stage with her cane and came bumping over to me and said, "Dr. Stern. I don't know when I have ever been so insulted by anyone." Then she turned on her heels, left the stage, and sat in the center seat of the first row. I thought *Hell, I've antagonized her! This is going to be difficult!* I gave my talk, which, in fact, was not so much about her.

That evening there was a cocktail party honoring her and Erickson. Helen Meyers took me by my arm and said, "You really should talk to Margaret. You have a lot to talk about."

I said, "I'm really afraid of her."

She said, "You needn't be. She's really very nice." She took me by the arm and led me to the table where Mahler was seated. She was all alone at that point. She said, "I'm glad we meet. We have many things to talk about. We can start right now." I said, "We'll get interrupted, this is not the best place to talk."

She said, "No, no. This is fine."

I said, "Why not wait till New York when we get back? This is a party for you."

She said, "No, we can really begin now."

I said, "OK. Dr. Mahler, I have a lot of problems with your work." She leaned towards me, put her arm on my shoulder, and with a wonderful and charming smile, said, "Dr. Stern, I've spent my entire life helping people with problems." We both broke up laughing.

I felt totally charmed by her, which I didn't expect at all. She said, "Now, would you be nice enough to get me a glass of that very nice Porto." I went after her Porto like a puppy dog wagging its tail. Then we sat down and made a date to talk in New York. From that time on I had a really nice feeling about her. We had a mutual seduction going on.

Later on she invited me, Anni Bergman, and Berry Brazelton to come to meetings with her and John McDevitt and Annamarie Weil. Brazelton and I tried to convince Mahler that the baby wasn't so autistic in the beginning. Brazelton had good things to show about it in his films.

Mahler said, "Maybe I shouldn't have called it autistic, but awakening." She was very good with making up names for things. I met with her on several occasions and we started talking about symbiosis, which I also disagreed with her about. We maintained this relationship in spite of our disagreements. I didn't feel bad about what I said in my books about her work because there was nothing in my books I hadn't told her first.

The last couple of times I went there to see her, she really was getting much older, actually she was close to dying. The last two times we met we really talked about music and life things, not about baby stuff. We couldn't talk long, she would get too tired. It was about a year before her death.

I could see times where she could be absolutely dreadful to people like Anni Bergman, but she could also be terrific. She never was awful to me. I grew to love her, I felt seduced by her. She was such a funny little lady and so strong, but somehow it didn't matter that we disagreed. Part of our attitude was that here were two hypotheses about something neither of us knew would turn out to be right in the long run. We were not in deadly competition. I don't think she felt we were either. She was very nice with me.

I said, "I was told she loved you, that she called you Danny." He seemed touched, and said, "I called her Margaret, not Dr. Mahler, after a while." One other possible reason for that," he added, "at the end of her life she moved on to other things, not that she didn't care deeply about her work. I was very surprised that she left her money to the Gray Panthers, that it was not going to the New School or Mahler Foundation. I sort of feel like my relationship was special, extraordinary to her and me. I really cherish and admire her a lot. I can't say it was truly intimate, we never talked about our private lives."

"Where do you think her work stands today?" I questioned, "or are you not the right person to ask?" (We laugh.)

He answered:

She was a real pioneer. I think she was always dealing with the right issues, even though she came up with some of the wrong answers. I hate anthropromorphizing, but she was not totally wrong. There are moments in the infant's life where he passes through states like impermeability and looks autistic-like. There were other moments where she was right in part and I was right in part.

The image of symbiosis and fusion is a truly complicated one. But I think even when you feel symbiotic and fused you never lose sight of the implicit sense that you are a separate person. That is a condition of life. You don't lose that, even when you look at some of these fused psychotic phases in hospitals. No matter how sick they are, they know there is never a state of complete fusion. I feel we both were talking about different sides of the same issue. In that sense the real difference between us is that I was taking a very normative even optimizing position in regard to children and infants, what their best capacities were, the best way to measure them. The idea behind this is that if an infant can be seen to do something even rarely, he has the capacity. She was looking at them with a different sense of lenses, more in search of the origins of pathology. I think it is a question of what you are looking for and how you are looking. In our discussions, this was kind of the feeling we had; it wasn't that anybody was truly wrong. Maybe that's why she could tolerate me.

I said, "This is very interesting, Dr. Stern, in that it brings together your theories and those of Dr. Mahler. Does anyone else know your thinking on it?"

"The only time I've ever talked about it was in Italy, and it was written up in Italian," he answered. "I don't know if it was ever published there. It's never been published in English."

"Thank you very much, Dr. Stern, for your very valuable interview. I've enjoyed talking with you," I said. Our conversation ended with Dr. Stern saying he would like a copy of the book, which I promised to send him on its publication.

Blum[32] agrees with Stern on the young infant's interest in the outside world. Blum says, "The baby on the basis of a variety of experimental research and evidence clearly differentiates between self and non-self almost from day one. If so, there was never an undifferentiated merger. The innate capacity for differentiation, therefore, demonstrates that there is no symbiotic phase or need for mother and child to separate, because they were never merged in the first place."

As a member of the Professional Advisory Board of the Mahler Foundation, Judith Smith was fortunate enough to sit in on a dialog between Mahler and Dan Stern, at Mahler's apartment. Smith said, "They sort of talked through their differences. At the time we were working on the film about 'The Emergence of the Sense of Self.' Stern came in with his diagrams of the mother and child dialogue. Mahler said, 'That's symbiosis!' He answered, 'You say it starts at five months, I say it starts at birth.' She really listened to him and dropped the autistic phase.

"Yes," Smith continued. "She really listened. She acknowledged that video allowed you to see things she you couldn't see when she was doing her work with naturalistic observation. She must have been seventy-five at the time. It is really remarkable that a woman of that age could be so open to new ideas."

"Was she angry with Stern?" I asked, thinking that with her temper one would expect her to be. Smith's answer was surprising. "No," she said softly. "She was seemingly very sweet and used to called him 'Danny.'"

Smith was right in her comment that Mahler listened to Stern, and as a result, changed her thinking about the autistic and symbiotic stages of development. According to Linda Gunsberg,[33] Mahler held on to her original position on normal autism and symbiosis, but grew to believe that the infant in the early stages experienced differentiation and an interest in the outside world as well. Her new thinking emphasized the *relative* emotional lack of differentiation between the infant and the mother. Where Mahler and Stern agreed was in their interest in how the complex inner world of object relations begins to establish itself in infancy.

Summary

In *Love's Labour's Lost*, William Shakespeare wrote,[34] "They have been at a great feast of languages and stolen the scraps." Sometimes I think that is what has happened to the work of Margaret Mahler. Occasionally one can find more truth in fiction than in the hallowed halls of academia. In Helen Fogarassy's interesting novel,[35] *Mix Bender*, Bernie, a house builder who feels the old analyst in the book looks down on him, says, "I ain't impressed with 'er coming up with this theory an' that one, and then have one o' her friends come up an' prove it was wrong to begin with. Hell, people don't know; they're just guessin'. An' on top o' that," Bernie sat up, "they get paid fer that. They get paid a lot o' money for that stuff they come up with that's all wrong, and in the end, what do they get? Worship. That's why they c'n go 'round thinkin' they're better'n house builders." I can't help but think of Bernie's remarks when I read some of the rebuttals of Mahler's work.

So where *does* the work of Margaret Mahler stand today in the hierarchy of psychoanalytic thinking? The consensus is that her contributions, like those of Freud's, are on a slippery slope. Her theories are still taught in analytic schools as part of the developmental process, but because of newer hypotheses such as attachment theory, are rarely given the central position they once held. Nevertheless, some analysts continue to view Mahler's contributions as fundamental to the understanding of psychic life. The jury, however, is still out on the subject. The pendulum swings back and forth, and it is entirely possible that separation-individuation, like the work of the master himself, will return to the central position it occupied in psychoanalytic thinking during Mahler's days of glory. But whether her views are in vogue or not, Margaret Mahler was a great pioneer who singlehandedly changed the theory and practice of child psychology forever.

Postscript:
"Ve Are Vun" (The Present)

This "postscript" is really a preamble to the story of the life of Margaret S. Mahler. Or perhaps it is all the same thing. In the beginning is the ending, in the ending is the beginning. Shortly after the fiasco at Masters Children's Center, I had a dream that a huge figure of Margaret Mahler loomed before me, covering the entire dream screen. She looked boldly into my eyes and

In 1983, five years before her death, Margaret traveled in France with some dear friends. She is pictured here in Cannes (photograph courtesy Maria J. Nardone).

said in her inimitable Hungarian accent, "Ve are vun." I thought, *If I am she and she is me, what better person could there be to write her biography?* I decided to do that one day. Yet with a busy practice, a husband, and three children, it took me a long time to get to it. Many times I wanted to say, "Go away, Margaret! Go haunt someone else's dreams." But how could I do that, any more than leaving myself? Dr. John McDevitt, Mahler's chief associate, inadvertently helped me decide to go ahead with the project.[1] When interviewing him, I asked "What do you think Mahler would say about my writing her biography?" He answered, "I think she would be delighted. I thank you for Margaret." So this book is your story, Margaret Mahler, as "ve" see it. I hope you like it.

Glossary

The following definitions were taken partly from psychiatric and psychoanalytic dictionaries, partly from my knowledge of Freud's works, and partly from the understanding I gained from practicing psychoanalysis for 37 years.

Acting-out Repeating actions that have undergone repression instead of remembering them. Acting-out occurs when the individual deals with emotional conflict or internal or external stressors by actions rather than reflections or feelings.

Analysand A patient in analysis.

Attachment theory Attachment theory, developed by John Bowlby (Bowlby, 1969; Bowlby, 1973; Bowlby, 1980), hypothesizes a pervasive human need to form close affectional bonds. The reciprocity of early relationships, a precondition of normal development in all humans beings, is basic to Attachment Theory. Biologically, attachment gives survival advantage to the infant, in that it protects the child from harm.

Autism A psychotic state in which the individual lives within his or her own world. They retreat from social or interpersonal situations, and substitute internal fantasy for the stresses of relating to others.

Borderline An infantile type of personality organization in which the individual is subject to rages and destructive behavior. They have difficulty sublimating powerful urges and using conscience to guide behavior.

Cognitive theory Cognitive theory postulates that the individual's thoughts determine their emotions, behavior, and personality. Many cognitive theorists believe that without thought processes, we could have neither emotions nor behavior and therefore would not function. In the philosophy of Cognitive Theory, thoughts always come before any feelings or actions.

Defenses Unconscious mechanisms by which people control instincts.

Differentiation The period when the child begins to realize that he and mother are separate people.

Drive theory Freud viewed the psyche as an energy system dominated by a particular drive he called "eros," or "libido," which serves as the motor force behind all physical and psychic activity. Drives are attached to various objects during different stages of a person's life, such as babies' attachment to their mothers' breasts. Freud believed the drive, for example, for oral gratification is much more important than the actual attachment.

Dual unity A symbiotic state in which two people perceive themselves as one.

Ego ideal That person in an individual's life who supplies him or her standards, ideals and ambitions.

Ejaculatio praecox Premature ejaculation in sexual intercourse.

Emotional refueling The need of toddlers to return to their mothers from time to time to reaffirm their relationship.

Ethology The scientific study of animal behavior, especially as it relates to their habitat.

Individuation The development of the individual personality as a being apart from any other.

Identification The patterning of an individual's behavior or thoughts after some person he or she admire. Identification plays a crucial role in ego development, but may also serve as a defense against anxiety or pain that accompanies separation from the object.

Libido The energy of the sexual drive.

Narcissism Self-love, in which the libido is invested in the self and not the external world.

Neurosis A type of character structure in which repression is used to keep anxiety-provoking thoughts and feelings out of awareness.

Object constancy The state attained when an individual is able to keep in mind the good aspects of a relationship, even when angry with or feel abandoned by the other person.

Object relations A libidinized relationship with a person outside of the self.

Passive-aggression The act of expressing aggressive hostile impulses through inactivity, such as failures, procrastination, not following through on tasks, and illnesses which are more of a problem for others than oneself.

Practicing subphase The period when the attainment of skills such as locomotion is uppermost in importance in the infant's world.

Psychopath A type of personality characterized by amoral and antisocial behavior, an individual who is not guided by his or her conscience.

Psychosis A type of character structure in which the individual is overwhelmed by material from the unconscious. The psychotic person reshapes external reality to suit his or her inner needs, and to sustain delusional feelings of superiority, megalomanic beliefs, grandiosity, and entitlement.

Rapprochement The period of infancy in which the child becomes aware of his powerlessness and fights to establish domination over his mother.

How the child masters this phase determines his or her future emotional health.

Regression An unconscious return to earlier means of satisfaction, when unbearable anxiety or insufficient satisfaction is experienced in the here and now. A symbolic reversion to infantile methods of reacting and thinking.

Repetition compulsion The tendency of an organism to repeat a trauma over and over in order to master it.

Repression The process by which offensive feelings or impulses are pushed out of awareness. Dealing with emotional conflict or external stress by expelling disturbing wishes, thoughts, or experiences from conscious awareness.

Resistance An involuntary defense erected by patients to ward off frightening urges or feelings.

Return of the repressed Affect or an idea from the unconscious breaks through the individual's defenses and is reexperienced in a new setting.

Splitting Compartmentalizing opposite emotional states, failing to integrate positive and negative qualities of the self or others into cohesive images. When ambivalent affects cannot be experienced simultaneously, balanced views of self and others are impossible to maintain.

Sublimation Dealing with emotional conflict or internal or external stressors by channeling unacceptable feelings or impulses into socially approved behavior. Analysts consider that sublimation is the only "successful" manner of dealing with unacceptable drives and desires.

Symbiosis the state of merged identities in which two organisms feel they are one being. According to Mahler, a normal phase of development in infancy.

Transference The patient's response to the analyst as if the analyst were an important figure from the past.

Chapter Notes

Preface

1. John Steinbeck. *Journal of a Novel: The East of Eden Letters* (New York: Penguin Books, 1990), 4.
2. Marc Pachter, "The Biographer Himself," Introduction, in *Telling Lives,* Marc Pachter, ed. (Philadelphia: University of Pennsylvania Press, 1979), 5.
3. Darline Levy. Letter to Margaret Mahler, March 28, 1978.
4. Pachter, 5.
5. Linda Hopkins, *False Self: The Life of Masud Khan* New York: Other Press, 2006).

Prologue

1. Paul E. Stepanski, *The Memoirs of Margaret Mahler* (New York: Free Press, 1988), 96.

Chapter 1

1. Bluma Swerdloff. Interview with Alma Bond.
2. Sigmund Freud, *Beyond the Pleasure Principle.* SE Vol. 18 (1920G), 1834–1844. The Repetition Compulsion is the tendency of an organism to repeat a trauma again and again in order to master it.
3. Karen Berberian. Interview with Alma Bond.
4. Jeremy Berberian. Interview with Alma Bond.

5. Interview with Margaret Mahler, Bluma Swerdloff, October 25, 1969, Columbia University Oral History, personal copy.
6. Jenny Unglow, "Goya: Bringing Forth Monsters," *New York Times,* November 23, 2003.
7. Columbia University Oral History. Unpublished manuscript by Lucy Freeman, pp. 29–30.
8. Margaret S. Mahler, "Pseudoimbecility: A Magic Cap of Invisibility," in *The Psychoanalytic Quarterly* 11, no. 2 (1942): 149–64. Reprinted in *The Selected Papers of Margaret S. Mahler,* vol. 1, *Infantile Psychosis and Early Contributions* (New York and London: Jacob Aronson, 1979), 3–16.
9. Margaret S. Mahler, "Les Infants Terrible," in *The Selected Papers of Margaret S. Mahler,* vol. 1, *Infantile Psychosis and Early Contributions* (New York and London: Jacob Aronson, 1949), 17–33). Reprinted from *Searchlights on Delinquency,* edited by K. R. Eissler (New York: International Universities Press), 77–89.
10. H.L. Mencken. Reprinted in *A Mencken Crestomathy* (New York: Vintage), 82.
11. Columbia University Oral History. Unpublished interview by Lucy Freeman, p. 33.
12. Paul E. Stepansky, *The Memoirs of Margaret S. Mahler* (New York: The Free Press, A Division of Macmillan, Inc., 1988).
13. Swerdloff interview with Bond.
14. Lotte Koehler. Interview with Alma Bond.
15. Anni Bergman and Caroline Ellman.

Discussion for Sacrificial Daughters Conference, Nightingale-Bamford School, March 23, 2003, p. 9.

16. Dr. Joseph Noshpitz, Unpublished interview with Margaret Mahler, May 2, 1981.

17. Interview with Margaret Mahler, by Lucy Freeman, October 25, 1969, p. 5.

18. Interview with Alma Bond. Leo Madow, former chairmen of the Department of Psychiatry at the Womens Medical College (now the Medical College of Pennsylvania).

19. Bluma Swerdloff interview with Bond.

20. Swerdloff interview with Bond, 5.

21. *Vaci Utca* is the name of the street, not a separate name for the school. In Hungary, educational facilities are often referred to after the street where they are located, thus the "*Vaci Utca* High School" is equivalent in meaning to, e.g., North Miami High School. I am grateful to Frank Hernadi for this information.

22. Interview with Margaret Mahler, Bluma Swerdloff, October 25, 1969, Columbia University Oral History, personal copy, p. 2.

23. Kovacs is the Hungarian equivalent of Cohen.

24. Freeman interview, October 25, 1969, p. 3.

25. Diethelm Library Interview, by Doris Nagel, April 8, 1981, pp.1–2.

26. Interview: Margaret S. Mahler, by Nancy Chodorow, p. 10, March 26, 1981, used by permission of Schlesinger Library, Radcliffe Institute, Harvard University.

27. Noshpitz interview, p. 4.

28. Chronology of the Holocaust, http://www.MTSU. EDU/_ Baustin/holokron.html. For all further Nazi chronology, see this reference.

Chapter 2

1. Swerdloff, personal copy, p. 4.

2. William Shakespeare, *Macbeth* 1, 7.

3. Columbia University Oral History, Swerdloff, p. 6.

4. Eugene L. Pogany, *In My Brother's Image* (New York: Penguin Books, 2000), 14.

5. Frank Hernadi. Personal communication.

6. Pyloric stenosis is the narrowing of the pyloric sphincter that blocks the passage of food from the stomach into the duodenum (webdictionary.co.uk, 1999–2005).

7. Rumination is a common problem among the developmentally disabled. It has been defined as "regurgitation of previously ingested food and its re-consumption and/or drooling from the mouth" (N.N. Singh, P.J. Manning & M.J. Angell "Effects of an Oral Hygiene Punishment Procedure on Chronic Rumination and Collateral Behaviors in Monozygous Twins," *Journal of Applied Behavior Analysis* 15 (1982)).

8. Columbia University Oral History, Swerdloff.

9. The modern projection planetarium was invented at the Carl Zeiss factory. In August 1923, a 16 meter dome was set up on the roof of the factory in Jena, and the first Model I projector was installed. The "Wonder of Jena" had its first unofficial showings there.

10. *A Dictionary of Architecture and Landscape Architecture* (Oxford University Press, 2006), 880. *Wikipedia: The free encyclopedia*, http://www.wikipedia.org (accessed 2006, February 13). Bauhaus is the common term for the *Staatliches Bauhaus*, an art and architecture school in Germany that operated from 1919 to 1933, and for its approach to design that it publicized and taught. The most natural meaning for its name (related to the German verb for "build") is *Architecture House*. Bauhaus style became one of the most influential currents in Modernist architecture, and one of the most important currents of the New Objectivity. The Bauhaus art school had a profound influence upon subsequent developments in architecture and interior design.

11. *Nostrification* is the validation of a diploma.

12. Noshpitz interview with Mahler, p. 12.

13. Nagel interview, pp. 9–10.

14. Richard Wagner, *Clemens Von Pirquet: His Life and Work* (Baltimore: Johns Hopkins Press, 1968), 179–181.

15. Unpublished interview. Doris Nolan, p. 8.

16. Freud, *Beyond the Pleasure Principle,* 39.

17. *Goethe: His Life and Times,* translated by Richard Friedenthal (Cleveland: World Publishing Co., 1965). Reprinted in *Clemens von Pirquet*, by Richard Wagner, 198.

18. Interview. Milton J.E. Senn, December 1, 1977, p. 4.

19. Nagel interview, p.11.

Chapter 3

1. Columbia University Oral History, Swerdloff, p. 17.

2. Abby Adams-Silvan, *A Biographical Sketch of Elizabeth Gero-Heymann,* Newsletter, *IPA* 9, no. 2 (2000).

3. Noshpitz interview.

4. Transference is an inappropriate reaction to the analyst, as though he or she were the person's parents as they were experienced in childhood.

5. Columbia University Oral History, Swerdloff.

6. Ibid.

7. Dr. Harold Blum, in his interview with Alma Bond, gave a conflicting account. According to him, Mahler never got over Deutsch's rejection.

8. Nolan interview, p. 12.

9. Stepansky, *The Memoirs of Margaret S. Mahler,* xxxv.

10. D. Kirsner, *Unfree Associations: Inside Psychoanalytic Institutes* (London: Process Press, 2000).

11. Letter to Alma Bond, July 1, 2005.

12. Paul Roazen, *Helene Deutsch: A Psychoanalyst's Life* (New York: Garden City, 1985).

13. Paul Roazen. Letter to Alma Bond, July 1, 2005.

14. "Women's Intellectual Contributions to the Study of Mind and Society," http://www.webster.edu/~woolflm/deutsch.html.

15. Helene Deutsch, *The Psychology of Women,* vols 1 and 2 (New York: Grune & Stratton, 1944, 1945).

16. Helene Deutsch, *Neuroses and Character Types* (New York: International Universities Press, 1965), 204–205.

17. August Aichhorn, *Wayward Youth* (London: Putnam, 1936).

18. Stepansky, *The Memoirs of Margaret S. Mahler,* 68–69.

19. Chodorow interview, March 26, 1981, p.30.

20. Noshpitz interview.

21. Irving Sternschein. Interview with Alma Bond.

22. William Langhorn. Interview with Margaret Mahler, April 4, 1980.

23. Noshpitz interview.

24. Freeman interview with Mahler, p. 13.

25. Oral History Columbia University, Swerdloff, 1977, personal copy, p. 41.

26. Bernard Pacella. Personal interview with Alma Bond.

27. The writer would like to express her gratitude to Thomas Aichhorn, grandson of August Aichhorn, for sending me this letter, among many others.

28. The letter was translated from the German by Dory Knoll and edited by Alma Bond.

29. Ferdinand Lundberg and Maryya Farnum, *The Modern Woman: The Lost Sex* (1947).

30. August Aichhorn, *Wayward Youth.*

31. Kurt R. Eissler and Paul Federn, eds, *Searchlights on Delinquency; New Psychoanalytic Studies* (dedicated to Professor August Aichhorn on the occasion of his seventieth birthday, July 27, 1948) (New York: International Universities Press, 1949).

32. Interview with Margaret Mahler. Nancy Chodorow, May, 1981, pp. 55–57, used by permission of Schlesinger Library, Radcliffe Institute, Harvard University.

33. Chodorow interview, March 26, 1981, p. 25.

34. Nagel interview, p. 11.

35. Judith Kestenberg and M.S. Mahler, "The Application of the Rorschach Test to the Psychology of the Organically Brain Damaged," in the *Schweitzer Archive fur Neurologie und Psychiatrie,* 1938.

36. Freeman interview with Mahler, p. 15.

37. Swerdloff interview with Bond.

38. Ruth Lax. Interview with Alma Bond.

39. Anni Bergman. Interview with Alma Bond.

40. Margaret S. Mahler and M. Furer, *On Human Symbiosis and the Vicissitudes of Individuation: Infantile Psychosis* (New York: International Universities Press, 1968).

Chapter 4

1. Oral History Columbia University, Swerdloff, personal copy, p. 39.

2. Swerdloff interview, p.58.

3. Chodorow interview, March 26, 1981, p. 49.

Chapter 5

1. Tax for those fleeing the Reich.

2. Ferenci's sculpture of Mahler is now in the possession of the Margaret Mahler Foundation in Philadelphia. A second copy was owned by the now deceased Bernard Pacella.

3. Columbia University Oral History, Swerdloff, personal copy, p. 71.

4. *Ejaculatio praecox:* Premature ejaculation.

5. Pogany, *In My Brother's Image* (New York: Penguin Books, 2000), 284.

6. Letter to Pista (full name unknown) from Margaret S. Mahler, New York, March 25, 1945.

7. Jennifer Tutak, "1996 Holocaust Remembrance Project," http://holocaust.hklaw.com/essays/1996/964.htm.

8. Joan Jackson. Interview with Alma Bond.

9. Interview with Margaret Mahler, Bluma Swerdloff, October 25, 1969, Columbia University Oral History, personal copy, p. 70.

10. Christabel Bielenberg, Obituary, *New York Times,* November 9, 2003.

11. Stepansky, *The Memoirs of Margaret S. Mahler,* 156–157. The data was obtained by Mrs. Bernice Apter, who attended a burial of Dr. Mahler's ashes in Sopron.

12. Alfred Kazin, "The Self as History: Reflections on Autobiography," in *Telling Lives: The Biographer's Art,* edited by Marc Pachter (University of Pennsylvania Press, 1981), 83.

Chapter 6

1. Stepanski, *The Memoirs of Margaret S. Mahler,* 94.

2. Columbia University Oral History, Swerdloff, p. 78.

3. Langford interview with Mahler, April 4, 1980.

4. Henri Parens. Interview with Alma Bond.

5. Ava Bry Penman. Interview with Alma Bond.

6. Raquel Berman. Interview with Alma Bond.

7. Columbia University Oral History, Swerdloff interview with Mahler, p 54.

Chapter 7

1. Columbia University Oral History, Swerdloff interview with Mahler, p 49.

2. Margaret Ribble, *The Rights of Infants: Early Psychological Needs and Their Satisfaction* (New York: Columbia University Press, 1943).

3. *The Research of Dr. Margaret S. Mahler: The Separation-Individuation Process,* 2nd ed. (Van Nuyes, CA: Child Development Media, Inc., 1977).

4. Noshpitz interview, p. 15.

5. Thomas Maier, *Dr. Spock: An Ameri-*

can Life (New York, San Diego, and London: Harcourt Brace & Co., 1998).

6. Margaret S. Mahler and L. Rangell, "A Psychosomatic Study of *Maladie des Tics* (Gilles de la Tourette's disease)," *Psychiatric Quarterly* 17 (1943): 579–603.

7. Mahler, Margaret S., and Jean A. Luke, "The Outcome of the Tic Syndrome," in *Journal of Nervous and Mental Disease* 103 (1946): 433–445.

8. Langford interview.

9. Morton Reiser. Interview with Alma Bond.

10. Stepansky, *The Memoirs of Margaret S. Mahler,* 129.

11. Oral History Columbia University. Swerdloff, personal copy, p. 57.

12. Margaret S. Mahler and M. Furer, *Psychoanalytic Quarterly* 29 (1960): 317–327.

13. Margaret S. Mahler, "The Clinical and Follow-up Study of the Tic Syndrome in Children," in *The American Journal of Orthopsychiatry* 15 (1945): 631–647

14. Ibid.

Chapter 8

1. Samuel Ritvo. Interview with Alma Bond.

2. Bluma Swerdloff. Interview with Alma H. Bond.

3. Personal communication to Alma Bond.

4. Letter to Arthur Bondi from Margaret Mahler, May 27, 1952.

5. Letter from Margaret Mahler to Paul Mahler, July 27, 1951.

6. Letter from Margaret Mahler to Paul Mahler, October 23, 1951.

7. Memorandum from Margaret Mahler to Paul Mahler, October 29, 1951

8. Letter from Margaret S. Mahler to Paul Mahler, November 7, 1951.

9. Letter from Arthur Bondi to Margaret Mahler, May 22, 1952.

10. Letter from Margaret Mahler to Arthur Bondi, May 22, 1952.

11. Pacella interview with Bond.

12. Letter from Margaret Mahler to Arthur Bondi, May 23, 1952.

13. Letter from Margaret Mahler to Arthur Bondi, May 27, 1952.

14. Letter to Arthur Bondi from Margaret Mahler, May 29, 1952.

15. Letter to Arthur Bondi from Paul Mahler, June 2, 1952.

16. Letter to Arthur Bondi from Paul Mahler, June 12, 1952.

17. Letter from Arthur Bondi to Paul Mahler, June 23, 1952.

18. Separation agreement between Margaret S. Mahler and Paul Mahler, July 1952.

19. Letter from Arthur Bondi to Paul Mahler, 1952. Exact date unknown.

20. Letter from Paul Mahler to Margaret Mahler, July 26, 1952.

21. Harold Blum. Interview with Alma Bond.

Chapter 9

1. Interview with Margaret Mahler and Selma Kramer, 1980, by Darline Levy.

2. Douglas Kirsner, *Unfree Associations: Inside Psychoanalytic Institutes* (London: Process Press, 2000), p. 1.

3. Stepansky, *The Memoirs of Margaret S. Mahler*, 122.

4. Noshpitz interview, p. 24.

5. Chodorow interview, March 26, 1981, p. 18.

6. Stepansky, *Memoirs of Margaret S. Mahler*, 75.

7. Margaret Mahler. Personal communication.

8. Freud, *Beyond the Pleasure Principle*.

9. Jacob Arlow. Interview with Alma Bond.

10. Fred Pine. Interview with Alma Bond.

11. Swerdloff interview with Mahler, personal copy, p. 44.

12. Douglas Kirsner, *Unfree Associations: Inside Psychoanalytic Institutes* (London: Process Press, 2000).

13. Manuel Furer. Personal communication.

14. Neubauer, Kramer, Mahler Interview, February 13, 1982. Margaret S. Mahler Papers, Manuscripts and Archives, Yale University Library, Tape reel 2, YT7-4298.

15. Levy interview with Mahler and Kramer, 1980.

16. Darline Levy interview. Date unknown, p. 7.

17 Chodorow interview, March 26, 1981.

18. Mahler and Furer, *On Human Symbiosis and the Vicissitudes of Individuation* (New York: International Universities Press, 1968).

19. Margaret S. Mahler, Fred Pine and Anni Bergman, *The Psychological Birth of the Human Infant* (New York: Basic Books, Inc., 1975).

20. Chodorow interview, p. 31–33.

21. Edward interview with Bond.

22. Chodorow interview, p. 37.

23. As reported by Raquel Berman. Interview with Alma Bond.

24. Berberian interview with Bond.

25. Freud, *Beyond the Pleasure Principle*.

Chapter 10

1. Berman interview with Bond.

2. Nerve, gumption.

3. Sternschein interview with Bond.

4. Mahler, Pine and Bergman, *The Psychological Birth of the Human Infant*, 8.

5. Margaret S. Mahler, "On the First Three Subphases of the Separation-Individuation Process," in *The Selected Papers of Margaret S. Mahler*, vol. 2, *Separation-Individuation* (New York and London: Jason Aronson, 1979), 119.

6. Fred Pine, "On the Separation Process: Universal Trends and Individual Differences," in *Separation-Individuation*, edited by J.B. McDevitt and C.F. Settlage (International Universities Press, 1971), 113.

7. Margaret S. Mahler, *On Human Symbiosis and the Vicissitudes of Individuation*, vol. 1 (New York: International Universities Press, 1968), 22–31.

8. Margaret S. Mahler, "On the Significance of the Normal Separation-Individuation Phase," in *Drives, Affects, Behavior*, vol. 2, edited by Max Schur (New York: International Universities Press, 1965), 164–168.

9. Margaret S. Mahler, "On the First Three Subphases," in *Selected Papers of Margaret S. Mahler*, 122.

10. Mahler, "Symbiosis and Individuation," in *Psychological Birth of the Human Infant*, 155.

11. Berman interview with Mahler, December 2, 1979.

12. Mahler, "Symbiosis and Individuation," in *Psychological Birth of the Human Infant*, p. 157.

13. Ibid. pp. 124–125.

14. Ibid. p. 158.

15. Ibid. p. 125.

16. Fred Pine, "On the Separation Process: Universal Trends and Individual Differences," in *Separation-individuation*, edited by J.B. McDevitt and C.F. Settlage (International Universities Press, 1971), 115.

17. Anni Bergman. Interview with Alma Bond.

18 Eleanor Galenson. Video interview with Margaret Mahler.

19. Mahler, "Symbiosis and Individuation," in *Psychological Birth of the Human Infant*, p. 127.

20. Martin Bergmann. Personal communication.

21. Anni Bergman. "Revisiting Rapprochement," Institute for Psychoanalytic Training and Research lecture, October 17, 2003.

22. Margaret S Mahler and Manuel Furer, "Certain Aspects of the Separation-Individuation Phase," in *The Psychoanalytic Quarterly* 32, no. 1 (1963): 1.

23. Margaret S. Mahler, "Development and Individuation," in the *Psychoanalytic Study of the Child* 18 (1963) (New York: International Universities Press): 309.

24. Pine, "On the Separation Process: Universal Trends and Individual Differences," in *Separation-Individuation*, 118.

25. Mahler, *The Selected Papers of Margaret Mahler*, vol. 2, *Separation-Individuation* (New York and London: Jason Aronson, 1979), 37.

26. Ibid. p. 161.

27. Anni Bergman, "Ours, Yours, Mine," in *Rapprochement and Developmental Issues: The Critical Subphase of separation-Individuation*, edited by Ruth F. Lax, Sheldon Bach and J. Alexis Burland (New York and London: Jason Aronson, 1980), 212–213.

28. Alma H. Bond, *Who Killed Virginia Woolf?: A Psychobiography* (New York: Human Sciences Press, a subsidiary of Plenum Press, 1989).

29. Milton J.E. Senn. Interview with Margaret Mahler, December 1, 1977, p. 18.

30. Margaret S. Mahler and Bertram J. Gosliner, "On Symbiotic Child Psychosis," in the *Psychoanalytic Study of the Child*, vol. 10 (New York: International Universities Press, 1955), 199.

31. Anni Bergman, "Revisiting Rapprochement," paper delivered at the Institute for Psychoanalytic Training and Research in New York City on October 18, 2003. I am grateful to Dr. Bergman for permission to use much of the material in her paper.

32. Ibid.

33. Justin Call. Interview with Alma Bond.

34. Margaret Mahler. Personal communication.

35. Margaret S. Mahler and Emanuel Furer, "Certain Aspects of the Separation-Individuation Phase," in *The Psychoanalytic Quarterly* 32, no. 1 (1963): 1.

36. Mahler, Pine and Bergman, *The Psychological Birth of the Human Infant*, 3.

37. Texas Roper, Texas Registry of Parent Educator Resources, 2001.

38. Margaret S. Mahler, *On Human Symbiosis and the Vicissitudes of Individuation*, vol. 1, *Infantile Psychosis* (New York: International Universities Press, 1968).

Chapter 11

1. Berman interview with Mahler, December 2, 1979.

Chapter 12

1. Lawrence Weinberg, *The Big Man*. The play opened at the Cherry Lane Theatre on May 19, 1966, at the Cherry Lane Theatre, New York City.

2. Freud, *Beyond the Pleasure Principle*, 15.

3. Margaret Mahler. Personal communication.

4. Benedict Carey, "Bullies in the Workplace," *New York Times*, June 22, 2004.

Chapter 13

1. D.W. Winnicott, *The Maturational Processes and the Facilitating Environment* (New York: International Universities Press, 1965), 56.

2. Bergman interview with Bond.

3. Arnold Richards. Personal communication.

4. Peter Neubauer. Interview with Alma Bond, June 12, 2003.

5. Swerdloff interview with Bond.

6. Walt Whitman, "There Was a Child Went Forth" (Harper & Brothers, 1943).

7. Pine interview with Bond, March 31, 2003.

8. Doris Nolan, Oral History, 8.

9. Ilo Milton. Interview with Alma Bond, May 9, 2004.

10. Pine interview with Bond.

11. Madow interview with Bond.

12. Jackson interview with Bond, July 28, 2002.

13. Lucia Wright. Interview with Alma Bond, March 15, 2003.

14. I hope Dr. Bergman is not offended for the inclusion of this material. Since so many people commented on her relationship

with Dr. Mahler, I thought it was necessary to incorporate material it in order to understand the paradoxical character of Margaret Mahler.

15. Kitty LaPerrière. Interview with Alma Bond.

16. Swerdloff interview with Bond.

17. Bergman interview with Bond.

18. Blum interview with Alma Bond.

19. Ibid.

20. Karen Berberian interview with Bond.

21. Karen Berberian. Phone conversation.

22. Neubauer, Kramer, Mahler interview of February 13, 1982, tape 2.

23. Not her real name.

24. Anna-Marie Sandler. Telephone interview with Alma Bond, May 20, 2003.

25. Mahler, Pine and Bergman, *The Psychological Birth of the Human Infant*.

26. Pacella interview with Bond.

27. Darline Levy. Letter July 20, 1979.

28. Darline Levy. Letter to Margaret Mahler, March 28, 1978.

29. Darline Levy. Interview with Alma Bond, October 8, 2003.

30. Milton interview with Bond.

31. Pacella interview with Bond.

32. Call interview with Bond.

33. Madow interview with Bond.

34. Swerdloff interview with Bond.

35. Judith Smith. Interview with Alma Bond.

36. LaPerrière interview with Bond, July 28, 2003.

37. Milton interview with Bond.

Chapter 14

1 Meyers interview with Bond.

2. Koehler phone interview with Bond.

3. Sternschein interview with Bond.

4. Arlow interview with Bond, June 8, 2003.

5. Madow interview with Bond.

6. Swerdloff interview with Bond.

7. Parens interview with Bond.

8. Rangell interview with Bond.

9. Manuel Furer. Interview with Alma Bond.

10. Milton interview with Bond.

11. Edward interview with Bond.

12. Lax interview with Bond.

13. Louise Kaplan. Interview with Alma Bond.

14. Louise Kaplan, *Oneness and Separation* (New York: Simon and Schuster, 1978).

15. Louise Kaplan. Personal communication.

16. Louise Kaplan. Letter dated May 22, 1980.

17. Jackson interview with Alma Bond

18. John McDevitt. Interview with Alma Bond, June 12, 2003.

19. Ernst Abelin. Interview with Alma Bond.

20. Lax interview with Bond.

21. Edgar Lipton. Interview with Alma Bond, October 8, 2003.

22. Levy interview with Bond.

23. Koehler interview with Bond.

24. Pine interview with Bond.

25. Robert Frost, "Fire and Ice."

26. J.P. Kalman, http://lp.soc.hit-u.ac.jp/kalman.

27. Olympia Dukakis, *Ask Me Again Tomorrow,* (New York: HarperCollins).

28. Swerdloff interview with Bond.

29. Helen Fogarassy. Interview with Alma Bond.

30. Paul Hoffman, *The Man Who Loved Only Numbers* (Hyperion, 1998), 145.

31. *Extra Hungariam non est vita, if est viat non est ita.*

32. Meyers interview with Bond.

33. Arline Zatz. Personal communication.

34. Swerdloff interview with Bond.

35. Madow interview with Bond.

36. Levy interview with Bond.

37. Anita Kolek. Telephone Interview with Alma Bond, 2003.

38. Mahler, Pine and Bergman, *The Psychological Birth of the Human Infant.*

39. Calvin Settlage. Interview with Alma Bond, July 16, 2003.

40. Unpublished letter from Margaret Mahler to Castilo de Padro, March 11, 1971.

41. Darline Levy. Interview with Margaret Mahler and Selma Kramer, 1980, p. 10.

42. Darline Levy interview with Bond.

43. Margaret Mahler. Personal communication.

44. Pine interview with Bond.

45. Madow interview with Bond.

46. Senn, Oral History, December 1, 1977, p. 18.

47 Sam Vaknin. http://samvak.tripod.com/acquirednarcissism.html

48. Kathleen S. Krajco, 2004.

49. Nagel, Diethelm Library, April 8, 1981, p. 4.

50. Ibid., 8.

51. Chodorow, Oral History, 17.

52. Nerve, gumption.

53. Blum interview with Bond.
54. Furer interview with Bond.
55. Anni Bergman. Eulogy for Margaret Mahler, October 6, 1985, p. 3.
56. Walt Whitman, "Song of Myself." I am grateful to AnnieLaura Jaggers, who referred me to the poem.

Chapter 15

1. Wright interview with Bond.
2. Richards interview with Bond.
3. Milton interview with Bond.
4. Lax interview with Bond.
5. Arnold Richards. Personal communication.
6. Chodorow, Oral History, March 26, 1981.
7. Yahoo, Directory Past Storms, Hurricane Gloria.
8. McDevitt interview with Bond.
9. Fogarassy interview with Bond.
10. Ibid.
11. Arlow interview with Bond.
12. Patricia Nachman. Interview with Bond.
13. Richards interview with Bond.
14. Rangell interview with Alma Bond.
15. Sternschein interview with Bond.
16. Sternschein interview with Bond.
17. Patsy Turrini. Interview with Alma Bond.
18. Ernst Abelin. Telephone interview with Alma Bond, May 18, 2003.
19. Settlage interview with Alma Bond.
20. Pine interview with Bond.
21. Margaret Mahler. Personal communication.
22. Judith Smith. Interview with Alma Bond, March 27, 2003.
23. Call interview with Bond, September 28, 2003.
24. Lotte Koehler. Interview with Alma Bond, November 19, 2003.
25. Ibid.
26. Mahler., Pine and Bergman, *The Psychological Birth of the Human Infant: Symbiosis and Individuation*, 227.
27. Nachman interview with Bond.
28. Susan Schwartz. Interview with Alma Bond, July 2003.

Chapter 16

1. This information is on Public Record and is taken from the will of Margaret Mahler, filed in New York State after her death on October 2, 1985.
2. Denise Galatas. Personal communication.
3. Ibid.
4. Bergman interview with Bond.
5. Smith interview with Alma Bond.
6. Darline Levy. Telephone interview with Alma Bond, October 7, 2003.
7. Abelin interview with Bond.
8. Blum interview with Bond.
9. Neubauer interview with Bond.
10. Bernice Apter. Interview with Alma Bond, October 13, 2003.
11. Furer interview with Bond.
12. R. Lax, S. Bach and J.A. Burland, *Rapprochement: The Critical Subphase of Separation-Individuation* (New York: Jason Aronson, 1993).
13. R. Lax, S. Bach and J.A. Burland, *Self and Object Constancy: Clinical and Theoretical Perspectives* (New York: Guilford Press, 1985).
14. Kaplan interview with Bond.
15. Sternschein interview with Bond.
16. Madow interview with Bond.
17. Fogarassy interview with Bond.
18. Pacella interview with Alma Bond.
19. Sylvia Brody. Interview with Alma Bond.
20. Meyers interview with Bond.
21. D. Kirsner, *Unfree Associations: Inside Psychoanalytic Institutes* (London: Process Press, 2000). Kirsner states that these figures were among the findings of a survey of members by Francis Baudry published in the *Newsletter of the New York Psychoanalytic Society and Institute* 20, no. 3 (November, 1983).
22. Frank Hernadi. Personal communication.

Chapter 17

1. Call interview with Bond.
2. Neubauer interview with Bond.
3. Parens interview with Bond.
4. Sternschein interview with Bond.
5. Smith interview with Bond.
6. Koehler interview with Bond.
7. Helen Gediman. Personal communication.
8. Blum interview with Bond.
9. Pine interview with Bond.
10. Fred Pine, *Journal of the American Psychoanalytic Association* 52 (2004): 511–533.

11. Bergman, "Revisiting Rapprochement."

12. J. Bowlby, *Attachment and Loss,* vol. 1, *Attachment;* vol. 2, *Separation;* vol. 3, *Loss, Sadness, and Depression* (New York: Basic Books, 1969–1980).

13. Peter Fonagy, "Transgenerational Consistencies of Attachment: A New Theory." Paper given before the Developmental and Psychoanalytic Discussion Group, American Psychoanalytical Association Meeting, Washington, D.C., 13 May 1999.

14. John Bowlby, *A Secure Base-Parent-Child Attachment and Healthy Human Development* (New York: Basic Books, 1988), 35–36. I am grateful to Anne Mansfield for bringing this comment to my attention.

15 See p. 56–57 of this book: "It was when she became the head of a well-baby clinic at the Mauthner-Markoff Hospital that Mahler was struck by the great insight that was to make psychoanalytic history and to change the course of countless lives to come. Once a week, she treated average mothers with their normal babies at the clinic. There she made the profound observation that these well babies were in a twilight state of existence. Although they were fully developed physically they had not really been *born psychologically,* in that they were not tuned in to the external world. Psychologically, the infants were still in the womb state. In the midst of her infantile psychosis studies at the Masters Children's Center much later, Mahler came to the conclusion that these infants were very similar to two psychotic latency children she had treated privately. In her child psychosis studies, Mahler observed that a symbiotic child psychosis occurs through arrest of the mother-infant relationship in the symbiotic stage of development. Through her observations of these children, and her parallel project with normal infants at the Masters Children's Center, she became more and more convinced of the *symbiotic origin of human existence,* that the emotional birth of the human child occurs *in duo* with the mother or not at all."

16. E. Peterfreund, "Some Critical Comments on Psychoanalytic Conceptions of Infancy," in *International Journal of Psycho-Analysis* 59 (1978): 427–441.

17. Karlen Lyons-Ruth, "Rapprochement or Approchement: Mahler's Theory Reconsidered from the Vantage Point of Recent Research on Early Attachment Relationships," in *Psychoanalytic Psychology* 8, no. 1:1–23.

18. Ibid., 4.

19. Fonagy, "Transgenerational Consistencies of Attachment: A New Theory."

20. Bergman, *Revisiting Rapprochement.*

21. Quoted by Bergman, *Revisiting Rapprochement.*

22. http://www.science-spirit.org/articles/Articledetail.efm?article_ID=329.

23. E. Tronick, H. Als and L. Adamson, "Structure of Early Face-to-Face Communicative Interactions," in *Before Speech: The Beginning of Interpersonal Communication,* edited by M. Bullowa (New York: Cambridge University Press, 1979).

24. Gyorgy Gergely, "Reapproaching Mahler: New Perspectives," in *Journal of the American Psychoanalytic Association* 48, no. 4. I am grateful to Dr. Gergely for sending me his paper.

25. Lyons-Ruth, "Rapprochement or Approchement: Mahler's Theory Reconsidered from the Vantage Point of Recent Research on Early Attachment Relationships."

26. Ibid., 19.

27. Allan Souter, "Who's Afraid of Jessica Benjamin?: Some Comments on Her "Recognition and Destruction," http://psychematters.com/papers/asouter.htm.

28. Bergman, *Revisiting Rapprochement.*

29. Janna Malamud Smith, *A Potent Spell* (Boston and New York: Houghton Mifflin, 2003), 147–152.

30. Daniel Stern, *The Interpersonal World of the Infant* (New York: Basic Books, 1985), 70.

31. Daniel Stern. Telephone conversation with Alma Bond, May 17, 2004.

32. Blum interview with Bond.

33. *Psychoanalytic Inquiry,* prologue, p. 1 (Hillsdale, NJ: The Analytic Press).

34. William Shakespeare, Moth in *Love's Labour's Lost* 5, 1:36–37.

35. Helen Fogarassy, *Mix Bender* (Lakewood, OH: Quality Publications, 1987), 108.

Postscript

1. McDevitt interview with Bond.

References

Many articles and newspapers were consulted for this book, but its major sources were Bluma Swerdloff's *Oral History* (Columbia University Oral History Research Office, interviews of 1969 and 1974, of which Dr. Swerdloff was kind enough to lend me her own personal copy), the *Memoirs of Margaret Mahler,* by Paul E. Stepansky (New York: The Free Press, 1988); and interviews the writer personally conducted with many of Mahler's friends and associates. The author also examined the 187 boxes of material from the Margaret Mahler Collection in the Yale Archives, including the following videos: *The Research of Dr. Margaret S. Mahler, second edition, The Separation-Individuation Process,* including two 10-minute updates; *Continuity of Conflict* and *Compromise Formation from Infancy to Adulthood: A Twenty-five Year Follow-up* by John B. McDevitt, M.D.; and *Separation-Individuation and Object Constancy,* by Harold Blum, M.D. The videos of Mahler conducted by Raquel Berman were first presented at the "First Symposium Margaret S. Mahler: The Separation-Individuation Process in Childhood Development — Preventative Aspects," held in Mexico D.F. Mexico, with the participation of Dr. Margaret Mahler (by video), Dr. Anni Bergman, Dr. Louise Kaplan and Dr. Calvin Settlage, on November 30 through December 2, 1979. Numerous written interviews were also consulted at the Columbia University Oral History Research Office and the Yale University Library of Manuscripts and Archives, including those by Darline Levy, Nancy Chodorow, Doris Nagel, Lucy Freeman, Eleanor Galenson, William Langford, Raquel Berman, Joseph Noshpitz, Peter Neubauer, Selma Kramer, and Milton Senn.

Bibliography

Aichhorn, August. *Wayward Youth*. London: Putnam, 1936.

Bergman, Anni. "Ours, Yours, Mine." In *Rapprochement and Developmental Issues: The Critical Subphase of Separation-Individuation*, edited by Ruth F. Lax, Sheldon Bach and J. Alexis Burland. New York and London: Jason Aronson, 1980.

Bond, Alma H. "Sadomasochistic Patterns in an 18-Month-Old Child." *The International Journal of Psychoanalysis* 48, no. 4 (1967): 597–602.

_____. *Who Killed Virginia Woolf? A Psychobiography*. New York: Human Sciences Press, 1989; reprinted in 2000 by Excel Press.

Bowlby, J. *Attachment and Loss*. 3 vols. *Attachment*, vol. 1; *Separation*, vol. 2; *Loss, Sadness, and Depression*, vol. 3. New York: Basic Books, 1969–1973.

Cohn, J., E. Tronick, R. Matias, and K. Lyons-Ruth. "Face-to-face interactions of depressed mothers with their infants." In *Maternal Depression and Infant Disturbance*, edited by E. Tronick and T. Field. San Francisco: Jossey-Bass, 1986.

Chronology of the Holocaust: (1930–1945), http://www.MTSU.EDU/_Baustin/holo kron.html.

Deutsch, Helene. *Neuroses and Character Types*. New York: International Universities Press, 1965.

_____. *The Psychology of Women*. 2 vols. New York: Grune & Stratton, 1944–1945.

Dukakis, Olympia. *Ask Me Again Tomorrow: A Life in Progress*. New York: HarperCollins, 2003.

Eissler, Kurt R., and Paul Federn, eds. *Searchlights on Delinquency: New Psychoanalytic Studies*. New York: International Universities Press, 1949.

Fogarassy, Helen. *Mix Bender*. Lakewood, OH: Quality, 1987.

Fonagy, Peter. "Transgenerational Consistencies of Attachment: A New Theory." Paper given to the Developmental and Psychoanalytic Discussion Group, American Psychoanalytical Association Meeting, Washington, DC, May 13, 1999.

Freud, Sigmund. *Beyond the Pleasure Principle*. SE Vol. 18 (1920G). 1834–1844.

Gergely, Gyorgy. "Reapproaching Mahler: New Perspectives." In *Journal of the American Psychoanalytic Association* 48, no. 4 (2000).

Hartmann, H. "The Mutual Influences in the Development of Ego and Id." In *Essays on Ego Psychology*. New York: International Universities Press, 1964. (The original work was published in 1952.)

Hoffman, Paul. *The Man Who Loved Only Numbers.* New York: Hyperion, 1998.

Hopkins, Linda. *False Self: The Life of Masud Khan.* New York: Other Press, 2006.

Kalman, J.P. http://lp.soc.hit-u.ac.jp/kalman.

Kazin, Alfred. "The Self as History: Reflections on Autobiography." In *Telling Lives: The Biographer's Art,* edited by Marc Pachter. Philadelphia: University of Pennsylvania Press, 1981.

Kestenberg, J., and M.S. Mahler. "The Application of the Rorschach Test to the Psychology of the Organically Brain Damaged." In *Schweitzer Archive fur Neurologie und Psychiatrie* (1938).

Kirsner, D. *Unfree Associations: Inside Psychoanalytic Institutes.* London: Process Press, 2000.

Klein, M. "On Mahler's Autistic and Symbiotic Phases, an Exposition and Evolution." In *Psychoanalysis and Contemporary Thought* 4, no. 1 (1980).

Krajco, Kathleen. www.operationdoubles.com.

Lax, Ruth F., Sheldon Bach and J. Alexis Burland, eds. *Rapprochement: The Critical Subphase of Separation-Individuation.* New York and London: Jason Aronson, 1980.

Lax, Ruth F., Sheldon Bach and J. Alexis Burland. *Self and Object Constancy: Clinical and Theoretical Perspectives,* New York: Guilford Press, 1985.

Lundberg, Ferdinand, and Maryya Farnum. *The Modern Woman: The Lost Sex.* N.p., 1947.

Lyons-Ruth, K. "Rapprochement or Approchement: Mahler's Theory Reconsidered from the Vantage Point of Recent Research on Early Attachment Relationships." In *Psychoanalytic Psychology* 8, no. 1 (1991).

Mahler, Margaret S. "The Clinical and Follow-up Study of the Tic Syndrome in Children." In *The American Journal of Orthopsychiatry* 15 (1945).

_____. "Development and Individuation." In *Psychoanalytic Study of the Child* 18. New York: International Universities Press, 1963.

_____. "Les Infants Terrible." In *The Selected Papers of Margaret S. Mahler.* Vol. 1, *Infantile Psychosis and Early Contributions.* New York and London: Jacob Aronson, 1949. (Reprinted from *Searchlights on Delinquency,* edited by K.R. Eissler. New York: International Universities Press.)

_____. *On Human Symbiosis and the Vicissitudes of Individuation.* New York: International Universities Press, 1968.

_____. "On the Significance of the Normal Separation-Individuation Phase." In *Drives, Affects, Behavior.* Vol. 2, edited by Max Schur. New York: International Universities Press, 1965.

_____. "Pseudoimbecility: A Magic Cap of Invisibility." In *The Psychoanalytic Quarterly* 11, no. 2 (1942): 149–64. (Reprinted in *The Selected Papers of Margaret S. Mahler.* Vol. 1, *Infantile Psychosis and Early Contributions.* New York and London: Jacob Aronson, 1979.)

_____. *The Selected Papers of Margaret Mahler.* 2 vols. New York and London: Jason Aronson, 1979.

_____. "A Study of the Separation-Individuation Process and Its Possible Application to Borderline Phenomena in the Psychoanalytic Situation." In *Psychoanalytic Study of the Child* 26 (1971).

Mahler, M.S., and Manuel Furer. (1960). "Observations on Research Regarding the Symbiotic Syndrome of Infantile Psychosis." In *Psychoanalytic Quarterly* 29 (1960).

Mahler, Margaret S., and B.J. Gosliner. "On Symbiotic Child Psychosis." In *Psychoanalytic Study of the Child* 10 (1955).

Mahler, Margaret S., and Jean A. Luke. "The Outcome of the Tic Syndrome." In *The Journal of Nervous and Mental Disease* (1946).

Mahler, Margaret S., Fred Pine and Anni Bergman. *The Psychological Birth of the Human Infant: Symbiosis and Individuation.* New York: Basic Books, 1975.

Mahler, Margaret S., and L. Rangell. "A Psychosomatic Study of *Maladie des Tics* (Gilles de la Tourette's disease)." In *Psychiatric Quarterly* 17 (1943).

Maier, Thomas. *Dr. Spock: An American Life*. New York, San Diego, and London: Harcourt Brace & Co., 1998.

Pachter, Marc. *Telling Lives: The Biographer's Art*. Washington, DC: New Republic Books, 1981.

Peterfreund, E. (1978). "Some Critical Comments on Psychoanalytic Conceptions of Infancy." In *International Journal of Psychoanalysis* 59.

Pine, Fred. "Some Refinements of the Separation-Individuation Concept in Light of Research on Infants." In *Psychoanalytic Study of the Child* (1992).

Pogany, Eugene L. *In My Brother's Image*. New York: Penguin, 2000.

_____. "Separation-Individuation Revisited." In *Psychoanalytic Inquiry* (1994).

Ribble, Margaret. (1943). *The Rights of Infants: Early Psychological Needs and Their Satisfaction*. New York: Columbia University Press.

Smith, Janna Malamud. *A Potent Spell*. New York and Boston: Houghton Mifflin, 2003.

Stepansky, Paul E. *The Memoirs of Margaret S. Mahler*, New York: The Free Press, A Division of Macmillan, Inc., 1988.

Stern, Daniel. *The Interpersonal World of the Infant*. New York: Basic Books, 1985.

Tronick, E., H. Als and L. Adamson. "Structure of Early Face-to-Face Communicative Interactions." *Before Speech: The Beginning of Interpersonal Communication*, edited by M. Bullowa. New York: Cambridge University Press, 1979.

Vaknin, Sam. "Malignant Self Love: Narcissism Revisited." http://samvak.tripod.com.

Wagner, Richard. *Clemens Von Pirquet: His Life and Work*. Baltimore: The Johns Hopkins Press, 1968.

Winnicott, D.W. *Collected Papers*. London: Tavistock, 1958.

_____. *The Maturational Processes and the Facilitating Environment*. New York: International Universities Press, 1965.

"Women's Intellectual Contributions to the Study of Mind and Society." http://www.webster.edu/~woolflm/deutsch.html.

Index

DUE